BRIEST

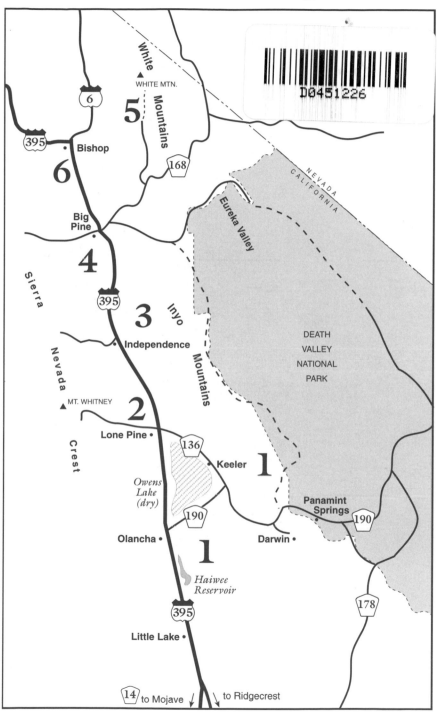

White Mountains

▲ WHITE MTN.

6

5

395

• Bishop

168

6

Big Pine

395

4

Sierra

NEVADA
CALIFORNIA

Eureka Valley

Inyo

3

• Independence

Mountains

DEATH
VALLEY
NATIONAL
PARK

Nevada

▲ MT. WHITNEY

2

Lone Pine •

136

• Keeler

Crest

Owens
Lake
(dry)

1

190

Panamint
Springs

190

Olancha •

1

• Darwin •

Haiwee
Reservoir

178

395

Little Lake •

14 to Mojave ↓   • to Ridgecrest ↓

The beginning of mountain biking in the Owens Valley

MOUNTAIN BIKING
The Eastern Sierra's
BEST 100 TRAILS

by Réanne Hemingway-Douglass,
Mark Davis, Don Douglass

MOUNTAIN
BIKING
PRESS™

FINE EDGE
Productions

IMPORTANT LEGAL NOTICE AND DISCLAIMER

Mountain biking is a potentially dangerous sport, and the rider or user of this book accepts a number of unavoidable risks. Trails by nature have numerous natural and man-made hazards; they are generally not signed or patrolled and they change with time and conditions.

While substantial effort has been made to provide accurate information, this guidebook may inadvertently contain errors and omissions. Any maps in this book are for locator reference only. They are not to be used for navigation. Your mileages will vary from those given in this book. Contact land managers before attempting routes to check for suitability and trail conditions.

The authors, editors, contributors, publishers, distributors, and public and private land managers accept no liability for any errors or omissions in this book or for any injuries or losses incurred from using this book.

Credits:

book design: Melanie Haage
copy editing: Cindy Kamler
cover design: Laura Patterson
diagrams: Sue Irwin
front cover photo: © John Dittli
back cover photo: courtesy of Mammoth Mountain Ski Area
all other photos by the authors, except as noted
BLM photos courtesy Bishop Resource Area

Library of Congress Cataloging-in-Publication Data

Hemingway-Douglass, Réanne,
    Mountain biking the Eastern Sierra's best 100 trails / by Réanne Hemingway-Douglass, Mark Davis, and Don Douglass.
       p. cm.
    Includes bibliographical references and index.
    ISBN 0-938665-42-1
    1. All terrain cycling—Sierra Nevada (Calif. and Nev.--Guidebooks. 2. Trails--Sierra Nevada (Calif. and Nev.)--Guidebooks. 3. Sierra Nevada (Calif. and Nev.)--Guidebooks.
I. Davis, Mark   II. Douglass, Don   III. Title.
GV1045.5.S56H45   1997
796.6'3'097944--DC21   97-2342
                                                    CIP

Address requests for permission to
Mountain Biking Press™
Fine Edge Productions; Route 2, Box 303, Bishop, CA 93514
www.fineedge.com

TABLE OF CONTENTS

Preface 9
Index to Topographical Maps 10
Welcome to the Eastern Sierra 11
Letter from BLM 12
Letter from USFS 13
Know Before You Go: Special Considerations for the Eastern Sierra . . . 14

Chapter 1: Southern Inyo County
1. Haiwee Reservoir Ride 20
2. Cactus Flat Ride 21
3. Darwin Loop 22
4. Tour De Joshua Loop 25
5. Cerro Gordo/Swansea Loop 27

Chapter 2: Lone Pine
1. South Alabama Hills Loop 32
2. Movie Road Loop 32
3. Hogback Loop 34
4. Lone Pine Station Ride 35

Chapter 3: Independence
1. Reward Loop 39
2. Independence Historical Tour 40
3. Mazourka Canyon Ride 43
4. Taboose Creek Loop 44
5. Tinemaha Loop 46

Chapter 4: Big Pine
1. Crater Mountain Loop 49
2. McMurry Meadows Loop 50
3. Baker Creek Loop 52
4. Westgard Pass Road Ride 54
5. Andrews Mountain Loop 55
6. Keough's Hot Ditch Loop 58

Chapter 5: White Mountains
1. Black Mountain Ride 60
2. Grandview Mine Ride 61
3. Silver Canyon Ride 62
4. Patriarch Grove Ride 64
5. White Mountain Ride 67
6. Wyman Canyon Ride 69

Chapter 6: Bishop South
1. Coyote High Sierra Traverse 74
2. Buttermilk Country Loop 77

3. Tungsten Hills Loop 79
4. Horton "Roubaix" Ride 81
5. Geiger Canal Loop 83
6 Artesian Wells Loop 84

Chapter 7: Bishop North
1. Pleasant Valley Loop 87
2. Volcanic Tableland Ride 89
3. Mount Tom Loop 90

Chapter 8: Benton
1. Banner Ridge Loop 93
2. Red Rock Canyon Ride 95
3. Blind Spring Valley Ride 97

Chapter 9: Rock Creek
1. Lower Rock Creek Trail Ride 101
2. Rock Creek Loop 102
3. Owens Gorge/Rock Creek Loop 104
4. Sky Meadow Loop 105
5. Sand Canyon Loop 107

Chapter 10: Crowley Lake
1. The Great Wall of Owens Gorge Ride 110
2. Crowley Lake Loop 111
3. McGee Canyon Ride 114
4. Tobacco Flat Ride 115
5. "Cabo San Crowley" Ride 116

Chapter 11: Mammoth Lakes
A. Shady Rest Staging Area 119
1. Town Bike Path 119
2. Shady Rest Park Loop 120
3. Shady Rest Forest Loop 120
4. Knolls Loops 121
5. Knolls Blue Diamond Loop 123
6. Knolls Triangle Loop 124
7. Sawmill Road/Mammoth Creek Loop 125
B. North Village Staging Area 126
1. Uptown/Downtown Singletrack Loop 126
2. Mountain View Ride 127
3. Minaret Vista Ride 128
4. Hard Core Ride (San Joaquin Ridge) 130
5. Scenic Loop Ride 131
6. Inyo Craters Loop 132

C. Mammoth Creek Park Staging Area 133
1. Town Bike Trail Loop 134
2. Mammoth Creek Trail Loop 135
3. Sherwin Creek Loop 135
4. Laurel Canyon Ride 136
5. Old Mammoth Road Ride 138
D. Lakes Basin Staging Area 139
1. Panorama Dome Loops 140
2. Lake Mary Loop 142
3. Horseshoe Lake Loop 143
E. Mammoth Mountain Bike Park 144
F. Geothermal Staging Area 145
1. Geothermal Loop 146
2. Hot Creek Ride 147
G. Smokey Bear Flat Staging Area 149
1. Little Smokey Loop 149
2. Big Smokey Loop 151
3. Lookout Mountain Loop 151

Chapter 12: Glass Mountain Ridge
1. Bald Mountain Lookout Ride 154
2. Sagehen Summit Loop 156
3. Sawmill Meadow Ride 157
4. Glass Mountain Ridge Ride 159
5. Wildrose Canyon Loop 160

Chapter 13: June Lakes Basin
1. Glass Flow Ridge Loop 163
2. Hartley Springs Loop 165
3. June Lake Loop 167
4. Panorama Trail Loop 169

Chapter 14: Mono Basin
1. Moraines and Meadows Loop 172
2. Tioga Pass Road Ride 174
3. Bennettville Ride 175
4. Log Cabin Mine Loop 176
5. Lee Vining Loop 177
6. Black Point Ride 179

Chapter 15: Bodie Hills
1. Aurora Canyon/Geiger Grade Ride 182
2. Bodie Peak Loop 183
3. Cottonwood and Bridgeport Canyons Loop 185

Chapter 16: Conway Summit & Bridgeport Valley

1. Copper Mountain Loop 188
2. Sinnamon Meadow Loop 189
3. Travertine Geologic Ride 190
4. Masonic Mountain Ride 193
5. Twin Lakes Loop 193
6. Buckeye Hot Springs Ride 195

Chapter 17: Sonora Pass

1. Kirman Lake Loop 200
2. Poore Lake Ride 201
3. Leavitt Lake Ride 202
4. Summit Meadow Ride 203

Chapter 18: Walker-Coleville Area

1. Burcham Flat/Walker River Loop 208
2. Little Antelope Valley Loop 210
3. Slinkard Valley Ride 211
4. Monitor Pass Ride 213
5. Leviathan Loop Ride 214

Appendix

References. 218
Eastern Sierra Agencies and Resources 219
Basic Skills & Equipment *by R. W. Miskimins* 221
Care and Feeding of a Mountain Bike *by R. W. Miskimins* 225
Roadside Repairs *by R. W. Miskimins*. 229
Index 232
Acknowledgments 235
About the Authors. 237
FEP Books 238

PREFACE

Much of the early history of mountain biking in the remote and sparsely settled Eastern Sierra began in 1980 when Réanne and I became the first fat-tire bike users to ride the hundreds of miles of outstanding dirt roads and trails that thread this mountain and high desert country. At that time, the hand-made Ritchie mountain bikes we brought to our home overlooking the Owens Valley were a strange novelty.

The threat of new fat-tire technology and opposition to the increasing use of trails by mountain bikers led to the closing of over 10,000 miles of trails across the United States to bikes for several years during the 1980s. As Land Access Director of the National Off-Road Bicycling Association (NORBA) and later a board member, I began the fight to keep trails open. In the late 1980s Réanne and I founded the International Mountain Bicycling Association (IMBA) which was based in our home during its formative first three years. We developed the IMBA Rules of the Trail and key strategic alliances with other trail users, helping to dissipate trail closure problems. Education of both mountain bike riders and other trail users about the need for multiple use trails and cooperation in their building and maintenance has been one of our major accomplishments.

Drawing on our first-hand mountain biking experiences in the Eastern Sierra, in the early 1980s Réanne and I published our *Mountain Biking Owens Valley and Inyo County* (Guide 1) and *Mountain Biking Mono County* (Guide 2), the first such guidebooks published in the country.

In 1985, I suggested staging the Kamikaze Mountain Bike Race on Mammoth Mountain. Bill Cockcroft, Director of Mammoth Mountain Operations, liked the idea and that same year Mammoth Mountain hosted its first Kamikaze. I served as promoter and race director, and we had the biggest turnout of mountain bikers at that time—300 riders! Bill has gone on to make the annual Kamikaze at Mammoth Mountain the biggest and most exciting mountain bike event in the nation.

In 1987, Cindy Whitehead won the women's mountain bike championship by riding the grueling 60-mile Sierra 7500, staged above Bishop, in 6 hours and 1 minute, *standing up 98% of the way because of a missing seat and broken, jagged seat post*. Velo News called this "one of the greatest bicycle triumphs of the decade, if not the half century." Bill, Cindy and I have received the honor of being inducted into the Mountain Biking Hall of Fame. The three of us continue to live and play in the Eastern Sierra.

Mountain Biking Eastern Sierra's Best 100 Trails is an all-new version of what Réanne and I began over a decade ago. We have been joined by Mark Davis, a Mammoth Lakes resident, who has extensive knowledge of the local trail systems. His interests include trail development and maintenance, and representing the cycling community in working with various agencies to maintain access for mountain bikes on both public and private land.

Réanne and I have benefited greatly from the challenges for exploration available in the Eastern Sierra and from our involvement with the growth and promotion of mountain biking. We invite you to share and care for this special place and encourage you to write your own history of mountain biking into the 21st Century.

Don Douglass, Eastern Sierra, 1997

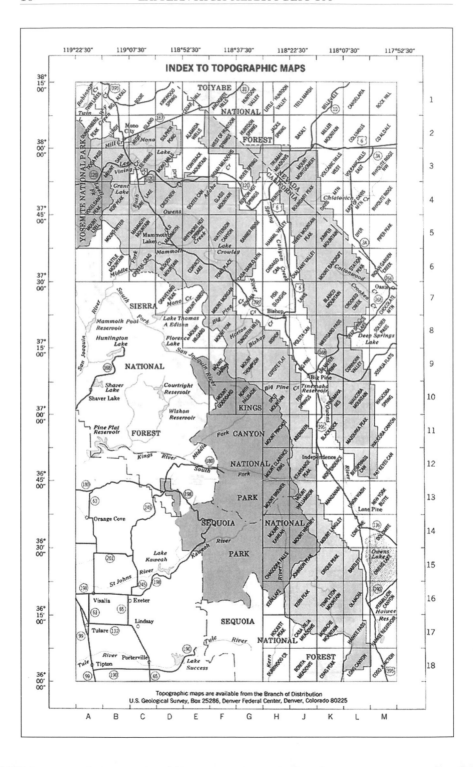

WELCOME TO THE EASTERN SIERRA . . .

one of the most scenic and least populated areas in the entire United States. Here you will find a flat, high desert corridor that runs from the Mojave Desert on the south to the Nevada border on the north. The western wall of this corridor is formed by the magnificent peaks and slopes of the Sierra Nevada; the eastern wall by the rugged Inyo-White Mountains. Highway 395 runs up this corridor and offers you easy access to these beautiful and unique ranges.

The Eastern Sierra encompasses natural wonders found nowhere else—bristlecone pines, the oldest living trees on earth, and Mono Lake with its tufa towers—as well as volcanic craters, hot springs, earthquake faults, and glaciers.

Imagine riding under sunny skies in the high desert while the rest of the country is overcast, frigid and raw. Imagine pedaling along secluded dirt roads at the foot of Mt. Whitney, the highest peak in the continental United States, or on a remote doubletrack in the White Mountains at 14,000 feet, with golden eagles soaring in an azure sky.

Imagine encountering a Basque sheepherder in a remote alpine meadow or downhilling Mammoth Mountain. Imagine riding along the route of the famous Kamikaze—the granddaddy of all mountain biking events—or cycling through Bodie, one of the best preserved ghost towns in the West.

If solitude, natural beauty, pure air, and unique biking terrain appeal to you, try some of the best 100 trails listed in this guidebook for unforgettable cycling experiences.

Réanne Hemingway-Douglass, Mark Davis, and Don Douglass

Backcountry Ethics

All cultural resources on Public Lands are protected for the enjoyment and scientific analysis of present and future generations by federal laws, including the Antiquities Act of 1906 and the Archeological Resources Protection Act of 1979. Please take only pictures and memories, leaving our historic heritage for others to enjoy.

United States Department of the Interior

BUREAU OF LAND MANAGEMENT
Bishop Resource Area
785 North Main Street, Suite E
Bishop, California 93514-2498
760-872-4881

Summer 1997

Dear Mountain Bike Enthusiast,

Think of *Mountain Biking the High Sierra's Best 100 Trails* as better than a guidebook; see it as a treasure that leads you to places and experiences to lift your spirit. Cherish it as a storehouse of gems where each ride sparkles with a life and brilliance that captivates your imagination. Think of it as a beacon of semi-primitive landscapes where you can ride continuously for days.

Many of the rides that follow are on public lands administered by the Bureau of Land Management (BLM). The Bishop Resource Area cares for 3/4 million acres of land throughout the eastern Sierra; thousands of miles of routes are available for all experience levels. A few of these routes are described in this book.

The eastern Sierra's popularity with mountain bikers has grown throughout the years. Visitors have discovered the subtle to the sublime, and the excitement of self-exploration. Now you can experience the remote majesty these lands offer. Imagine exploring the scenic Alabama Hills where old westerns and science fiction movies were filmed. Imagine riding to a historic mining town frozen in time. Imagine cruising down an old road and feeling like a kid again!

During the past several years I have had the pleasure of working with many individuals in the mountain bike community. I have watched the rapid evolution and growth of this outdoor activity. Don and Reanne Douglass, pioneers of the mountain bike movement, have contributed greatly to raising public awareness of access issues. Their sensitivity to the environment and their dedication to mountain bike ethics has been exemplary.

While you are out enjoying our many eastern Sierra gems, the courtesies you extend to others on the trail will be returned with some of our rural hospitality. Your consideration will increase your acceptance into our home, where locals take pride in our quality of life.

With this book, I invite you to some of the most spectacular scenery and riding adventures in California. When you are in Bishop, contact us at our office for more information about the BLM or how you can become a partner in our many programs. Your interest and involvement in your public lands is invaluable.

Sincerely,

Genivieve D. Rasmussen
Area Manager

United States	Forest	Inyo	873 N. Main St.
Department of	Service	National	Bishop, CA 93514
Agriculture		Forest	(760) 873-2400
			(760) 873-2538 TTY

Reply to: 2300

Date: April 25, 1997

Dear Mt. Bike Enthusiast:

As you may know, one of the fastest growing outdoor recreational activities on public lands is mountain biking. The Forest Service recognizes that some of the best riding opportunities exist within National Forests. Here, in the Eastern Sierra the Inyo National Forest offers a wide variety of riding opportunities in one of the most scenic areas of the state. Don and Reanne Douglass' new guidebook "Mountain Biking the High Sierra's Best 100 Trails" highlights some of the outstanding trails open to mountain bikes on the forest.

Mountain biking can be a recreational use that is light on the land when responsible riding habits are employed. During all of your rides, please practice good mountain bike ethics by following the **IBMA Rules of the Trail**, particularly by staying on existing roads and trails that are open for mountain bike use. Be considerate of other users, leave gates as you found them, control your speed, and pack out your trash. Remember, you are responsible for your own personal safety, use proper safety equipment, orient yourself to the land using topographic maps and guidebooks, and contact the nearest ranger station for local trail information and regulations before you start your ride.

We care about your experience and encourage you to share your ideas with us on how we can improve our services and facilities. Please feel free to contact us if your group or club would like to participate in a partnership to enhance riding opportunities on the forest.

Sincerely,

BILL BRAMLETTE
Deputy Forest Supervisor
Inyo National Forest

Caring for the Land and Serving People

FS-6200-28b(4/88)

KNOW BEFORE YOU GO

Special Considerations for the Eastern Sierra

The Eastern Sierra is a land of extremes—in climate, elevation, trail and road conditions, and remoteness. Good preparation provides opportunities for pleasure; poor preparation can bring disaster. As a guide for exploring the Eastern Sierra by mountain bike, we offer the following suggestions:

1. **Courtesy.** Extend courtesy to all other trail users and follow the IMBA Rules of the Trail. The trails and roads of the Eastern Sierra are popular with many user groups: hikers, equestrians, fishermen, ranchers, enthusiasts, hunters, and pack outfits. Mountain bikers are the newest user group, so set a good example.

2. **Preparation.** Plan your trip carefully; develop and use a check list. Know your equipment, your ability, and the area in which you are riding. Prepare accordingly and be self-sufficient at all times. Wear a helmet, keep your bicycle in good repair, and carry necessary supplies for changes in weather or other conditions.

3. **Mountain Conditions.**

High Elevation: To minimize the possibility of altitude sickness, allow time for your body to acclimate. You may need 3 days or more before attempting a strenuous trip or one at high elevation. If you have symptoms of nausea, headache, dizziness or shortness of breath, descend to a lower elevation to rest and recover.

Intense Sun: Protect your skin against the sun's harmful rays by wearing light-colored, long-sleeved shirts or jerseys. The higher you go, the more damaging the sun becomes. Use sunscreen with a sufficient rating. Wear sunglasses that offer adequate protection. Guard against heatstroke by riding in early morning or late afternoon when the sun's rays are less intense.

Water and Low Humidity: The climate is dry. Surface water is a precious commodity and potable water is unfortunately even more scarce these days. To avoid headaches or cramps, start each trip with a minimum of two or more full quart water bottles. (*Gallons* of water may not be sufficient for really hot weather or hard rides.) Force yourself to drink *before* you feel thirsty. Carry water from a known source or treat water gathered from springs, streams and lakes. Untreated drinking water may cause Giardiasis or other diseases.

Temperatures and Weather Conditions: High desert and alpine sun can be very hot, but conditions can change rapidly, bringing wind, cold, and rain or snow. Carry extra clothing—a windbreaker, gloves, stocking cap—and use the multi-layer system so you can quickly adapt to changing weather conditions. Afternoon thundershowers occur frequently in the high country, so keep an eye on changing cloud and wind conditions and prepare accordingly. For the latest information on weather and trail conditions, check with local authorities before setting out on an overnight ride. Be prepared to deal with dehydration, hypothermia, altitude sickness, sunburn and heatstroke.

Fatigue: Sluggish or cramping muscles and fatigue indicate the need for calories and liquids. Carry high-energy snack foods such as granola bars, dried fruits and nuts to maintain strength and warmth. To conserve energy, add clothing layers as the temperature drops or the wind increases.

Closures: Many mountain areas are closed to the public during times of high fire danger. Other areas may be temporarily closed during hunting season or

Horton Creek Campground

because of logging activity or other reasons. Please check ahead of time with local authorities and observe *all* such closures.

4. **First Aid.** In your first aid kit, include bandages and ointment for cuts and scrapes, and aspirin for aches that won't go away. In addition, include antiseptic swabs, moleskin, a single-edged razor blade, a needle, elastic bandage, anti-acid tablets, and waterproof matches. If you have allergies, be sure to include your medicine, whether it's for pollen or bee stings. Sunscreen saves your skin, and insect repellent increases your comfort in many seasons. Ticks are very common; avoid contact with brush as much as possible. Check your extremities periodically and remove ticks before they bury themselves in your skin.

For expedition trips, consult mountaineering texts on survival for additional suggestions.

5. **Horses and Pack Animals.** Many of the trails in the Eastern Sierra are used by recreational horse riders and commercial pack trains, as well as cyclists and hikers. Some horses are spooked easily, so make the riders aware of your presence with a friendly greeting or a bell *well in advance of the encounter;* a startled horse can cause serious injuries to an inexperienced rider, to itself, *or to you!*

As you first become aware of an approaching horse or pack train, stop and ask the riders how they would like you to proceed. If you come upon horses moving toward you, yield the right-of-way, even when it seem inconvenient. Do not attempt to pass until you have received permission from the rider in charge. Carry your bike to the downhill side and stand quietly, well off the trail in a spot where the animals can see you clearly. If you come upon horses *moving ahead of you in the same direction,* stop well behind them. Then, pass on the downhill side of the trail, talking to the horse and rider as you do. It is your responsibility to ensure that such encounters are safe for everyone. Do not disturb grazing sheep or cattle.

6. **Respect the Environment.** Minimize your impact on the natural environment. Be sure to pack out at least as much as you packed in. Stay on established roads and trails and do not create any new ones. Practice low-impact cycling and leave plants and animals alone, historic and cultural sites untouched. Follow posted instructions and use good common sense. Do not enter private property. Remember, *mountain bikes are not allowed in Wilderness Areas and in certain other restricted areas.*

If you wish to camp, you may need a permit; contact the nearest land management agency for current information. (Please see Agencies & Resources in the Appendix.)

7. **Control and Safety.** Control your mountain bike at all times. Guard against excessive speed. To protect yourself from scrapes and impacts with rocks, dirt, and brush, wear protective gear—helmet, gloves and glasses. Avoid overheating your rims and brakes on long or steep downhill rides. Lower your center of gravity on downhills by lowering your seat. Decrease your tire pressure on rough or sandy stretches. Carry first aid supplies and bike tools for emergencies. Avoid the opening weekends of hunting and fishing season. In spring or fall, inquire at the appropriate land management agency about areas open to hunting. *Avoid solo travel in remote areas.*

It's easy to get lost. Before you leave, tell someone where you are going, when you expect to return, and what to do in case you don't return on time. Ask them to contact the County Sheriff's Department with full details about your vehicle and trip plans if you are more than six hours overdue. En route, keep track of your position on your trip map(s); record the time you arrive at a known point on the map. Look back frequently in the direction from which you came, in case you need to retrace your path. Don't be afraid to turn back when conditions change or if the going is rougher than you expected. If you find an emergency phone, dial 911 for help.

8. **Trailside Bike Repair.** Minimum equipment: pump, spare tube, patches, 2 tubes of patch glue, 6-inch adjustable wrench, Allen wrenches, chain tool and spoke wrench. Wide tires, the correct tire inflation, and avoiding rocks prevent most flats. Grease, lube, and proper adjustment prevent most mechanical failures. Frequent stream crossings wash out chain lube, so carry extra.

9. **Maps & Navigation.** Everyone who enjoys exploring by mountain bike should carry maps and a compass and know how to use them. The maps in this book are not designed for navigation, are not to scale, and should be used with U.S. Forest Service maps, U.S. Geological Survey maps (USGS topo maps) and FEP's *Eastern High Sierra Recreation Topo Map.* Please see Index to Topographical Maps, page 13. USGS has now converted its 15-minute series maps to 7.5 minute for the Eastern Sierra. In many cases, the rides in this book may require three to four topo maps. We have listed the necessary maps for expedition trips only. *Warning:* Not all the roads on the USFS maps are on the guidebook maps, and not all the roads found on the maps in this guidebook are on the USFS maps!

Studying Eastern Sierra petroglyphs

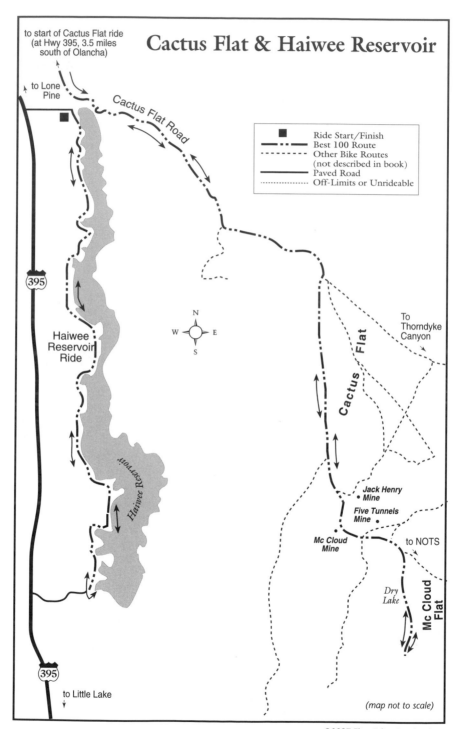

Cactus Flat & Haiwee Reservoir

to start of Cactus Flat ride
(at Hwy 395, 3.5 miles
south of Olancha)

to Lone
Pine

Cactus Flat Road

■ Ride Start/Finish
—··— Best 100 Route
········ Other Bike Routes
(not described in book)
——— Paved Road
············· Off-Limits or Unrideable

395

Haiwee
Reservoir
Ride

N
W · E
S

To
Thorndyke
Canyon

Cactus Flat

Haiwee Reservoir

Jack Henry
• Mine

Five Tunnels
Mine •

Mc Cloud
Mine

to NOTS

Dry
Lake

Mc Cloud Flat

395

to Little Lake

(map not to scale)

CHAPTER 1

Southern Inyo County

The word *Inyo* translated from the Paiute language means "dwelling place of a great spirit," and both the Inyo mountain range and the county that it borders live up to that definition. The Inyo Mountains, and their northern extension, the White Mountains, consist of high, dry peaks of complex folded and faulted rocks, some of which are more than 600 million years old. Inyo County consists of a long river valley, bordered by the Sierra Nevada on the west and the Inyo-White Mountains on the east. It is a "land of little rain" that embraces mountains, snowfields, water-carved gorges, frozen lava flows, volcanic cinder cones, marshes, ponds, and hot springs.

The dry Owens Lake bed, at the south end of the Owens Valley, is one of the most prominent geologic features of southern Inyo County. Once a vast inland sea, the lake covered over 100 square miles and was 30 feet deep when settlement of the area began in the 1860s. Owens Lake quickly became a hub of activity. Wagons full of silver from the Cerro Gordo mines in the Inyos traveled around the lake and, later, an 85-foot steamboat ferried silver from Swansea's smelter on its northeast shore to Cartago on the southwest. Water diversion by upstream farmers and ranchers began the shrinkage of Owens Lake. By the mid-1920s, after ten years of diversion by the City of Los Angeles, the lake was essentially dry.

During the late 1800s Cerro Gordo, one of the richest silver mining areas in California, helped build Los Angeles into a commercial center. Silver was transported to Los Angeles, and provisions were carried from Los Angeles to Swansea, Cartago, and Cerro Gordo. Darwin was also the site of an extensive silver mine.

Rides in southern Inyo County bring you in touch with this history. The Haiwee Reservoir ride covers a moderate route along twin reservoirs, part of the Los Angeles Aqueduct. The Darwin Loop includes historic Darwin mine and offers a side trip to beautiful, remote Darwin Canyon. The Tour de Joshua, on the west side of Death Valley National Park, features a forest-like profusion of Joshua trees—the largest continuous stand of these trees in the area. The Cerro Gordo/Swansea Loop is an expeditionary ride along the crest of the Inyo Mountains, with outstanding views of the Sierra and the Owens Valley.

Note: Some of the rides in this chapter use roads that are access corridors to wilderness areas where bicycles are not allowed. Please respect these areas. If you are interested in camping opportunities, contact the BLM prior to your ride.

1 Haiwee Reservoir Ride

Distance: 16 miles round trip.
Difficulty: Moderate, non-technical.
Elevation: Lowest point: 3,700'; highest point: 3,900'.
Type: Out-and-back on gravel road.
Season: Year-round. (You may want to avoid summer riding when temperatures soar.)
Facilities: Parking, toilets, trash cans, and a kiosk. Carry a minimum of 3–4 pints of water.
Features: Take a cool ride along the green shoreline of the twin reservoirs. Marsh birds and waterfowl are abundant, especially in fall, and views are spectacular.
Access: From the junction of Highways 395 and 190 (Death Valley Junction) in Olancha, head south for 5 miles on Highway 395. About a hundred yards after the highway becomes a divided freeway, take the first left (east) to North Haiwee Road and drive to a parking area by the reservoir.

Note: This ride crosses private property belonging to Los Angeles Department of Water and Power (DWP). Day-use is permitted. Please remain on existing roads.

Begin your ride at the entrance to the parking area at a gated road. Take this road down to Haiwee Reservoir with its shores of lush foliage. Cross a flat area near a big metal building. It is pleasantly cool here, and birds sing amid the tule and aspen. The road follows the shore south around three small coves lined with cottonwood trees. Joshua trees dot the hillsides above.

At 2.7 miles, you cross a big wash. Stay on the lakeside road as it climbs a hill. Ahead are a parking area and buildings belonging to DWP. Follow the road downhill to the parking lot and through the gate.

Haiwee Reservoir looking south

Ride to the building at the parking area exit. On the far side of the building a bridge crosses the cement aqueduct. Take this bridge and bear right on the road along the aqueduct. The road runs through a flat section between the cement riverbank and the outlet of the power station. After a couple of miles, the road cuts through a hill and away from the water for 1.5 miles. Continue toward the dam.

At 7.8 miles, the road ends at a paved road near the dam. Just to the right and up the hill is another parking area and toilets. Return the way you came for a total ride of 16 miles.

2 Cactus Flat Ride

Distance: 27.2 miles round trip.
Difficulty: Easy to moderate.
Elevation: Owens Valley floor 3,700'; Jack Henry Mine 4,800'; McCloud Flat 5,200'.
Type: Out-and-back on dirt roads.
Season: Year-round, depending on snow conditions or flash floods.
Facilities: No water. Carry several gallons in your vehicle to refill your water bottles. Primitive camping at Jack Henry Mine or along the route.
Features: Scenic high desert surrounded by mountains; beautiful stands of Joshua trees and cactus.
Access: Go 3.5 miles south of Olancha on Highway 395 to Cactus Flat Road (sign on west side of highway reads *Butterworth Ranch Rd).* Turn east onto Cactus Flat Road at the Olancha Highway Maintenance Yard and park at the side of the road.

Note: The area north of Cactus Flat lies within the Coso Wilderness. Please remain on existing roads and do not enter the wilderness.

Begin your ride from the parking spot and head east on the paved road. The pavement ends at 1.4 miles and the road turns to dirt. At 2.6 miles, you pass Haiwee Reservoir and start uphill, heading southeast. At 6.6 miles you reach the top of the hill where you have a view of Cactus Flat. Continue south on the level road among Joshua trees and cholla cactus, ignoring any trails that lead to Thorndyke Canyon.

At 9.0 miles, there are roads to the west that lead to a mine on the ridge. A mile later, a side road leads 3.5 miles up a large box canyon to the southwest. (If you feel like adding some mileage, this is an interesting side trip.)

At 10.3 miles, take the fork that heads due east to Jack Henry Mine and a primitive campsite where you can see the foundation and fireplace of an old cabin. This is a good base camp for exploring on foot or by bicycle. [**Option:** From the cabin foundation at Jack Henry Mine you can make a beautiful loop trip leading directly northeast toward Thorndyke Canyon on any of three jeep trails that lead down through Joshua trees and eventually rejoin the main road.]

The main road continues southeast toward the McCloud Flat turnoff and, although it is sometimes subject to wash-outs, preventing vehicle passage, you shouldn't have trouble negotiating it. There are excellent views of the high desert and Cactus Flat. At about 11.0 miles, a half-mile walk south up the canyon takes you to the McCloud mine where a rock cabin still stands. (Be cautious of the deep hole here.) Just past the McCloud mine, you can head northeast to the Five Tunnel Mine, then easterly up a beautiful draw. The main road continues east to a dry lake bed and the turnoff to McCloud Flat at 11.6 miles. Go south for about 2 miles to a large area of boulders.

McCloud Flat, one of the most scenic high desert areas you will find, is worth hours of exploration. The valley is entirely surrounded by desert mountains and, although extensive mining was once carried on at its north end, it is now unusually serene.

Note: The Naval Ordinance Training Station (NOTS) lies to the east; entry is prohibited. This is strictly enforced.

3 Darwin Loop

Distance: 35.5 miles.
Difficulty: A strenuous, technical expedition.
Elevation: Start: 4,000'; Darwin: 4,746'; highest point: 4,975'.
Type: Loop ride on paved road, graded road, and jeep roads.
Season: Spring, fall and winter. Due to elevated temperatures, riding in summer is not recommended. Occasional flash floods thunder down Darwin Wash, so avoid this ride in unsettled weather.
Topo maps: (7.5-minute series) Talc City Hills; Darwin.
Facilities: Museum (not always open) and water available in Darwin. Carry minimum of 3-4 pints of water with you.
Features: See the historic Darwin silver mine where dozens of buildings still stand. Huge piles of tailing stand as a testament to the trainloads of silver ore, zinc, lead, and other minerals that were shipped from this once-busy mine. Darwin Canyon contains fantastic rock formations and several mines. An optional side trip to China Spring features goldfish, shady cottonwoods, ruins and mines. Darwin Falls is a beautiful oasis with diverse plant and bird life, gorgeous rock slabs, and a swimming hole at the base of the falls.
Access: From the Interagency Visitor Center at the south end of Lone Pine, go east on Highway 136. Continue 7 miles to its junction with Highway 190. Go east on Highway 190 for 26 miles to Darwin Road on the right. Park off the road by the historic marker. Please cycle on existing roads.

Start your ride at the junction of Darwin Road and Highway 190. Ride south on the paved Darwin Road up a long, straight incline to an obvious saddle. Look carefully and you will see an old railroad grade and the ruins of several mines.

At the crest (4,975'), you can see down into Darwin Basin with the Coso Range behind it. Drop into the desert basin and enjoy a mild climb. At 5.0 miles you come to the main entrance to Darwin mine. This is *private property.* Please keep out.

The road continues into "downtown" Darwin. The museum is quite interesting when you can gain access. Darwin is home to a number of people, so please remain on the roads and keep off private property.

Your route goes left at the T-intersection. Take a broken pavement road steeply up to a gap in the ridge. At the crest you can see Darwin Canyon and the Coso Mountains. You then continue downhill for three miles, passing mines, ruins, a water pipe, and wrecked cars.

Desert vegetation along the Darwin Loop

At 9.8 miles the road joins a sandy route in the wash. Go left down the Darwin wash where the rock is fantastic. You pass some mines and a ranch with several water tanks; scraps of wood and metal are scattered everywhere. Continue past two small side canyons as you ride down Darwin Wash. At 12.3 miles, the road climbs a side canyon.

[**Side trip:** A road left leads down the canyon to China Springs from where a stream flows to Darwin Falls. Mileage for this side trip is not included.]

Continue up and out of Darwin Canyon, climbing steeply onto a ridge where, at the crest, you have a great view of Darwin Canyon, the Darwin Hills, and old mines.

The road is steep, stony, and rutted on the downhill section—a technical descent that you may want to walk. There are occasional overlooks into Darwin Canyon along this section, and the mill and mine near the road are interesting ruins. An old wagon road with handmade stone

walls parallels the route.

At the bottom of the downhill, back in Darwin Canyon, a spur road on the left leads to a parking area from where a difficult but fascinating hike of 1.5 miles takes you to Darwin Falls. Although this area seems too remote to worry, lock up your bike before hiking to the falls.

For the main bicycle route, continue on the dirt road 1.5 miles to Highway 190, where you turn left onto the pavement. This fantastic road climbs for several steep miles around endless curves, circling higher and higher and rewarding you with ever-expanding views of Panamint Valley. The colorful rock is strangely shaped, and Joshua trees and cactus dot the landscape. The brutal ascent is offset by the beauty of the mountains, valleys, and canyons. Near the crest of the hard climb, stop at Father Crowley Overlook to look out over brilliant Rainbow Canyon and Panamint Valley. The overlook honors Father J. J. Crowley, a Jesuit, known as the

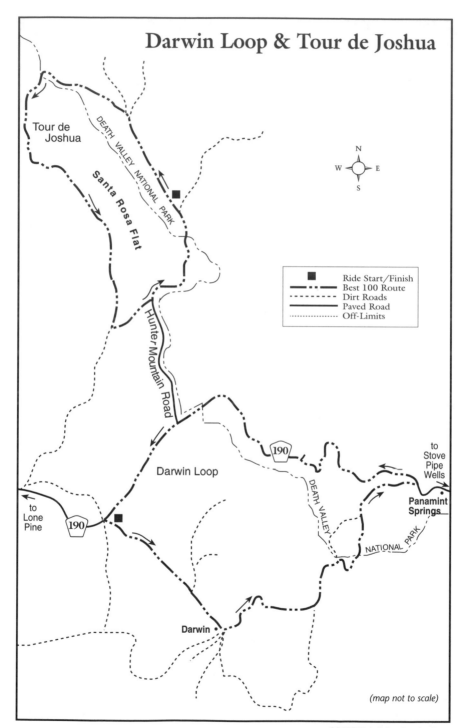

Darwin Loop & Tour de Joshua

Tour de Joshua

Santa Rosa Flat

DEATH VALLEY NATIONAL PARK

Hunter Mountain Road

N
W E
S

■ Ride Start/Finish
▬▬▬ Best 100 Route
‑‑‑‑ Dirt Roads
▬▬▬ Paved Road
········ Off-Limits

190

Darwin Loop

DEATH VALLEY

to
Stove
Pipe
Wells

Panamint Springs

to
Lone
Pine

190

NATIONAL PARK

Darwin

(map not to scale)

Eastern Sierra's traveling priest (1930s and '40s).

Past the overlook the road is less steep. The curving road traverses the Darwin Hills and climbs across a high desert basin. You pass Saline Valley Road junction on your right, climb to a crest on Highway 190, and continue downhill to Darwin Junction—a total of 35.5 miles.

4 Tour de Joshua Loop

Distance: 21.6 miles.
Difficulty: Moderately difficult; minimally technical.
Elevation: Starting point: 1,500'; highest point: 1,850'.
Type: Loop ride on gravel roads and jeep roads.
Season: Year-round.
Topo maps: (7.5-minute series) Santa Rosa Flat; Lee Wash; Jackass Canyon; Harris Hill.
Facilities: None. Carry at least 2 quarts of water.
Features: Two spectacular high desert basins with views of the Inyo and Coso mountain ranges. The desert flora includes a vast forest of Joshua trees, cacti, and spring wildflowers.
Access: From the Interagency Visitor Center at the south end of Lone Pine, go east on Highway 136 seven miles to Highway 190. Continue east on Highway 190 for 30 miles to Hunter Mountain Road. Go left on this broken pavement road, follow it across the desert basin for 8 miles to a Y-junction and park. Please stay on existing roads.

Begin the Tour de Joshua at the Y-junction. The Joshua trees throughout this area, larger than most, look like something from a Dr. Seuss book. These bizarre-looking trees bloom with brilliant white flowers in spring. The seed pods, about 3 inches long and resembling small coconuts, prompted early miners to call them palmettos.

Santa Rita Flat, Tour de Joshua

View north of Hunter Mountain

Take the left gravel road that heads north through the Joshua tree forest and a broad basin, Lee Flat. The road runs straight for about 3.5 miles. Continue on the wide graded road as it curves and ascends to the north end of the basin. The Joshua trees thin out as the road heads toward Cerro Gordo Peak.

At the junction at 6.7 miles, take a narrower road to the left up a small drainage toward the Inyo Mountains. In a mile there is a split in the canyon and the road forks. Take the left fork, where a sign marks the road, up the drainage and into a pinyon forest. In a quarter-mile there is a third junction. Take a left here also and follow an unlikely jeep road, signed 1S88, that leads up a dry gully through the pinyon trees toward a saddle.

At 8.2 miles you come to the crest of the saddle and the high point of the ride. Across a basin there are views of the Coso and Inyo mountains. The jeep road now makes a long, gradual descent in a gully through juniper and pinyon. The road is faint in many places, but signs assure you of the route. The wash leads into the desert basin and returns to the Joshua trees. As it continues down the wash across the broad basin of twisted trees, the road is very bad. Cacti and flowers grow amid the Joshua trees as you parallel a long, low ridge for miles. Continue past a spot where the road splits, then rejoins a bit farther on.

At 16.4 miles, the jeep road ends at a graded road near the center of the vast basin. Go left and take the road toward a low ridge. A road ahead runs along the base of that ridge. In 2 miles you come to a junction with a broken pavement road (the road on which you came in). Go left again.

Follow the road over the crest of the ridge and down into another basin. The road climbs to a second saddle and drops into Lee Flat. Follow it back to the Y-junction and the start of your ride for a total of 21.6 miles.

5 Cerro Gordo/ Swansea Loop

Distance: 33.5 miles.
Difficulty: Extreme; expeditionary. An overnight stay breaks the ride into two difficult days; a one-day ride demands extremely difficult riding.
Elevation: Owens Valley floor: 3,600'; Cerro Gordo: 8,400'; highest point: 9,400'.
Type: Loop on jeep roads with a pavement finish.
Season: Spring, summer, and fall. Avoid in unsettled weather.
Topo maps: ((7.5-minute series) Cerro Gordo Peak; Dolomite.
Facilities: None. Be totally self-sufficient. Carry a minimum of 3-4 pints of water.
Features: This ride features a challenging and incredibly scenic traverse of the southern Inyo Mountains. The Saline Valley Salt Tram, completed in 1913, was an engineering marvel, carrying salt from evaporators at Saline Dry Lake, at about 1,000 feet, to the station in the gap, 8,800 feet, then down to Swansea in the Owens Valley at 4,000 feet. Materials for dozens of towers were packed in by mule and the towers were built by hand. Salt was the only food preservative in use at the time, and government price supports helped keep this operation afloat. Cerro Gordo is one of the best preserved ghost towns in California; many historic mine buildings, hotels, and stores still stand. To inquire about a tour, contact Jodi Stewart at 760-876-4154. (See Appendix for additional information.)
Access: Take Highway 395 south of Lone Pine; turn east on Highway 136 and go about 11 miles to Keeler. Park near the Cerro Gordo historic marker on the highway. Please remain on existing roads.

From the historic marker, bike up the road to the base of the mountains. The road takes you up the Yellow Grade (named for the color of the rocks), following the towers of the old salt tram. This steep, relentless climb curves up and around the side of the mountain. You pass hundreds of mine pits as you climb, and some sections of the

Sunrise on Mount Whitney

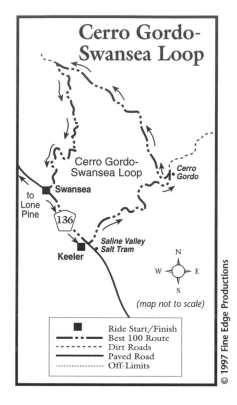

Cerro Gordo-Swansea Loop

to Lone Pine

Swansea

136

Keeler

Saline Valley Salt Tram

Cerro Gordo

Cerro Gordo-Swansea Loop

N
W — E
S

(map not to scale)

■ Ride Start/Finish
▬ ▬ Best 100 Route
‑ ‑ ‑ ‑ Dirt Roads
▬▬▬ Paved Road
⋯⋯⋯ Off-Limits

© 1997 Fine Edge Productions

good view of Cerro Gordo.

Follow the road as it contours around the peak. Spectacular views of Owens Lake, more than a vertical mile below you, reveal fantastic colors that vary with the salt concentrations in the lake—from brilliant reds and purples to light blue or dazzling white. Continue on the shale road to the first saddle at 9.0 miles.

> *Note:* Once you leave the shale section of the road and climb out of the ravine, this road becomes an access corridor, bisecting the Inyo Wilderness all the way to Swansea. The wilderness boundary parallels the road at a distance of 30 feet from the centerline of the road, creating, in effect, a 60-foot-wide corridor where mountain bikes and vehicles are allowed to traverse. Mountain bikes and vehicles are limited to the main road. Although there are many lateral roads that take off from the main road, entry on these roads is restricted to foot travel.

original, steeper road are visible. The final approach rounds several steep switchbacks. The ghost town of Cerro Gordo lies in a saddle at the crest of the Inyo Mountains, 7 road miles and 5,000 feet up from Keeler. From Cerro Gordo, you can see the towers of the old salt tram most of the way back down to Keeler.

Continue through the old town 200 yards above the museum and turn left, passing a private property sign. About fifty yards beyond the sign, turn left (west) onto a faintly visible jeep road and go a quarter mile to a gate where a weathered BLM sign reads *Swansea/Cerro Gordo Road, Caution Dangerous grades, 4WD only, do not disturb mining facilities, Salt Tram, or cut any trees.* Keep the gate closed. From this point you have a

Stay on the main road that heads left and down into the canyon, dropping 500 feet. Then take a sharp right and climb a ravine. At 11.5 miles the road crests a second saddle and traverses the east side of the ridge; you can see Saline Valley and Saline Dry Lake 7,000 feet below you to the east. The road then crosses back to the west side of the ridge where you again have a view of Owens Dry Lake and the Sierra. At 13.1 miles and 9,400-foot elevation, you arrive at Pleasant Peak.

From Pleasant Peak the road contours down to a knife-edge ridge with incredible views in both directions. The road descends gradually to the

Whitney Portal

low part of the saddle and the salt tram at 15.3 miles. If you want to explore the many bits and pieces of the tram, please leave your bicycle at the side of the road and proceed on foot. Be cautious and do not disturb this historic site.

Back on your bike, continue northwest along the ridge. The road descends gradually through a small saddle then follows the ridge to a junction where you take the right. At 17.7 miles you come to a second junction. Take the left-hand road toward Swansea which crosses the ridge again with even more panoramic views.

At 20 miles you begin a steep, technical, and dangerous downhill. *Be cautious. If you have any doubts about your ability to control your downhill speed, walk.* If you have a problem or are on your own, it could be weeks before anyone found you here. Even with friends who could go in search of an ambulance, this could turn out to be an expensive ride!

You now leave the Inyo Crest and head south down the small ridge to the west. At 22.0 miles the road descends a ravine. Walk a washed out section along the bottom of this ravine. In another mile, you drop into the creek bed. (This downhill seems endless.) Pass under the salt tram at about 24.4 miles.

At 26.8 miles the road goes up and out of the wash, passing a tram tower. At 27.7 miles a jeep road offers a side trip of about a mile to a transfer station with good views of the Owens Valley.

Follow the main road down the ridge. At 28.9 miles the road drops into a steep, rocky canyon, then climbs an even steeper side canyon. In a half-mile you cross under the salt tram again. Below there is a series of dry waterfalls. You pass under the tram one last time as the canyon opens up onto the alluvial fan back to Highway 136. When you reach Swansea at 32.8 miles, take a left and head south on the paved road to Keeler at mile 33.5.

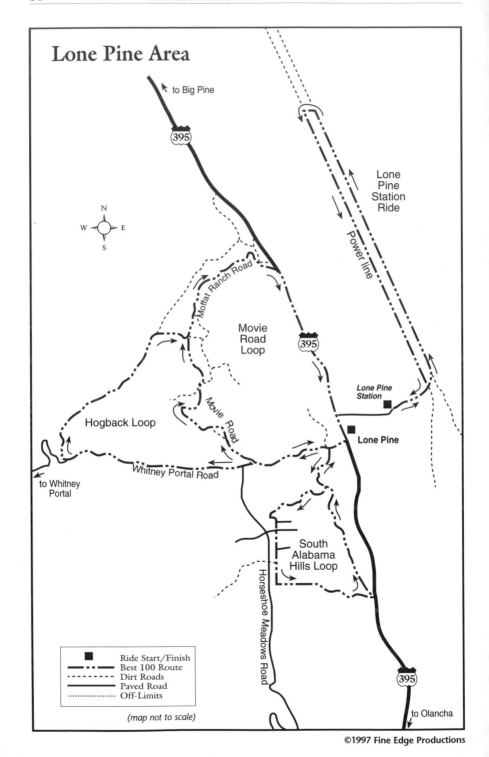

Lone Pine Area

to Big Pine

395

Lone Pine Station Ride

Power line

Moffat Ranch Road

Movie Road Loop

395

Lone Pine Station

Movie Road

Hogback Loop

Lone Pine

Whitney Portal Road

to Whitney Portal

South Alabama Hills Loop

Horseshoe Meadows Road

■   Ride Start/Finish
—··— Best 100 Route
······ Dirt Roads
——   Paved Road
·········· Off-Limits

(map not to scale)

395

to Olancha

©1997 Fine Edge Productions

CHAPTER 2

Lone Pine

Lone Pine, the second largest town in Inyo County, is the gateway to Mount Whitney, the highest peak in the 48 States. In its past, Lone Pine was the supply center for many area mines. Nearly leveled in the powerful earthquake of 1872, only seven buildings remained standing. The quake created numerous scarps—short cliffs formed by vertical faulting, a tidal wave on Owens Lake, and avalanches in the Sierra. Springs dried up, new ones were created, and Diaz Lake was born. At the north edge of town you can visit a mass grave and memorial on top of a small ridge that is the earthquake fault.

West of Lone Pine, blocks of granite, separated and rounded by millions of years of weathering, form the Alabama Hills, used extensively as movie backgrounds, especially western films.

Ranching has been continuous in this area for over a century, and ranchers and packers have been here for a long time. Please show respect by yielding to horses and by being courteous and pleasant.

photo courtesy BLM

Alabama Hills, Lone Pine, California

1 South Alabama Hills Loop

Distance: 14 miles.
Difficulty: Moderate.
Elevation: Lowest point: 3,700'; highest point: 4,800'.
Type: Loop ride on paved roads and dirt roads.
Season: Year-round.
Facilities: All amenities available in Lone Pine. Carry at least 2 quarts of water.
Features: There are fantastic, extensive views of the Sierra south to Owens Dry Lake.
Access: This ride begins at the junction of Whitney Portal Road and Highway 395 (traffic light) in Lone Pine.

Take Whitney Portal Road a half-mile west and go left on Tuttle Creek Road past Portagi Joe County Campground. Parallel the Los Angeles Aqueduct along the base of the Alabama Hills.

Cross the aqueduct and ascend the slit of a canyon in the rough, weathered Alabama Hills. Cross Tuttle Creek and climb a series of steep curves out of the drainage. Dramatic views of the Sierra open as the road curves past a subdivision and onto a wide, paved road.

At 5.9 miles, Tuttle Creek Road ends at Lubkin Canyon Road, where you turn left and head downhill. The road runs between two fences, then down to wide meadows at the south end of the Alabama Hills. Descend along Lubkin Creek to the Los Angeles Aqueduct, a dramatic contrast to the endless high desert.

Just past the aqueduct, take a left onto a rough jeep road, head north across a gully, and continue over a mild rise. Take a right where the road forks and head downhill toward Lone Pine. Just before Highway 395, go left through a green gate, past a wooden platform. Follow the dirt road north, parallel to the aqueduct.

On the west side of Diablo Lake, cross a small creek. Follow the road for several miles paralleling the power line and the aqueduct. Pass behind the golf course to the road's end at Tuttle Creek Road. Turn right on Tuttle Creek Road, and right again on Whitney Portal Road downhill to Lone Pine and your starting point.

2 Movie Road Loop

Distance: 17 miles.
Difficulty: Moderate.
Elevation: Lowest point: 3,700'; highest point: 5,000'.
Type: Loop ride on paved and gravel roads.
Season: Year-round.
Facilities: All amenities available in Lone Pine. Carry plenty of water.
Features: The Alabama Hills, a fantastic, rocky maze, have served as locations for many movies. Give yourself time to explore the many side roads in this maze. There are great views of Mount Whitney.
Access: Start at the junction of Whitney Portal Road and Highway 395 (traffic light) in downtown Lone Pine.

Alabama Hills—Mount Whitney

From the junction, head west on Whitney Portal Road, past the Los Angeles Aqueduct, up a small canyon in the Alabama Hills, and alongside Lone Pine Creek.

At the top of the canyon, Mount Whitney comes into view. You will see a parking area and brass plaque on the right at 3.0 miles. Turn right here at the wooden sign marking Movie Road. The colorful, weathered rock formations form a maze for miles, and many of the dead-end roads invite exploration.

Head north, paralleling the main ridges. Climb over a gap and past a wide pullout. The road gradually climbs in a series of dips and rolls. A gap in the Alabama Hills offers a great view of the Inyo Mountains.

At 6.6 miles, you crest a saddle at the highest point of the ride. Twin buttes are on your left and you can see where the outwash from the Sierra has almost buried the Alabama Hills. Continue down the wide grav-el road, passing another gap that allows views of the Inyos. Ignore the road to the right and continue downhill toward the north end of the Alabama Hills where you can see Hogback Road below.

At 8.4 miles, Movie Road ends at Hogback Road.

At the intersection of Movie Road and Hogback Road go left downhill alongside the creek. When you reach Moffat Ranch Road, veer left again. The road runs between the Alabama Hills and the meadows of the creek bottom—a green strip in stark contrast to the vast high desert.

The road ends at a junction with a broken pavement road. Go right onto this road and immediately cross the Los Angeles Aqueduct. The road parallels the aqueduct and Highway 395 for 0.75 mile where you make a quick left to the highway.

Go right on Highway 395. The Alabama Hills are on your right; to the left is a vast marsh, a reserve for tule elk. Ride on the wide shoulder for 3.3 miles to the edge of Lone Pine and the historical marker for the victims of the 1872 earthquake. The 15-foot-high ridge at the site is the fault scarp; a short trail leads to the mass grave.

Continue south on Highway 395 into Lone Pine, past the City Park to your starting point.

3 Hogback Loop

Distance: 22.2 miles.
Difficulty: Strenuous and minimally technical.
Elevation: Lowest point: 3,700'; highest point: 6,450'.
Type: Loop ride on pavement and gravel roads.
Season: Year-round.
Facilities: All amenities in Lone Pine. Carry 2 quarts of water or more.
Features: A challenging loop that tours the Alabama Hills and passes a memorial to the victims of the 1872 Earthquake.
Access: Start at the junction of Whitney Portal Road and Highway 395 (traffic light) in downtown Lone Pine.

From the starting point, go west on Whitney Portal Road, crossing the Los Angeles Aqueduct before entering a small canyon into the Alabama Hills. The road follows the creek where fantastic weathered granite surrounds you. Where the canyon opens up, there is a natural amphitheater to the right.

Continue up the road toward the Sierra, past Movie Road and Tuttle Creek Road. You can soon see switchbacks winding uphill toward Whitney Portal.

A long, steep climb up the alluvial plain leads past the Cuffe Ranch and around granite knolls. Stay on the paved road to Lone Pine Creek Campground at 7.0 miles. Cross the wash of Lone Pine Creek and begin the brutal climb toward the canyon.

Just before you reach the switchbacks there is a wide gravel road to the right (north)—Hogback Road—marked by a sign that reads *Not recommended for Trailers*. Turn right onto Hogback and drop down into the trees where you have magnificent views of Owens Valley. The road descends the crest of a lateral moraine, "the Hogback." Enjoy this long, beautiful downhill across wide-open high desert.

You parallel willow-lined Hogback Creek for miles, passing several camps along the creek. At a small depression, you pass a dirt road to the left, curve right on the graded road and head for the Alabama Hills.

At the intersection of Movie Road and Hogback Road (13.7 miles), go left downhill alongside the creek. When you reach Moffat Ranch Road, veer left again. The road runs between the Alabama Hills and the meadows of the creek bottom—a green strip in stark contrast to the vast high desert.

At 17.1 miles, the road ends at a junction with a broken pavement road. Go right onto this road and immediately cross the Los Angeles Aqueduct. The road parallels the aqueduct and Highway 395 for 0.75 mile where you make a quick left to the highway.

Go right on Highway 395. The Alabama Hills are on your right; to the left is a vast marsh, a reserve for tule elk. Ride on the wide shoulder for 3.3 miles to the edge of Lone Pine and the historical marker for the victims of the 1872 earthquake. The 15-foot-high ridge at the site is the fault scarp; a short trail leads to the mass grave.

Continue south on Highway 395 into Lone Pine, past the City Park to your starting point.

Mass Grave, 1872 Earthquake, Lone Pine

4 Lone Pine Station Ride

Distance: 20 miles.
Difficulty: Long, moderate, flat ride.
Elevation: 3,700'.
Type: Loop ride on dirt roads and parallel to an historic railroad grade.
Season: Year-round.
Facilities: All amenities available in Lone Pine.
Features: Visit the Lone Pine Station on the grade of the old Southern Pacific Railroad, the center of transportation in Owens Valley before the turn of the century. The Carson and Colorado Railroad ran from Carson City, Nevada, to Keeler on the shores of Owens Lake. In about 1900, a Quaker colony was established at Owenyo. Although the Quakers built 42 miles of canals on their 13,000 acres, they were among the first to sell their property to Los Angeles City. In 1910, when the Southern Pacific Railroad built a branch from Mojave to Owens Valley, Owenyo was the junction point for the standard and narrow gauge lines. During the period when Los Angeles hauled materials for the aqueduct, Owenyo was a busy settlement.
Access: From the City Park at the north end of Lone Pine, head north on Highway 395 for a half-mile. Go right (east) on the Lone Pine Narrow Gauge Road, take a sharp left, then a quick right. Park here off the road. On the left is Lone Pine Station.

Lone Pine Station

The ride begins at the Station. You are welcome to park, but please respect this private residence. Take the paved road east, over Owens River bridge, cross the flat, and ride past a radar installation.

At a Y-junction, take the paved road to the left. Go right at the second junction and follow this to a third T-junction at a gravel road. This was the site of the Mt. Whitney Station (the Lone Pine stop) on the Carson and Colorado narrow-gauge railroad.

Go left onto the county road and head north. As you roll along past a couple of old ranch sites and mines, the county road and railroad grade trade sides. Please remain on the county road.

At 5.3 miles you come to the extensive ruins of Owenyo Station where the two railroads joined. There are many foundations and ruins, as well as a long pit with rows of pilings—the elevated track where cars of the narrow-gauge railroad transferred ore into standard-gauge railroad cars for shipment to Los Angeles.

Continue north along the increasingly sandy county road. The railroad grade is almost nonexistent at this point. Keep heading north past several mines and some low dunes. Cross a big ditch.

At 10 miles you come to a wide gravel road and the site of Manzanar Station, an area famous for its apples around the turn of the 19th Century. Take a left turn and head west toward the Sierra. In a quarter-mile, take a second left and follow the power line south.

Follow the power lines parallel to the Owens River for 8 miles along the river. There are marshy areas covered with tule. Keep a sharp eye out for tule elk. You cross the old Southern Pacific Railroad grade near Owenyo Station. At 18.3 miles, turn right at a paved road. Ride past the radar installation, across the Owens River, and back to your starting point at Lone Pine Station.

CHAPTER 3

Independence

Camp Independence, originally established by the U.S. Cavalry on July 4, 1862 at a site north of town, is now an Indian Reservation. The area was the focus of fighting between U.S. troops and the Paiutes, and the town later took its name from the camp.

Independence has been the Inyo County seat for 125 years. It is one of the most historic towns in the Owens Valley, boasting many well-preserved buildings over a century old. It is also the home of the Eastern California Museum which features natural and cultural history of the area. The museum houses one of the finest collections of Paiute and Shoshone artifacts, mementos of the area's pioneers, and an exhibit chronicling the story of the World War II Manzanar Relocation Camp. Outdoor displays include a Paiute dwelling, a reconstructed pioneer town, antique wagons, tractors and mining implements. There is also a nature walk that interprets the Indian culture which once thrived along Independence Creek.

View of Sierra from valley floor, Independence

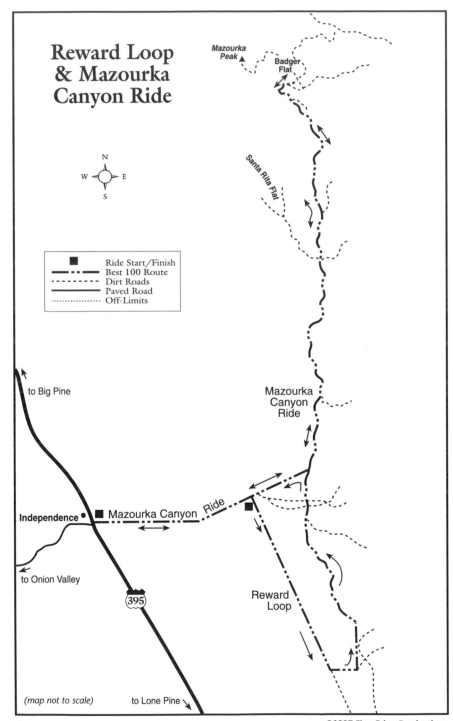

Reward Loop
& Mazourka
Canyon Ride

Mazourka
Peak

Badger
Flat

Santa Rita Flat

N
W · E
S

■   Ride Start/Finish
▬·▬·▬   Best 100 Route
--------- Dirt Roads
━━━━   Paved Road
········· Off-Limits

to Big Pine

Mazourka
Canyon
Ride

Independence ● ■ Mazourka Canyon Ride

to Onion Valley

⑳ 395

Reward
Loop

(map not to scale)   to Lone Pine

©1997 Fine Edge Productions

The five rides described in this chapter reflect the rich history of the area. Tinemaha and Taboose Creek Loops, west of Highway 395, lead through lava flows and cinder cones. East, of Highway 395, you can ride along the old narrow-gauge railroad on the Reward Loop, or take an expedition ride up Mazourka Canyon into the mining past of the Inyos. The Independence Historical Tour is an easy ride that leads past a number of historical buildings. [Not listed is a scenic and challenging road ride, 17 steep miles up Onion Valley Road to the alpine zone of the Sierra. Start at the flashing light in town.]

Some rides in this chapter use roads that are access corridors to wilderness areas where bicycles are not allowed. Please respect these areas. If interested in camping opportunities, contact BLM prior to your ride.

1 Reward Loop

Distance: 12 miles.
Difficulty: Easy and flat.
Elevation: 3,800'.
Type: Loop on railroad grade, dirt and gravel, and an old irrigation ditch.
Season: Year-round.
Facilities: None. Carry a minimum of 3-4 pints of water.
Features: Ride alongside the historic Carson and Colorado grade from the site of Kearsarge Station to Reward Station and the site of the Reward and Brown Monster Mines. The Reward produced small amounts of gold, silver and lead, while the Brown Monster, once known as The Eclipse, may have been the earliest mine located in Owens Valley. The return leads along the Owenyo ditch, an irrigation project built by the Quakers at the turn of the century.
Access: Start at the south end of Independence at the junction of Highway 395 and Mazourka Canyon Road (Citrus Road on some maps). Park well off the highway. Remain on existing roads at all times.

Start at the end of the pavement on Mazourka Canyon Road. Several foundations mark the site of the Kearsarge Railroad Station. Follow the dirt county road, which parallels the Carson-Colorado grade, south across the desert with the Inyo Mountains towering above you to the east. This is an easy-going ride except for a couple of small washouts.

At 4.9 miles you come to a wide gravel road across the old railroad grade, the site of Reward, from where—in the 1860s—ore from the Reward Mine was shipped to Carson City. Take a left toward the big mine

and a three-way junction.

[**Side trip:** Take one of two roads on the right that loop to the Reward Mine—a 1.3-mile side trip.]

To continue, take a left and ride along the base of the Inyos past the remains of several ranches. Rows of stumps are signs of the Quaker Colony founded here at the beginning of the 20th Century. Try to imagine this sparse desert once as green as Bishop.

At 7.0 miles, you begin to follow the Owenyo Canal which contours across the base of alluvial fans. The road crosses the ditch and continues north. Part of the road lies within the old canal and can be very sandy at times.

At 9.4 miles the road leaves the ditch and heads toward the crest of an alluvial wash. Continue northeast toward the base of the Inyo Mountains.

At 10.6 miles you reach a gravel road at the Monte Verde Mill— *Private Property—keep out!* Go left toward a small hill.

In about a mile and a half you reach Mazourka Canyon Road. Take a left and head downhill to Kearsarge Station and the start of your ride.

2 Independence Historical Tour

Distance: 1.5 miles.
Difficulty: Easy and flat.
Elevation: 3,900'.
Type: A short road ride.
Season: Year-round.
Facilities: Some amenities available in Independence.
Features: This short ride features several historic buildings in the town of Independence: the Mary Austin Home, Fort Independence Hospital, and Commander's House, which was moved from Camp Independence. The oldest house in the county dates to 1865 and others date to the 1880s. The historic Slim Princess locomotive, the Winnedumah Hotel, Elks Hall, and County Courthouse are all located along Highway 395. The Pioneer Church and the Eastern Sierra Museum round out the ride. Before or after your ride, take time to visit the museum.
Access: In Independence, turn west on Center Street and drive a couple of blocks to the end of the road and the Eastern Sierra Museum and parking. A map published by the museum serves as a guide for this ride.

Mary Austin home, Independence

Begin by riding a block back on Center Street toward the County Courthouse on Highway 395. Go right on Webster Street for one block, then left on Market Street.

On the corner is the Mary Austin Home. Mary Austin was a naturalist who wrote several books about the desert. She was observant and intuitive, blending history, ecology, and geology into a portrait of the Owens Valley in her best-known book, *Land of Little*

Rain. Her house is now a private home.

Continue east on Market Street, then right on Washington Street. Go south one block to Kearsarge and turn left. On your left is a big white house, once the Fort Independence hospital, now a private home. Take the next left off Kearsarge, a narrow alley, ride one block north back to Market Street, and turn right.

On the corner is the Edwards House, the oldest structure—just a

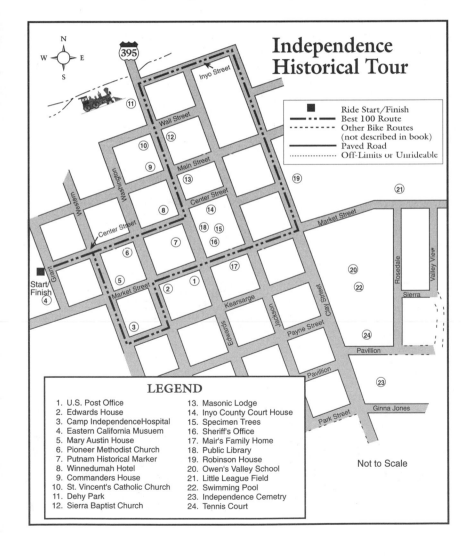

Independence Historical Tour

■ Ride Start/Finish
━ ･ ━ ･ ━ Best 100 Route
- - - - - Other Bike Routes
(not described in book)
━━━━━ Paved Road
⋯⋯⋯⋯ Off-Limits or Unrideable

LEGEND

1. U.S. Post Office
2. Edwards House
3. Camp IndependenceHospital
4. Eastern California Musuem
5. Mary Austin House
6. Pioneer Methodist Church
7. Putnam Historical Marker
8. Winnedumah Hotel
9. Commanders House
10. St. Vincent's Catholic Church
11. Dehy Park
12. Sierra Baptist Church

13. Masonic Lodge
14. Inyo County Court House
15. Specimen Trees
16. Sheriff's Office
17. Mair's Family Home
18. Public Library
19. Robinson House
20. Owen's Valley School
21. Little League Field
22. Swimming Pool
23. Independence Cemetery
24. Tennis Court

Not to Scale

small shack—in Inyo County. A marker here tells how the original owner laid out the streets of Independence when it became the county seat in 1866; the cottage was built a year earlier.

Next, continue east on Market Street past the Post Office which was once a bank. Cross Highway 395 and pass the Sheriff's Office. Half a block beyond is a mustard-colored house— the Mairs Home—built in the 1880s and now a private home.

Go east on Market Street to the school, then left on Clay Street for two blocks to the Robinson House. This large two-story home, built in the 1880s, is partially made from wood taken from Camp Independence. Follow Clay Street to its end on Inyo Street, go left to Highway 395 and cross to the City Park where the *Slim Princess* locomotive sits. This narrow gauge train ran up and down

Owens Valley from Carson City to Keeler shipping trainloads of ore and produce from mines and farms along this route for over 30 years. Later a rail line from the south operated along parts of the old track until the 1950s.

Along Highway 395 are several other historic buildings. The Commander's House, moved from Fort Independence, dates from the early 1870s. Nearby Elks Hall is a late 1800s building, and the Winnedumah Inn, an impressive building, still operates as a bed-and-breakfast. The courthouse on the east side of Highway 395, built in the 1930s, is the third since 1866—the previous two were destroyed in earthquakes.

Take Center Street west of Highway 395 one block to view Pioneer Church; the main building dates to the late 1870s. Follow Center Street back to the Eastern Sierra Museum, the end of your ride.

Owens Valley and Inyo Mountains, Independence

3 Mazourka Canyon Ride

Distance: 36 miles round trip.
Difficulty: A strenuous ride into the remote Inyo Mountains.
Elevation: Lowest point: 3,900'; highest point: 9,000'.
Type: Out-and-back on good dirt roads and jeep roads, with many optional side trips.
Season: Spring, summer, and fall; lower elevations are possible in winter.
Facilities: Some amenities available in Independence. Carry at least 2 quarts of water.
Features: Ride from the desert floor of the Owens Valley to the alpine meadows at the crest of the Inyos. Many mines, located in this area, provide opportunities for side trips if you want to see them. Please stay off posted property.
Access: Start at the south end of Independence at the junction of Highway 395 and Mazourka Canyon Road (Citrus Road on some maps). Park well off the highway. Remain on existing roads at all times.

Head due east on Mazourka Canyon Road. Just beyond the Los Angeles Aqueduct at 1.9 miles, the road drops down a 15-foot fault scarp formed by the 1872 earthquake. Cross the Owens River at 3.8 miles. At 4.4. miles, the pavement changes to gravel. Cross the old Carson & Colorado railroad right-of-way where Kearsarge Station once stood. Climb an alluvial fan eastward, then head north on a well-graded gravel road and begin your climb.

[**Side trips:** At 5.8 miles, the Snow Cap Mine Road goes off to the left. The mine is about 7 miles away. At 7.2 miles, the Copper Queen Mine is to the west. At 8.3 miles, Lead Gulch Road (with gate) leads east for several miles to the Betty Jumbo Mine at 7,500 feet.]

Short of 9 miles, you enter Inyo National Forest. At 9.3 miles, pass Squares Tunnel and two cabins east of the road. Paiute Monument (also called Winnedumah), an 8,369-foot granite monolith, lies 3 miles due east along the Inyo Ridge.

At 11.7 miles, you pass some houses, mining equipment, water tank, and wrecked cars. *This is private property; do not enter.* At 12.1 miles,

cross a cattle guard and go 0.2 mile to a sign: *Santa Rita Flat to the left. Badger Flat straight ahead.*

[**Side trip:** At this point you can add a loop west to Santa Rita Flat, rejoin your ride, then continue to Badger Flat. About 14 miles long, this loop is not included in total mileage.]

As you continue on your ride, Sunday Canyon enters from the west at 12.8 miles. You pass a seldom-used jeep road on the right, staying left on the main road that enters Rose Canyon.

At Pop's Gulch, 14.3 miles, a gravel road offers an additional route to Santa Rita Flat. At 18 miles, you reach Badger Flat, a large, bowl-shaped area surrounded by tree-covered ridges where mining and hunting trails lead off in many directions. In the spring, this area is bright with wildflowers.

[**Side trips:** Tamarack Canyon trail leads 3 miles east to the north side of an unnamed peak, elevation 10,724 feet. From the east side of Badger Flat, you can head northwest to the Blue Bell Mine complex, 1.5 miles.]

For your return, retrace the route, controlling your speed and guarding against heat buildup on your brakes and rims. The trail descends nearly 5,000 feet in one swoop!

4 Taboose Creek Loop

Distance: 12.5 miles.
Difficulty: Difficult, strenuous, and technical.
Elevation: Lowest point: 3,800'; highest point: 5,861'.
Type: Loop ride on pavement, dirt road, and jeep road.
Season: Spring, summer, and fall.
Facilities: Parking, phone, store, water and a cafe at Aberdeen.
Features: A challenging ride through a fascinating volcanic area with views of the Sierra, Inyo Mountains, and Owens Valley. Aberdeen was once a stop on the Owens Valley stage route.
Access: From Independence, take Highway 395 north about 15 miles. Turn left on Goodale Creek Road and continue one mile to the junction with Tinemaha Road. Turn left (west) and go 100 yards. Park near the Aberdeen store/restaurant, being careful not to block access.

From the four-way stop at Aberdeen, go north on Tinemaha Road toward the Poverty Hills along old highway 395. Cross under two big power lines and continue north toward a line of trees.

At 1.4 miles you cross a bridge in Taboose Creek Campground. Continue north 0.75 mile to Taboose Creek Road, then turn left and head uphill toward the Sierra, paralleling Taboose Creek. Stay on the graded road.

As you climb, there are expanding views of the eerie volcanic landscape. Red Mountain, to the north, has extensive lava flows. To the south are several cinder cones and a massive lava field. Taboose Creek crosses a big alluvial fan between the two lava flows.

At 2.7 miles you cross a gate and enter BLM land. Take a left at the next junction and follow the jeep road close to Taboose Creek which

Taboose Creek near Aberdeen

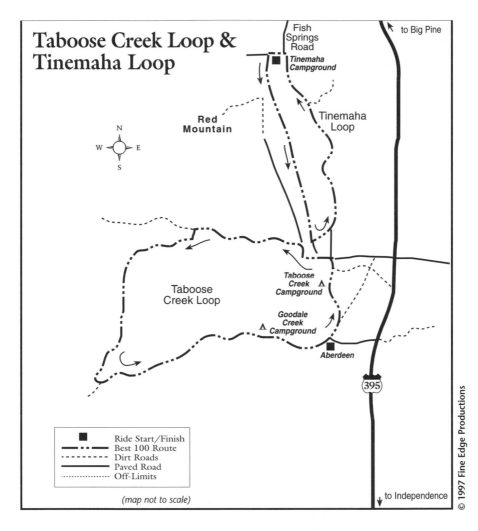

Taboose Creek Loop &
Tinemaha Loop

to Big Pine

Fish
Springs
Road

Tinemaha
Campground

N
W — E
S

Red
Mountain

Tinemaha
Loop

Taboose
Creek
Campground

Taboose
Creek Loop

Goodale
Creek
Campground

Aberdeen

395

■	Ride Start/Finish
▬▬▬▬▬	Best 100 Route
— · — · —	Dirt Roads
───────	Paved Road
················	Off-Limits

(map not to scale)

to Independence

© 1997 Fine Edge Productions

is lined with willows and tall grasses.

At 4.5 miles is a junction by the creek. Go left across Taboose Creek, up its opposite side, then along the edge of the black lava field. At the next junction, go left and ride along the base of the Sierra.

You cross a gate near three volcanic cones. Continue along the edge of the lava flow to a saddle—a long climb in coarse sand. The crest of the saddle at 6.9 miles is close to a red cinder cone. Descend toward Goodale Creek, cross it, and climb. At a junction, go left on 11S02 and climb to a crest on the alluvial fan, the apex of the ride.

Now you begin a 3-mile-long, rugged and technical downhill on a "road" that is nothing but rock. When you can risk a look, there are outstanding views of Owens Valley. Stay on the road heading east toward Aberdeen. The last part, which is quite sandy, ends at Tinemaha Road. Go left to Aberdeen and your starting point, 12.4 miles.

5 Tinemaha Loop

Distance: 6.7 miles.
Difficulty: Moderate.
Elevation: Lowest point: 4,100'; highest point: 4,400'.
Type: Loop ride on dirt roads.
Season: Year-round.
Facilities: Water, parking, pit toilets, and camping at Tinemaha County Campground.
Features: Volcanic cones and lava flows of the Eastern Sierra. Views of the Inyo Mountains and the Sierra.
Access: Drive north from Independence on Highway 395 for about 19 miles, or 5 miles south from Big Pine, to just north of Tinemaha Reservoir. Turn west on Fish Springs Road, then south about 2.5 miles to the Tinemaha County Campground where you can park.

The ride starts at the county campground entrance. Take the narrow paved road through the camp and across the stone bridge, and begin climbing the alluvial fan toward the Sierra. At the junction with a utility road that accesses two big power lines, go left and follow this route south. Red Mountain is the largest of several highly visible volcanic cones in the area. Cross Tinemaha Creek and continue south up the wide road as it gradually climbs to the crest.

From the summit you have great views of Owens Valley, the Sierra and Inyos. Now you enter the ancient black lava flow and start downhill across inhospitable terrain. At the bottom of the hill, you cross a flat, sandy stretch of road; the line of trees you see beyond is at Taboose Creek Campground.

At a T-junction with a dirt road, go left toward the Inyos. Another quarter mile brings you to Tinemaha Road. Go left again and ride north toward the Poverty Hills. You cross a sandy flat, then reenter the black lava flow for a mild climb through rolling moonscape. Again you pass Red Mountain as you continue along the base of the Poverty Hills, past many old mine sites, and back to your starting point.

Poverty Hills, Tinemaha Loop

CHAPTER 4

Big Pine

Big Pine, the small town 15 miles south of Bishop, is a green oasis in the high desert, as was most of the Owens Valley in the early 1900s. The valley, which once supplied much of the food for the busy mines in Nevada and eastern California in the last half of the 1800s, rivaled the Central Valley in food production. Irrigation ditches brought water from Sierra creeks and the Owens River to local farms. Big Pine still has one of the last active irrigation ditches in the Owens Valley.

In the 1930s, the Civilian Conservation Corps planted 200 giant sequoia trees around Big Pine, 38 of which are still living. The Roosevelt Sequoia at the junction of Highway 395 and Highway 168 has become a landmark. The Palisades, a cluster of 14,000-foot peaks, stand to the west of Big Pine; volcanoes and vast lava fields lie to the south, and Zurich, east of town, was once a station on the Carson and Colorado Railroad. The famous mountain climber Norman Clyde, one of Big Pine's more illustrious names, lived along Baker Creek.

Lava flows, Crater Mountain

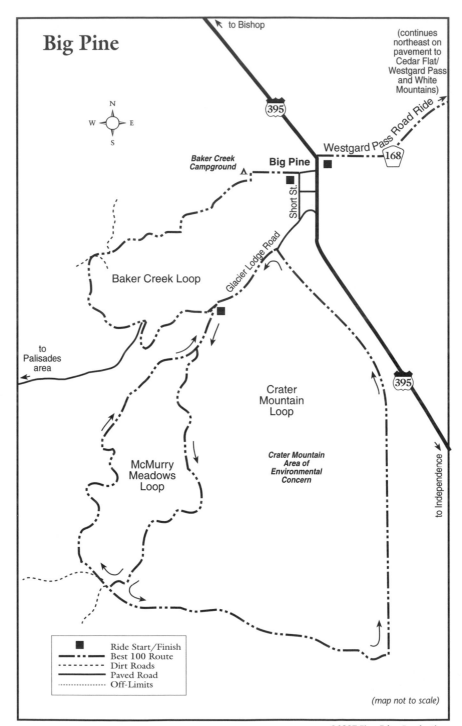

Big Pine

to Bishop

(continues northeast on pavement to Cedar Flat/ Westgard Pass and White Mountains)

395

Westgard Pass Road Ride

168

Baker Creek Campground

Big Pine

Short St.

Glacier Lodge Road

Baker Creek Loop

to Palisades area

Crater Mountain Loop

395

McMurry Meadows Loop

Crater Mountain Area of Environmental Concern

to Independence

Ride Start/Finish
Best 100 Route
Dirt Roads
Paved Road
Off-Limits

(map not to scale)

Since the beginning of the 20th Century, the Los Angeles Department of Water and Power (DWP) has bought most of the private land in the Owens Valley, putting an end to large-scale agriculture and a limit on private land use. However, it has benefited recreational users. The DWP allows almost unlimited access to its lands.

If you're heading directly into the White Mountains, the Sierra, or Death Valley from here, Big Pine is the last place to buy gas and supplies. The rides in this chapter include high mountains, a hot creek, and geological remnants of the valley's volcanic past.

1 Crater Mountain Loop

Distance: 19.2 miles.
Difficulty: Moderately strenuous and technical.
Elevation: 3,900' at Big Pine to 6,500' at McMurry Meadows.
Type: Loop ride on jeep roads.
Season: Spring, summer, and fall.
Facilities: None. Carry 3-4 pints of water. Amenities available in Big Pine.
Features: Travel through a fantastic volcanic landscape and view Crater Mountain, a young, recently active volcano, that rises abruptly 2,200 feet from the valley floor. This large cone is surrounded by a lava flow of over 12 square miles, but the ridge on which it sits is granite. On the slope of the cone itself are a number of lava tubes. The basaltic formations in this area range from 10,000 to 100,000 years old, young in a geological sense. Crater Mountain is an Area of Critical Environmental Concern managed by the BLM and a Wilderness Study Area.
Access: From the flashing light at Highway 395 in Big Pine, take Glacier Lodge Road west for 2.5 miles. Just past the bridge over Big Pine Creek turn left and park on the McMurry Meadows Road.

Start this ride just above Big Pine Creek on the left side of Glacier Lodge Road. Go downhill on Mc-Murry Meadows Road, around a curve, and under a power line. Go right at the first junction and head uphill toward Crater Mountain, crossing Little Pine Creek. The road runs along the black lava flow and at one point you can see an island of granite surrounded by rough black lava.

At 1.5 miles, as the road goes along the base of the granite ridge, you pass a sand pit. Cross the dry drainage and ascend toward the saddle. The road leads across a wide basin up to a second saddle.

At 3.1 miles, the top of the second saddle is close to Crater Mountain. Stay right on the road around the base of the granite ridge and climb over the shoulder of the ridge. From the second bowl, there is an amazing view of the Owens Valley. Climb to a crest by a granite point. McMurry Meadows lies at the base of the sheer granite mountains. Drop across a bowl and climb uphill toward McMurry Meadows.

At 5.6 miles there is an intersection above Birch Creek. Turn left on the primitive jeep track (road 903A) and start a downhill run across the alluvial fan parallel to the Birch Creek Draw. Continue down the primitive road toward Tinemaha Reservoir.

About 2 miles from the junction, a spur goes to the banks of Birch Creek Wash. Crater Mountain is just across the fantastic lava flows. Continue following the road downhill, passing another spur to the edge of the wash.

At 8.4 miles the jeep road comes to a T-junction with another dirt road. Go left toward Crater Mountain. In 0.5 mile there is a second junction. [**Side trip:** The road to the right leads down into the gorge where there was once an old water-powered stamp mill and washing operation. You can explore it if you want.]

To continue your ride, take the second left toward a granite outcropping. At another T-junction turn right toward the Poverty Hills. In one mile, you come to a small subdivision and a paved road where you turn left and continue downhill. Go left again at the power line and follow the utility road north toward the black lava flow. From here you can see Highway 395 below. Cross a big wash and continue the traverse of a high shelf toward the eastern slope of Crater Mountain.

At 11.6 miles you enter the lava flow. Continue north on the utility road, crossing rough terrain in a series of ridges formed by wrinkles of contracting rock.

At 14.4 miles a third power line joins the two big power lines and the road rolls over a low ridge continuing north. The lava flow continues toward Big Pine for two miles.

The road on the right at 16.8 miles leads to a graveyard and Highway 395, but keep riding straight on the road under the big power lines. Exit the lava flow into a sandy drainage and cross behind the dump. Cross another road with a single power line and keep going straight.

At the junction with the two-pole power lines, turn left up the slope and follow the road uphill for a mile and a half. At the next junction go right and uphill about 30 yards to the start of your ride.

2 McMurry Meadows Loop

Distance: 13 miles.
Difficulty: A challenging loop ride on jeep roads.
Elevation: 3,900' at Big Pine to 6,500' at McMurry Meadow.
Type: Loop ride on dirt road and jeep road.
Season: Spring, summer, and fall.
Facilities: Amenities available in Big Pine. Be sure to carry a minimum of 3-4 pints of water.
Features: Crater Mountain, 3 miles due south of Big Pine, is the highest of several volcanic cones. This ride includes views of a stunning volcanic landscape: the vaulted volcanic field, nearly 80 ft. high, which extends from the east side of Crater Mountain to Red Mountain, the fault scarp extending northward from Poverty Hills, and the extensive lava flows along the foothills of the Sierra and the Inyos. The Poverty Hills are not of volcanic nature but are built upon an uplifted block of granite and marble. Crater Mountain is an Area of Critical Environmental Concern and a Wilderness Study Area.
Access: From the flashing light at Highway 395 in Big Pine, take Glacier Lodge Road west for 2.5 miles. Just past the bridge over Big Pine Creek, turn left and park on the McMurry Meadows Road.

Start this ride just above Big Pine Creek on the left side of Glacier Lodge Road. Go downhill on Mc-Murry Meadows Road, around a curve, and under a power line. Go right at the first junction and head uphill toward Crater Mountain, crossing Little Pine Creek. The road runs along the black lava flow and at one point you can see an island of granite surrounded by rough black lava.

At 1.5 miles, as the road goes along the base of the granite ridge, you pass a sand pit. Cross the dry drainage and ascend toward the saddle. The road leads across a wide basin up to a second saddle.

At 3.1 miles, the top of the second saddle is close to Crater Mountain. Stay right on the road around the base of the granite ridge and climb over the shoulder of the ridge. In a second bowl, there is an amazing view of the Owens Valley. Climb to a crest by a granite point. McMurry Meadows sit at the base of the sheer granite mountains.

Drop across a bowl and climb uphill toward McMurry Meadows. At 5.6 miles there is an intersection above Birch Creek. Go right at this intersection onto the jeep road, ascending toward McMurry Meadows.

[**Side trip:** At a junction at 6.2 miles, a road to the left heads uphill to McMurry Meadows, a fantastic alpine meadow with a spectacular wall of granite above. This vast meadow is filled with flowers shortly after the snow melts. The road climbs through the meadow up to the mountain, providing spectacular views across Owens Valley. Distance for visiting the meadows is not included in this loop.]

To continue the loop, go right at the junction. Head north across the edge of a big bowl and along the

McMurry Meadows Loop

Photo courtesy BLM

Red Mountain cinder cone

base of a bare granite ridge. Stay right as you ride to the far side of the bowl. Take the third possible left and ride over a low saddle, cross into a new drainage, and begin a traverse.

At 8.1 miles, take the road to the right that leads down the gully to a narrow canyon where the road deteriorates into a primitive singletrack. Fol-

low the wash to the creek and climb the bank, where the road begins again.

The road exits the canyon and descends northeastward across the alluvial plain toward Big Pine. Parallel Little Pine Creek and cross it twice. Descend toward the lava flows and your starting point, with Crater Mountain to your right.

3 Baker Creek Loop

Distance: 9.4 miles.
Difficulty: Strenuous, technical ride.
Elevation: 3,900' to 4,500'.
Type: Loop ride on pavement, dirt road, and singletrack.
Season: Spring, summer, and fall.
Facilities: Parking, shade, restrooms, picnic tables, and water at Edith Mendenhall Park in Big Pine. Other amenities are available in Big Pine.
Features: A steep ride across three canyons with a fast, fun downhill return.
Access: At the north end of Big Pine, turn west off Highway 395 onto Baker Creek Road. Go west three blocks to Edith Mendenhall Park and park in the gravel lot.

From the four-way stop near Edith Mendenhall Park, head south on School Street and turn right on Glacier Lodge Road past the graveyard, and up the earthquake fault scar toward the Sierra.

Cross under two big power lines as you head toward Big Pine Canyon. At 2.5 miles, pass Sugarloaf Road, ascending toward Big Pine Creek. Just above the bridge, the road on the left leads to McMurry Meadows. [**Option:** Here you could add the McMurry Loop, for an additional 13 miles.]

For this ride, continue up Glacier Lodge Road as it becomes increasingly steep. Cross a second bridge at the mouth of Big Pine Creek Canyon. Follow the road around a big curve and up the lateral moraine. From the curve there is a beautiful view down toward Big Pine. Continue to the crest of the moraine.

At 4.5 miles a dirt track to the right drops down the other side of the moraine. Follow it into the wash of a short canyon, cross the wash, and climb a short, steep road up the other side. At the next crest, you drop to a second wash, then climb a second short, steep grade to a low saddle. The next descent takes you to Baker Creek at about 6.0 miles.

Cross Baker Creek and go right down the canyon on a steep, rough road. Ride past a couple of small meadows, cross Baker Creek a second

time at a culvert by a big cottonwood tree, and continue out of the canyon. Follow this dirt road down until you cross another creek.

Just past the second creek, and before the pavement, there is a green gate on your left. Turn left and go around this gate, following the new road which weaves downhill, in and out of the trees and across two meadows before fading to a primitive track. After crossing a dry creek bed, a trail on the right leads you across another meadow. After passing through a hole in the fence, turn left onto a primitive road.

Fault line near Crater Mountain

Courtesy BLM

At 7.9 miles, pass a turnaround and keep following the dirt road downhill, paralleling Baker Creek to Baker Creek Campground. Follow the road around the camp to the entrance, turn right, and cross the cattle guard.

Follow the paved road past a line of tall cottonwoods. This road leads back to the four-way stop and Edith Mendenhall Park, your starting point.

4 Westgard Pass Road Ride

Distance: 26 miles round trip.
Difficulty: Strenuous, non-technical road ride.
Elevation: 3,900' to 7,300'.
Type: Out-and-back on pavement.
Season: Spring, summer, and fall. (Check for road conditions in the spring and fall.)
Facilities: Seasonal water and restrooms at Triangle County Campground. Carry 2 quarts of water. Amenities available in Big Pine.
Features: This is a challenging road ride up to a mountain pass.
Access: Drive to the junction of Highways 395 and 168 at the north end of Big Pine and park at the Triangle County Campground marked by the Roosevelt Tree, a giant sequoia.

Head east on Highway 168, the Westgard Pass Road. Cross the Owens River and pass an historical marker near some foundations and a corral—all that remains of Zurich, a train station on the old Carson and Colorado Railroad. From this point you can see the old grade.

Continue toward the White Mountains, passing a road on the right at 2.3 miles. Bear left around a curve, staying on Highway 168. Use

Westgard Pass Road

extreme caution: the road has little or no shoulder, and what exists is gravel. Enter the foothills along the base of the mountains.

[**Side trip:** Just before the road turns uphill into the canyon, a short dirt road on the left leads to the top of a knoll where you get spectacular views across Owens Valley. Mileage for this side trip is not included.]

Your ride along Highway 168 follows the route of the old toll road up the desert slopes of a flat-bottomed canyon to White Mountain City, one of the first settlements in this area.

At the 5,000-foot marker, the canyon narrows and deepens; the climb grows steeper. At 7.8 miles you pass the site of the old toll station where fees were collected. There are foundations and a water trough near-

by. Just above the toll station is the 6,000-foot marker.

At 9.9 miles, the road narrows to a single lane; *use caution*. The rock in this narrows is striped and tilted. Above the narrows, you enter pinyon forest. You pass the 7,000-foot marker and ride through a smaller narrows. The canyon then widens and the road tops out in a vast bowl, Pinyon Flat. This broad saddle is the low crest of the White Mountains.

Pass White Mountain Road on the left and continue up Highway 168 to the saddle. This is Westgard Pass. To the north you can see the crest of the White Mountains. The tall white peak you see is the site of Schulman Grove.

Reverse your route and return the way you came to Triangle Campground, the start of your ride.

5 Andrews Mountain Loop

Distance: 25 miles.
Difficulty: A strenuous expedition across the crest of the Inyo Mountains.
Elevation: Start: 6,600'; crest: 9,126'.
Type: Loop ride on primitive roads.
Season: Late spring, summer, and early fall. (Check with local authorities before setting out.)
Topo maps: (7.5-minute series) Uhlmeyer Spring, Cowhorn Valley, Waucoba Mtn., and Waucoba Spring.
Facilities: None. Amenities available in Big Pine. Carry extra clothing, food, first aid and a minimum of 2 quarts of water. Treat all water from local sources.
Features: High elevation, alpine meadows, incredible vistas, old mines and cabins.
Access: Just north of Big Pine, turn off Highway 395 onto Highway 168. Go 2.3 miles and turn right onto the Saline Valley/Eureka Valley Road (9S18), formerly called Waucoba Road. Continue past Devils Gate to a dirt road (9S15) on the right at 13.6 miles. Park off the road.

Note: Some of the roads are access corridors to wilderness areas where bicycles are not allowed. Please respect these areas. If you wish to camp in this area, you must obtain a campfire permit in advance.

Begin this ride *only* in the morning.

Take the dirt road that parallels the main road for several hundred yards, then turns south. At 0.2 mile there is a fork and a sign reading *Papoose-Squaw Flat 4 x 4 advised*. Go right and south onto a sandy gravel road, passing through a wide flat valley of sagebrush.

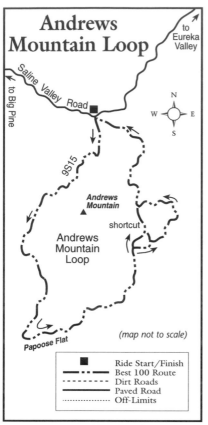

Andrews Mountain Loop

to Eureka Valley

Saline Valley Road

to Big Pine

9S15

N
W — E
S

Andrews Mountain ▲

shortcut

Andrews Mountain Loop

Papoose Flat

(map not to scale)

■ Ride Start/Finish
— ·· — Best 100 Route
- - - - - Dirt Roads
· · · · · · · Paved Road
················· Off-Limits

©1997 Fine Edge Productions

At 1.5 miles, the road makes a U-turn and drops into a wash. Pinyon and juniper appear. At 3.0 miles, the canyon narrows and the road becomes deeply rutted. Ignore a road to the left, and continue up a draw to a fork at 4.1 miles.

Go left up the switchbacks to the summit at 5.1 miles and 9,126 feet. Take a short walk northwest along the crest to examine some unusual vertical shale formations and enjoy the view directly across to Crater Mountain, and the full southern Sierra Crest.

From the summit, the descent into Papoose Flat passes through juniper and sage. At 6.8 miles, take the left fork. At 8.0 miles, you cross a major drainage—the wash to the east flows into Squaw Flat—and climb a shallow pass to a Y-junction at 9.0 miles. Go left and begin the steep descent east to Papoose Flat.

In the flat, at 10.3 miles, there are some primitive campsites. *If you wish to camp in this area, you must have a campfire permit and stay in established campsites near the road only.* Please keep this area clean by packing out all your trash.

A short walk to the west gives you an outstanding view of the Owens Valley and Sierra Crest. *Warning: If you are low on water, find the trip too taxing, or are running out of daylight, retrace your route now; it's much easier and faster to return from this point.*

If you choose to continue, you are committing to a major undertaking and must be fully prepared for a remote and strenuous trip. The road from here on passes through a number of sandy washes.

To continue your loop ride, go 200 yards south to a major junction at 10.4 miles. Go east toward Squaw Flat on an easy downhill. Ignore a jeep road at 11.5 miles and another that comes in from the south which lead to Mazourka Canyon.

At 12.1 miles, there is a granite monolith on the left. As the wash widens, you leave the granite formations behind. Stay in the middle of the wash, heading toward Squaw Peak (10,358 feet), and contour across upper Squaw Flat. Waucoba Mountain (11,123 feet) comes into view to the right of Squaw Peak.

Follow the wash to mile 14.1, where it narrows before opening up again at the 8,000-foot contour. Cross a wash at 15.3 miles where a road joins from the south.

Glacier Lodge Road

[**Option:** There is a three-way intersection at 16.4 miles. The route dead ahead climbs steeply to the north, passing close to an unnamed red peak. This is a shortcut if you wish to avoid the narrows.]

To continue the longer loop, go east (right) through the narrowing canyon. At 17.0 miles, you drop into a sandy wash due south of Peak 8173. The road narrows slowly and the ramparts of Squaw Peak close in on you. There are interesting red lava flows along the way.

At 17.8 miles, you leave the wash temporarily and climb a short ridge. At 18.6 miles you reach the narrows of Marble Canyon where there are two old mining cabins. Leave your bike and walk into the narrows of Marble Canyon for a look. Proceed carefully on foot. The descent into the canyon is steep, and there are mines all around. Since this canyon is so rarely visited, no one would find

you if you fell or had an accident.

Back on your bike, continue up the canyon to the left on a steep, rocky road composed of shale with poor traction. With perseverance, you reach a small flat area at 20.5 miles. Head north, ignoring a faint track to the west, and at 20.7 miles you intersect the main road from the southwest (the short cut).

At 21.2 miles, you reach the ridge where there are primitive campsites on the right. From here, you can see White Mountain directly to the north.

At 21.4 miles, pass three tunnels on the left. If you wish to explore on foot, *use caution*. At 22.7 miles, the canyon again narrows and becomes rockier. At 23.0 miles, the trail splits and you can take either fork as they rejoin around the bend.

Continue down the broad wash to the Papoose Flat sign (mile 24.8) and then back to your starting point.

6 Keough's Hot Ditch Loop

Distance: 11.5 miles.
Difficulty: Easy and flat.
Elevation: 4,000' to 4,100'.
Type: Loop ride on broken pavement and dirt roads.
Season: Year-round.
Facilities: All amenities available in Bishop.
Features: There is a natural hot creek at the start of this ride where a series of pools have been dug, the pools becoming cooler as they drop down the gradual slope. This public hot ditch has incredible views of the Sierra and Inyos. The ride also follows part of the Big Pine irrigation ditch.
Access: From Big Pine, take Highway 395 about 8 miles north. Turn left onto Keough's Hot Springs Road. Drive west 1.5 miles to a junction with a broken-pavement road. Park anywhere.

Begin your ride at the junction. (The broken-pavement road is old Highway 395.) Just north of the start is the flowing hot ditch where you can plan to take a soak after your ride.

Follow the old highway north and downhill, paralleling the freeway. At 1.8 miles, the old highway intersects Collins Road. Go right and cross Highway 395, heading east on Collins Road past irrigated fields, toward the towering White Mountains.

At 4.9 miles there is an intersection with the Big Pine Canal, close to the Owens River. Tall grasses and cattails line the ditch. Take the bridge across the canal, and turn right on the road that parallels it where you have fantastic views down the Owens Valley and along the Inyo Mountains. Occasionally you can spot tule elk in the vast, flat grasslands.

Follow Big Pine Canal for several flat miles to its intersection with Highway 395 at 9.3 miles. Cross the highway carefully. Go north 50 yards along the west side of the highway and through a gate where you pick up the old highway again. Follow it uphill across the alluvial fan to Keough's Hot Springs Road and your starting point.

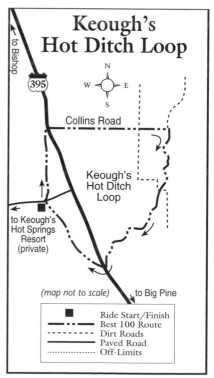

Keough's Hot Ditch Loop

Collins Road

Keough's Hot Ditch Loop

to Keough's Hot Springs Resort (private)

to Bishop

to Big Pine

(map not to scale)

■	Ride Start/Finish
—·■·—	Best 100 Route
- - - -	Dirt Roads
————	Paved Road
··········	Off-Limits

©1997 Fine Edge Productions

CHAPTER 5

White Mountains

The White Mountains, the northern extension of the Inyo range, rise sharply from the eastern edge of the Owens Valley. This range—one of the highest desert-mountain ranges in North America—has the largest expanse of rare alpine steppe, or tundra, in the western United States.

On the rocky, windswept slopes of the White Mountains grow the oldest continuously living trees in the world. Gnarled, twisted, and starkly beautiful, the bristlecone pine, with their stubby bottle-brush branches reaching for the sky, cling fiercely to the shallow and alkaline dolomite soil found on the higher slopes of the White Mountains. These unique trees grow at elevations between 9,500 and 11,500 feet, surviving the harsh elements for over 4,000 years and often growing less than one inch in diameter in 100 years. Their exceptional age makes them of scientific value in studying climatic fluctuations that have occurred over the past 40 centuries. The Ancient Bristlecone Pine Forest includes Schulman and Patriarch groves. Don't leave the White Mountains without visiting these ancient trees which offer an amazing experience and excellent photography. Note: Bicycles are not allowed on any of the trails within the Bristlecone Pine Area. You must stay on the roads and leave your bicycles in the parking areas.

If you are in good physical shape, consider riding to the summit of White Mountain (14,242 feet) where you have unparalleled views of the entire 200-mile-long Sierra Nevada crest. The elevation at the peak, California's third highest mountain, is just 250 feet less than that of Mt. Whitney, visible to the southwest.

While camping is not allowed inside the Ancient Bristlecone Pine Forest, there are two campgrounds nearby: Grandview Campground, 5 miles north of Highway 168 on White Mountain Road, and Cedar Flats, a group campground, located on Highway 168 at the White Mountain Road turnoff. If interested in camping opportunities, contact the White Mountain Ranger Station 760-873-2500.

The rides in this chapter are difficult. Elevation, uphill riding, steepness, and distance all combine to make these some of the most challenging mountain bike rides in the world. Silver Canyon and Wyman Canyon call for extreme climbs and descents. Grandview Mine and Black Mountain are less difficult and highly scenic. The ride from Schulman Grove to Patriarch Grove takes you through the ancient trees and along the crest of the White Mountains. Most of these rides are suitable only for advanced, experienced, self-sufficient cyclists in excellent physical shape.

The White Mountain crest is a place of unusual beauty and solitude. Please help keep it that way!

Note: Weather can be extremely variable, especially in late spring and early fall. Inquire ahead of time and be alert to weather patterns. There is no drinking water available in the White Mountains. Carry all you need. Please stay on existing roads. Some of the rides in this chapter use roads that are access corridors to wilderness areas where bicycles are not allowed. Please respect these areas.

1 Black Mountain Ride

Distance: 11 miles.
Difficulty: Moderately difficult.
Elevation: Cedar Flat: 6,900'; ridge: 8,750'.
Type: Out-and-back on primitive jeep road.
Season: Late spring, summer, and early fall.
Facilities: None. Carry at least 2 quarts of water.
Features: Travel through juniper and pinyon woodlands with great views of the Whites, Owens Valley and Sierra. Black Mountain Silver Mine, with three shafts still active, is on your route.
Access: At the north end of Big Pine, the junction of Highway 395 and Highway 168, take 168 (Westgard Pass Road) east to the summit and turn left on White Mountain Road. Continue past the entrance station one quarter-mile to a dirt road and park off the road at the sign reading *Black Mountain.* Please stay on existing roads.

Black Canyon

From the parking place, take the jeep road west through dense pinyon, a long climb with many spurs that soon grows steeper.

At a triangle junction on the crest of the ridge, the spur to the right leads to an overlook with views east to Deep Springs Valley. To continue the ride, go left, traverse the pinyon-covered ridge, and soak in the views of Owens Valley and Marble Canyon to the north.

At 2.5 miles the road crosses a saddle, then continues downhill along the south slope of the ridge. Follow the ridge down to a sandy gully and go right up the gully to the crest of the ridge.

Take a left and climb along the ridge. The road makes a wide curve up and along the crest of a knoll, with expansive views in both directions. Black Mountain, with its gray and black striations, is directly ahead where you can see the mine.

Continue following the road down the ridge to its end at Black Mountain Silver Mine (5.5 miles). This is a working mine so please do not disturb anything.

Reverse your route, returning the way you came in.

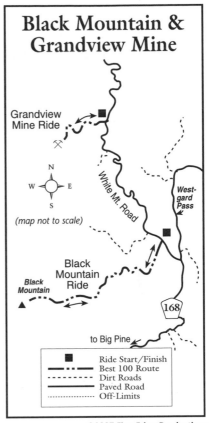

Black Mountain & Grandview Mine

Grandview Mine Ride

West-gard Pass

White Mt. Road

N
W ⟶ E
S

(map not to scale)

Black Mountain Ride

Black Mountain

168

to Big Pine

	Ride Start/Finish
—·—·—	Best 100 Route
---------	Dirt Roads
————	Paved Road
··············	Off-Limits

©1997 Fine Edge Productions

2 Grandview Mine Ride

Distance: 4 miles.
Difficulty: Short, moderate, and steep.
Elevation: 8,500' at Grandview to the mine at 9,200'.
Type: Out-and-back on jeep road.
Season: Late spring, summer and early fall.
Facilities: Toilets and parking at Grandview Campground. No water; carry a minimum of 3-4 pints.
Features: A spectacular view across Deep Springs Valley, Eureka Valley, Saline Valley, and Death Valley.
Access: From the junction of Highway 395 and Highway 168, take 168 (Westgard Pass Road) east to the summit, turn left on White Mountain Road, go five miles north to Grandview Campground and park. Please stay on existing roads.

From the campground entrance, take the road to the right that runs along the side of a bowl through sparse meadow. Pinyon trees grow on the hillsides and there are campsites along the way.

At a T-junction on the far side of the campground, take a left, then a quick right. The road ascends the ridge out of the basin to a crest. Walk to the rock point for an excellent view of Black Canyon.

Follow the road over the crest along the ridge and drop down a couple of switchbacks. At a junction, where there is evidence of some mining, take the sharp left and continue along the crest of the ridge.

At 2 miles is the Grandview Mine. There are two mine shafts and the scattered debris of shacks and mining equipment. This is the end of the recommended ride. There is truly a "grand view" from here. The ridge drops away on two sides to Marble Canyon on the south and Black Canyon to the north. You can see the Owens Valley below you; beyond, the Sierra Crest rises in a continuous wall from near Mount Whitney to the Mammoth Lakes area, and the vista is one of the finest. The crest of the White Mountains is to the north.

The return is simple. Just reverse your route!

3 Silver Canyon Ride

Distance: 23.2 miles round trip; 11.6 miles downhill with shuttle.
Difficulty: Extreme ride for advanced, self-sufficient riders only.
Elevation: Valley floor: 4,000'; highest point: 10,800'.
Type: Out-and-back on steep jeep road or long descent only with optional shuttle.
Season: Late spring, summer, and early fall.
Facilities: Parking, restrooms, and water at Laws Railroad Museum. For out-and-back trips, carry snacks, first aid and at least two quarts of water; there is none on your route.
Features: Silver Canyon, known for one of mountain biking's most insane rides, was the route of the Plumline Outback Ultimate Kamikaze Race held during the 1980s. During the race, unusual safety precautions were taken with full communication and rescue teams in place. In the late 1980s the Kamikaze was moved to Mammoth Mountain. Laws Railroad Museum features the history of Owens Valley, with emphasis on the railroad. Be sure to schedule time to visit it.
Access/Shuttle: At the Y-junction of Highways 395 and 6 in Bishop, take Highway 6 north for four miles. Just past the Owens River Bridge, go right on Silver Canyon Road to Laws Railroad Museum. Park across the road from the museum. To shuttle, leave a car at Laws Railroad Museum and drive another to Schulman Grove and park there. Please stay on existing roads.

To begin the downhill ride, head north from Schulman Grove for 3 miles along the White Mountain Road. Go left (west) at the saddle onto Silver Canyon Road, climbing several hundred yards over the Inyo crest proper, passing a radio relay station located on Peak 10,842 to the north.

To begin the round-trip ride (up and down), head east from Laws Museum on the wide road past fields and across two irrigation ditches. At the end of the pavement, follow the gravel road toward Silver Canyon. At 2.0 miles, you make your first creek crossing and enter Silver Canyon where the road

Bottom switchback, Silver Canyon

narrows and steepens. Ride up the deep canyon, crossing willow-lined Silver Creek several times. Aspen appear as you climb higher up the canyon. Ride through a narrows, cross the creek for the fifth time, and see the switchbacks ahead. This is your future! Continue up the road past a couple of mines.

After the eighth creek crossing (about 7.0 miles), there is a closure gate at the bottom of the first steep switchback. The impossible slope becomes merely difficult after the first switchback. After the road enters pinyon forest, the route is still steep, and rocks, ruts, and off-camber turns give it additional spice.

At a junction with a power line road, go right on the better road. Portions of the road are bare rock and it becomes extremely steep, rutted and technical, climbing 800 feet in the last mile to the top—a ride to the sky.

At the crest, 11.6 miles, there is a level pad from which you can enjoy the quintessential view of the Sierra—from the Palisades to Yosemite. Take time to rest and eat, because the ride down is difficult and dangerous.

On the way down, the steep and technical road is a constant workout. *Rims can heat up enough to melt tubes, so stop and rest your braking hands and let your rims cool.* Slow down before each sharp curve. The road, rough and uneven, is often solid rock or strewn with rocks, and its upper section requires skill and judgment. Walk, if you're in doubt or if fatigue sets in—remember, this is the Ultimate Kamikaze! From the top of the last switchback, stop to enjoy the view down Silver Canyon.

At the bottom of the last switchback the character of the ride changes. The road no longer has sharp turns and is much less steep and technical. This is the fastest part of your return and each of the many creek crossings is a refreshing splash. For over 5 miles the exhilarating downhill continues through Silver Canyon.

Once you reach the flats, follow the road to Laws Railroad Museum for a glimpse into the early history of Owens Valley.

4 Patriarch Grove Ride

Distance: 24 miles.
Difficulty: Difficult due to distance, steep climbs, and altitude.
Elevation: Start at 10,100' at Schulman Grove and climb to Patriarch Grove at 11,200' Although the difference in elevation is 1,100 vertical feet, you have about 3,700' with gain and loss (uphill and down).
Type: Out-and-back on good dirt road.
Season: Usually summer and fall. Conditions can be variable, so check with the White Mountain Ranger Station, U.S. Forest Service in Bishop, 760-973-2573.
Facilities: Parking and restrooms at Schulman Grove visitor center. Parking, picnic tables, and pit toilets at Patriarch Grove. No water available at either grove, so carry plenty—a minimum of 2 quarts.
Features: This traverse of the White Mountain Crest takes you from Schulman Grove, home of the Methuselah Tree, over 4,700 years old, to Patriarch Grove, where you can view the largest bristlecone tree alive. At Schulman Grove, you can walk the Discovery Trail and browse the interpretive displays for a better sense of these enchanted forests.
Access: From the junction of Highway 395 and Highway 168, take 168 (Westgard Pass Road) east to the summit, turn left on White Mountain Road, and go 10 miles to Schulman Grove. Park at the Visitors Center. Please stay on existing roads.

The ride starts and finishes at the visitor center. Let the ranger know your plans, since this is a difficult and extended ride.

At the entrance to the parking area, go right and uphill on the wide gravel road, climbing to a saddle. The white hill just south of the road is covered with bristlecone pines. At the crest is a bowl covered with tiny alpine plants.

Traverse the top of the bowl and climb to a second saddle from where you can see two more bowls and the crest of the White Mountains ahead. The thin line of the road ahead fades

White Mountain Peak from Patriarch Grove area

Top of Silver Canyon, looking toward Sierra

off along the ridge; this is your route. Drop down the side of a hill covered with bristlecone and limber pines, then climb to an intersection in a wide saddle at 3.0 miles. Silver Canyon is to the left; the road on the right leads to Wyman Canyon.

Continue straight along the crest toward the double peak. Ascend curves to the limber-pine-covered top of the first peak. Cross a saddle between the double peaks and climb a second set of curves to the higher peak which is covered with bristlecone pines.

Pass through a notch, through the marvelous forest of bristlecone pines, and drop along the ridge to a low saddle. Ahead you can see the road to Patriarch Grove. There is an excellent scenic overlook toward Owens Valley at the bottom of the saddle on the left side. At a junction, keep left and ride along an open area below a single power line.

At a crest on the north side of the mountain, the road drops across a wide, flat bowl, still paralleling the power line with White Mountain visible in the distance. Climb to an intersection, passing the road to Crooked Creek, and heading straight to a barren crest, then down into a drainage. Patriarch Grove is on the white mountain across the gully. Cross a dry, sandy wash and begin a brutally steep climb to the grove, ascending 700 feet in one mile.

As you head up to Patriarch Grove, the terrain becomes more barren and rugged, the trees larger and more grotesque. At the top of the steepest part there is a junction where you go right toward Patriarch Grove across a bowl for a mile, passing over a low saddle and entering the parking area.

Here you find pit toilets, picnic tables, an interpretive display, and a nature walk. *(No bikes are allowed on the trails.)* Leave your bicycle in the parking area and proceed on foot to

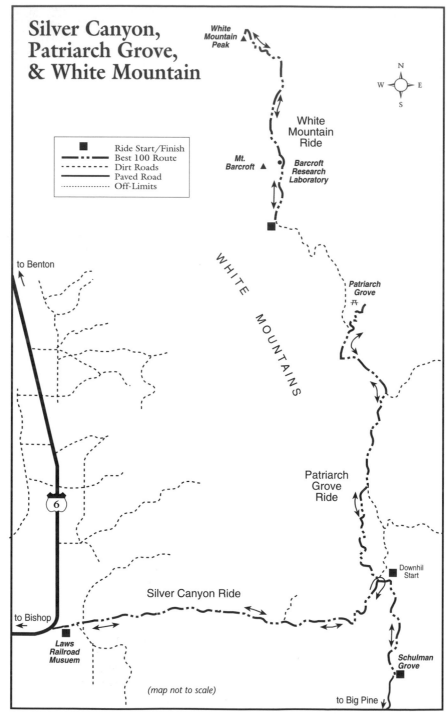

Silver Canyon, Patriarch Grove, & White Mountain

White Mountain Peak

White Mountain Ride

Mt. Barcroft

Barcroft Research Laboratory

■ Ride Start/Finish
Best 100 Route
Dirt Roads
Paved Road
Off-Limits

to Benton

WHITE MOUNTAINS

Patriarch Grove

Patriarch Grove Ride

Downhill Start

6

Silver Canyon Ride

to Bishop

Laws Railroad Musuem

Schulman Grove

(map not to scale)

to Big Pine

©1997 Fine Edge Productions

Patriarch Tree, located on a walking path just to the east. This tree has a circumference of 36 feet, 8 inches and is recognized as the world's largest bristlecone pine. As you walk along the nature trail past these living sculptures, it's fun to think about the age of these trees and compare them to humanity's brief recorded history.

The University of California maintains Crooked Creek High Elevation Research Laboratory a few miles southeast of Patriarch, where experiments are performed on plants, animals and humans to determine the effects of high elevation. Because of the need for carefully controlled conditions, visitors are not permitted.

The return is a simple reverse, but not an easy ride.

5 White Mountain Ride

Distance: 14 miles.
Difficulty: Extremely difficult ride. Very high elevation, remote, and technical. For well-prepared expert riders.
Elevation: From 12,000' to the summit of White Mountain at 14,280'.
Type: Out-and-back on difficult jeep road.
Season: Summer and early fall. Keep an eye on weather patterns!
Facilities: None. Barcroft Laboratory has an emergency phone only. Carry at least two quarts of drinking water.
Features: White Mountain Ride is the highest mountain bike ride in California, an epic ride through a remote alpine zone with panoramic vistas. Be aware that this is a fragile area. Deep snow, extreme cold, and hurricane-force winds define the life of the small plants that survive here, and crushing them causes irreparable damage. Stay on the road, be courteous to any hikers you encounter, and do your part to preserve this area in its natural state.
Access: From the junction of Highway 395 and Highway 168, take 168 (Westgard Pass Road) east to the summit, turn left on White Mountain Road. Drive 4.6 miles past Patriarch Grove to a locked gate and park.

View of Hammil Valley, Casa Diablo Mountain from White Mountain Peak

Start at the closure gate in the saddle. Go around the gate and up a steep graded road. Fragile alpine flowers and grasses grow in the poor soil alongside the road. *Remember:* This is a delicate and unique environment. Remain on the road at all times.

At 1 mile, the grade slackens. Patriarch Grove lies across the huge basin to the south, and Barcroft Laboratory is ahead. The laboratory, a huge Quonset hut that stands at 12,500 feet, is a high-altitude research area, property of the University of California. Do not disturb anything.

Follow the primitive jeep road uphill. The road is steep and rocky, leading through alpine tundra to the crest where there is an observatory and a tremendous view of White Mountain. From this point, you can see the road leading to the summit.

You drop down to a sandy bowl covered with sparse alpine grasses and flowers, cross a small rise, then drop into a second bowl, before starting up the technical rocky road that leads to the crest of a small peak within 1.5 miles. (You can see the road ahead across the saddle.)

Drop down the loose, technical road to the saddle, cross a sparse green meadow, and start up the final approach to White Mountain, where the terrain is steep and loose. Even if you are acclimated to the high elevation, you may find cycling slow going. Take one switchback at a time, breathe deeply, and drink plenty of fluids, no matter whether you feel thirsty or not! The air is dry and thin and your system needs those fluids to keep you going.

At the top of the third switchback, you leave the band of beige rock and enter black rock. Continue up the switchbacks across the east face of White Mountain. At the top of the seventh switchback, you crest the south ridge, then climb to a higher terrace. After you cross the top of the black ridge, you ascend several last switchbacks to the crest.

From the gate where you began, it is 7.0 miles to the summit of White

Schulman Grove walk

Mountain, where you'll find a small cement building, some solar panels, and a radio tower. Stay out of the building, but you may climb onto the roof of the building which makes a great sun deck and offers a 360-degree view. You can see most of the area described in this book—a panorama that includes the crest of the White Mountains, Owens Valley and the Sierra all the way from Independence to Bishop. To the north you can see Glass Mountain ridge, Mono Basin, and the Bodie Hills beyond. Nevada stretches east with lines of mountains and basins fading forever into the distance.

When you are ready, return down the road. Ride slowly on the steep and technical sections, yielding to hikers. Take some breaks to rest—this is no place to risk injury. At 8.6 miles you are back at the low saddle. Most cyclists walk the next section to the top of the smaller peak; the ride down the other side is also challenging. Cross the double bowl and climb to the observatory, then continue to Barcroft at 11.9 miles. The last part of the ride is good road and a fast downhill to the closure gate.

Note: To date, entry into this area has been open to foot traffic and mountain bikes, but closure could occur at any time if adverse impact is found on the fragile slopes. For information phone White Mountain Ranger Station 760-873-2500.

6 Wyman Canyon Ride

Distance: 21.8 miles one way with shuttle.
Difficulty: Difficult and technical with a long descent.
Elevation: From 10,800' to 5,600'.
Type: Downhill ride on dirt and gravel, water crossings.
Season: Summer and fall.
Topo maps: (7.5-minute series) Crooked Creek, Blanco Mtn., Chocolate Mtn.
Facilities: Restroom at Schulman Grove. Carry food and 2 quarts of water. Treat any water from local sources.
Features: Much of Wyman Canyon is surprisingly wet (you cross the creek 18 times), with abundant plant and animal life. There are petroglyphs along the side of the creek. Visit the ruins of White Mountain City, one of the oldest mining towns in this area. Westgard Pass Toll Road, built to serve these mines, was the last toll road to close in California (1916).
Access/Shuttle: Drive both vehicles from the junction of Highways 395 and 168 over Westgard Pass to Deep Springs Valley, about 25 miles. Park at the Cal-Trans station on the far side of the valley. Take the second vehicle back over Westgard Pass, go right on White Mountain Road 10 miles to Schulman Grove, and park at the visitor center.

Note: While visiting petroglyph sites, do not touch or walk on the sensitive traces of the past. Remember archeological and cultural resources are a non-renewable resource. Once disturbed or removed, they are gone forever. Please cycle on existing roads.

From Schulman Grove, go north on the White Mountain Road to a saddle where flowers abound in early summer. Drop into the bowl and traverse to a second saddle. From here you can see two vast bowls and the crest of the White Mountains. Drop down a hill that is covered with bristlecone and limber pines and

Cycling down Wyman Canyon

climb to a wide saddle

At 3.0 miles, go right at an intersection and follow the road along a single power line. At the next junction, go left along the power line down the drainage, and ride a half-mile to another intersection where a wooden sign reads: Wyman Canyon. Take the right here and drop steeply down switchbacks to a dry wash, following the road to a junction near a small cabin.

Continuing down upper Wyman Canyon, the single power line runs parallel to your route. Sagebrush and tall grasses grow along the bottom of the wash and the canyon walls become higher as you ride past the winter closure gate.

This section of the canyon provides a long, gradual descent. You pass several side canyons, each with a closed jeep road, and a pair of small tin shacks. The meadows become greener and willows grow in small patches as the canyon gradually widens.

Cross a dry creek, descend the other side of Wyman Canyon passing a sign marked Leaving the Ancient

Forest, and continue down the curving canyon. The chocolate-colored rocks along this section show evidence of extreme geologic forces.

Pass a big canyon to the left and at 11.0 miles you come to Roberts Ranch, with three cabins, a corral, and an old smelter. [Side trip: You can take the road up the side canyon leading to the crest of Roberts Ridge. Mileage is not included.]

As this middle portion of Wyman Canyon becomes steeper, its character changes. You pass through several meadows where willows and brush grow dense. You cross the creek 18 times and although there is running water, do not drink it.

The canyon is narrow and drops off in shelves. There are several small waterfalls; deer are common and dozens of species of birds live in this 5-mile-long oasis.

At 16 miles, the road climbs out of the canyon to a badlands of weathered granite rock with views of Deep Springs Valley. Next a rocky, technical section descends through the strangely shaped

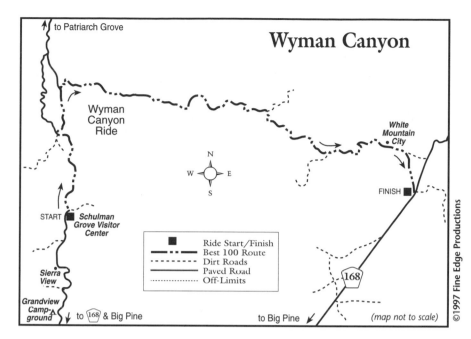

to Patriarch Grove

Wyman Canyon

Wyman
Canyon
Ride

N
W — E
S

White
Mountain
• City

FINISH ■

START ■ Schulman
Grove Visitor
Center

■ Ride Start/Finish
— Best 100 Route
---- Dirt Roads
Paved Road
·········· Off-Limits

Sierra
View

Grandview
Camp-△
ground ↓ to ⑯⑧ & Big Pine

to Big Pine ↙

⑯⑧

(map not to scale)

©1997 Fine Edge Productions

rocks down into Wyman Canyon.

At a junction in the canyon bottom, go right. Cross the creek one last time and follow it, passing a cattle guard and several signs. Cross Crooked Creek and head into Deep Springs Valley. Just below you can see the ruins of White Mountain City. Look for petroglyphs on the side of two boulders by the creek.

The ride continues down a wide gravel road for one mile. After you pass a gravel pit, take a right on the road by a single power line. Cross the desert toward a small square oasis. At Highway 168, go right toward the Cal-Trans station and your waiting shuttle vehicle.

Deep Springs Valley from Grandview Overlook

Courtesy BLM

Cool cycling near the Owens River

CHAPTER 6

Bishop South

Bishop, the largest community in the Eastern Sierra, traces its beginnings to Samuel Bishop who started the San Francis Ranch here in 1861. Due to conflict with the local Paiutes, he stayed only one season, but as relations improved with the Native Americans, others migrated to the area. In 1864, the first structure—a blacksmith shop—was built; the first church was built in 1869.

Bishop is surrounded on all sides by nature's playgrounds. A drive of an hour or two in any direction takes you high into the Sierra or Inyo-White Mountains, Yosemite, Mono Lake, and Mammoth Lakes. There are extensive trails and jeep roads used traditionally by hikers, hunters, fishermen, and pack trains. Since these recreational users have had almost a century of seniority over mountain bikers, please keep a friendly relationship with them by being courteous and yielding trails to hikers and horses.

Although ranching and farming, mostly alfalfa, were a mainstay of the community for over a century, tourism has become the principal source of income and employment over the past 40 years. Bishop, population 6,000, offers travelers

Reeds and cattails line the river

lodging, dining, and entertainment. Displays at the Paiute-Shoshone Cultural Center give us a picture of the life of the valley's early inhabitants. A few miles outside town, the Laws Railroad Museum records the history of early white settlers.

For a challenging road ride not described, you might want to tackle the South Lake/Sabrina route to the west of Bishop (Highway 168).

1 Coyote High Sierra Traverse

Distance: 21.7 miles with shuttle.
Difficulty: Expedition-level ride due to high elevation and remoteness; route-finding skills required.
Elevation: Average elevation about 10,000', with some elevations over 11,000'; 4,370' gain, 5,000' loss.
Type: Expedition-level trip; five miles of technical singletrack. Riders must be self-sufficient, fully prepared with topo maps, compass, clothing, first aid, and at least 2 quarts of water.
Season: June through fall, depending on snow. Keep an eye on the weather!
Facilities: Food, water, and toilets at Bishop Creek Lodge. Carry water and treat all water from local sources. All amenities in Bishop.
Features: This high traverse of the Coyote Flat area through high alpine meadows and stunted forests offers outstanding vistas of northern Owens Valley, the White Mountains, and the Sierra Crest. This is an excellent overnight adventure.
Map required: Coyote Flat 7.5 min for route-finding on the singletrack section.
Access/Shuttle: Leave a shuttle vehicle in downtown Big Pine and return to Bishop. Go west on West Line Street (Highway 168) for 13 miles, turn left onto South Lake Road, and drive about 6 miles. Park in the turnout to the right just beyond Bishop Creek Lodge.

From the parking area off the paved road, ride about 500 feet uphill to a dirt road on your left. Take this road and cross a bridge over Bishop Creek. The road becomes a doubletrack, curves north through an aspen grove, and climbs through loose sandy soil to a lateral moraine. At the top of the moraine, you round a corner and enter a hanging valley (elevation 8,800 feet). Ignore the faint road to the right.

After many switchbacks and sandy spots, you reach a T-intersection at 3.0 miles where you go left and climb to a minor ridge at 10,000 feet. You have now climbed 1,600 feet with another 1,100 feet to go to the top of Coyote Ridge.

A short descent and gentle climb bring you to the remains of an old log cabin at 3.5 miles. From this point, the road averages a 14 percent grade

to the top of 11,070-foot Coyote Ridge at 5.0 miles. Rest and enjoy the spectacular views.

You now begin a 1,500-foot descent through an alpine meadow where there are wonderful fields of lupine in springtime. At 7.0 miles, at an intersection, continue straight ahead. [**Side trip:** The right-hand trail leads to a pleasant camping area at the usually dry Coyote Lake.]

Another mile brings you to the first crossing of Coyote Creek at elevation 9,950 feet.

The road improves as you continue your descent. At 9.2 miles you reach a road junction and decision time. The described route to Big Pine Creek goes right (south) downhill and heads into Coyote Flat.

[**Option:** If you continue straight, the main jeep road will take you to

Reata Road west of Bishop. This route is easier, shorter, and less technical; a definite short way back.]

To follow the full route, go right and downhill, crossing Coyote Creek again. After 5.2 miles of easy riding, you reach the southern end of Coyote Flat, a plateau running north-south. At mile 14.4, cross Cow Creek, pass a cattle guard, and go to a junction and a ridge forming the edge of the Baker Creek drainage.

Go right (west) and climb to 10,290 feet and another junction at

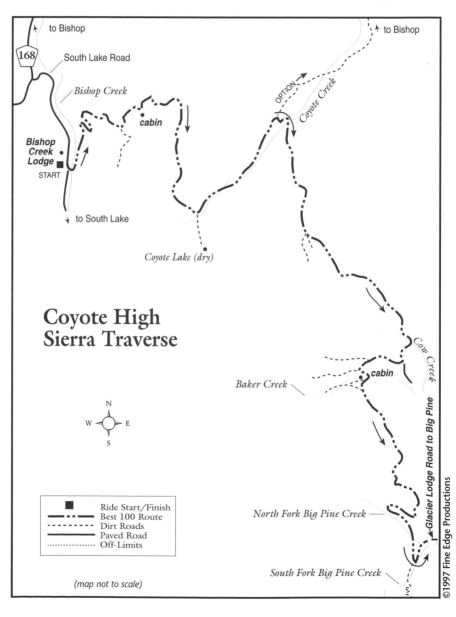

to Bishop

168

South Lake Road

Bishop Creek

cabin

Bishop Creek Lodge

START

to South Lake

Coyote Lake (dry)

to Bishop

OPTION

Coyote Creek

Cow Creek

cabin

Baker Creek

Coyote High Sierra Traverse

N
W — E
S

Glacier Lodge Road to Big Pine

North Fork Big Pine Creek

South Fork Big Pine Creek

■	Ride Start/Finish
▬▬	Best 100 Route
- - - -	Dirt Roads
▬▬	Paved Road
· · · · ·	Off-Limits

(map not to scale)

©1997 Fine Edge Productions

15.5 miles. Go left (southwest) and downhill to another junction, then left again. This brings you to Baker Creek and the Baker Creek Cabin at 16.0 miles. From here, elevation 10,070 feet, you find the last water until Big Pine Creek. *Treat any water.*

The next section, the start of the technically demanding singletrack, requires route-finding skills. Go upstream from the cabin about 500 feet and cross the stream; you should be in the trees and just upstream from a swampy meadow area. Avoid any trails that lead away from the north side of the stream.

Look for a trail that either parallels

the creek on its south side or goes up the hillside to the south. If the trail parallels the creek, go left and downstream. If the trail goes up the hill, follow it south. If you have trouble at this spot, you may not have gone far enough upstream from the cabin. (The Coyote Flat topo map helps at this point.)

In 0.3 mile, go left at a junction and to the top of the ridge at 16.4 miles. From here, the singletrack goes 0.6 mile downhill to High Meadow (10,020 feet), then climbs steeply to a rounded ridge at the edge of Big Pine Canyon. Views of 14,000-foot peaks and two of the largest glaciers in the Sierra unfold as you ride toward some

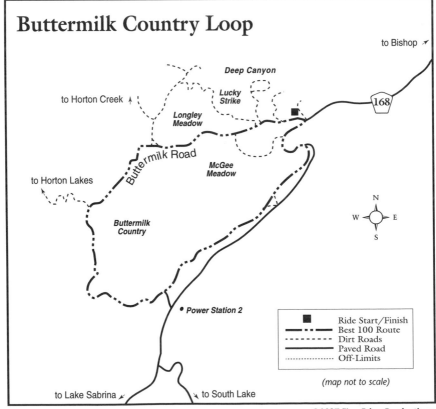

rocks at the southern end of the ridge at 17.7 miles.

Ahead is the South Fork of Big Pine Creek; to the right is the North Fork, into which you descend along a steep, technical route to Grouse Spring. Walk your bike if necessary.

Past Grouse Spring (there is little or no water here) the trail becomes easy to the end of Logging Flat. You then descend steeply through sand and several switchbacks before contouring around a draw and climbing to a minor ridge.

The trail now drops into Big Pine Canyon to a four-way junction at 20.0 miles (8,600 feet). Go straight downhill. Watch for hikers! You are now on a heavily-used hiking trail. In

0.5 mile you reach an abandoned road which you take across the creek. Within a few hundred yards a sign indicates that the hiking trail goes left. Your route continues straight down the abandoned road.

As you approach Big Pine Creek South Fork, watch for a trail at 21.3 miles that is not visible ahead of time. Turn left for 0.5 mile to the trailhead and paved Glacier Lodge Road, where you go downhill for a 9-mile descent into Big Pine.

Note: This ride follows the route of the Sierra 7500 mountain bike competition held in the mid-1980s. Billed as the most difficult mountain bike race course in the United States, the original route covered 50 miles.

2 Buttermilk Country Loop

Distance: 17.4 miles.
Difficulty: Difficult and sometimes technical. Strenuous climb.
Elevation: Lowest point: 5,100'; highest point: 8,240'.
Type: Loop ride on good dirt road and jeep roads.
Season: Spring, summer, and fall.
Facilities: None. Carry a minimum of 3-4 pints of water. Treat *all* water from local sources. All amenities available in Bishop.
Features: This loop takes you high into the foothills of the Sierra for views of the Bishop area. Wildflowers abound in spring and early summer. The name Buttermilk Country comes from the fact that a dairy, known among miners for its buttermilk, was once located along this route.
Access: From the junction of Highways 395 and 168 in Bishop, go west on Highway 168 (West Line Street) for 7.2 miles to the intersection of Buttermilk Road and park off the road. If interested in camping opportunities, contact BLM or USFS for information.

Ride west on dirt Buttermilk Road directly toward Mt. Tom, passing the Peabody Boulders ("Grandpa" and "Grandma" are the pair of boulders to the north). At 3.6 miles there is a cattle guard and the Horton Roubaix cutoff to your right. Keep going about 300 yards to where a short singletrack loop heads left and rejoins Buttermilk Road in 0.25 mile. Listen for the

sound of a waterfall. [**Side trip:** A 50-yard walk takes you to a deep-carved overlook above McGee Creek. Work your way carefully along this gorge to find a waterfall where birch, willows and ferns grow along stream.]

Back on the singletrack, ride west to rejoin Buttermilk Road which becomes narrow and rocky. [**Side trips:** Pass several turnoffs; the sec-

West Line Road to Buttermilk Country and the Sierra

ond jeep trail is the approach to Mt. Tom and a short road on the left heads to McGee Creek (4.9 miles) at the base of Grouse Mountain.]

Ride to the first stands of aspen at 5.7 miles, where your road levels off and heads south. Crossing the 7,600-foot contour, you can see Table Mountain to the south, Coyote Ridge to the southeast, and Grouse Mountain, a large granite outcropping, to the east.

At 6.1 miles, you pass a cattle crossing, and go through an area that is sometimes marshy. [**Side trip:** A small trail to the right of the road leads to a spring. *Treat all water.*]

Your road closes in on the ramparts of the Sierra at 6.9 miles where another trail leads up to another spring. Pass springs and marshes until you reach pines at 7.4 miles.

Climb a short ridge to the left, double back and head west, and climb to 8,240 feet (8.8 miles), the high point of this ride. Head easterly into aspen and pine, passing a jeep road on the right and the Birch Creek culvert. From here, the road is sometimes bladed and you have a fast downhill.

There are more primitive campsites at 9.0 miles. Continue due east to 10.4 miles where a road goes sharp right and up the ridge, south to Highway 168 (Power Station #2).

To complete the loop, turn left downhill along a narrow ridge, following the Aqueduct pipe and, at 12.7 miles, cross the left side of the ridge. You can see the upper end of Owens Valley and all the way to Montgomery Pass in Nevada.

[**Option:** There is a locked gate where an SCE service road heads west, paralleling the pipeline back to Highway 168. This short cut allows you to avoid the rocky, steep ascent ahead.]

Continue east out of the sandy wash and climb to a small ridge at 13.9 miles. You can see the USFS parking area below. *Caution: The next few hundred yards are the worst of the loop.*

At 14.5 miles you reach the USFS parking lot where there is room for about 15 cars. Take Highway 168 back to Buttermilk Road on your left at 17.1 miles. The highway descends steeply; watch for cars and guard against excessive speed.

3 Tungsten Hills Loop

Distance: 12 miles.
Difficulty: Moderate; challenging climb with a technical descent.
Elevation: Lowest point: 4,400'; highest point: 5,500'.
Type: Loop ride on dirt road, jeep road, and pavement.
Season: Spring, summer, and fall.
Facilities: Water, parking, restrooms, and shade at Millpond Park. All amenities available in Bishop.
Features: Tungsten mining was at its peak during World War I, and this area was extensively mined. From the top of the ride, you can see the roads and ranches in Round Valley, Mount Tom and Wheeler Crest, and Lower Rock Creek Canyon. The White Mountains rise behind the Volcanic Tableland and Casa Diablo Mountain.
Access: Take Highway 395 about 3 1/2 miles north of Bishop. Turn west on Ed Powers Road and take the first right toward Millpond Park. Park by the baseball fields. Many equestrians, motorcyclists, and four-wheel drive enthusiasts use this area, a popular spot with Bishop locals. Please extend appropriate courtesies and respect to these users.

Start from the three-way junction at Millpond entrance. Take the middle road past the ball fields to the log arch, bear right, and pass through the campground toward the Tungsten Hills.

At the back of the campground (western side), pass through the gate and continue up a jeep road parallel to McGee Creek. At a Y-junction, bear left close to the creek.

This road ends at Tungsten City Road where you go right uphill toward a gap, cross under three power lines, then take another right at the Y-junction. Climb into the McGee Creek canyon, following the

Tungsten Hills

Looking across Round Valley to Wheeler Crest

road toward the Tungsten Hills where you can see mines on the hillsides. Head toward the trees, ignoring several jeep roads, to a Y-junction just before the trees. Go right across the creek, then take a second right and climb a side canyon. Stay with the best road; this is steep and sandy.

After a steep ascent up the dry gully and a sharp curve, there is a junction to the right. Take a look into the Blue Monster Tungsten Mine, being careful to avoid the dangers in this area. Continue to the left toward the crest of the road. The road worsens as you roll through this weathered, rounded granite.

At 4.0 miles there is a junction at a low crest. Go left and ride into a basin, crossing it, and climb to a higher crest—the top of the ride.

Take time to admire the view there before you begin the downhill which starts off steep, loose and technical. Walking is allowed!

Traverse to a saddle and a four-way junction. Go left downhill along a ridge. As you break over the ridge, and before you drop north toward the creek, you can see Round Valley.

You come to a series of switchbacks where there was extensive mining. Drop down some steep, loose turns to the flats where there is a green metal building and mining equipment, then head east toward a rocky point.

At the next junction, go right. Follow the road downhill along the base of the Tungsten Hills, cross a wash, and pass under the power lines. Take left turns at the next two junctions.

At 8.5 miles, this road ends at a wide dirt road. Go left, head north 50 yards, then right onto paved Round Valley Road and head south. Cross under the big power lines and follow the road through a cut where a short downhill leads to another T-junction.

Take another right on Sawmill Road and head back to Millpond Park.

4 Horton "Roubaix" Ride

Distance: 19 miles, a half-day ride with lunch stop.
Difficulty: Moderate, technical, with strenuous climb.
Elevation: Lowest point: 4,100'; highest point: 6,450'.
Type: Loop, all on dirt, graded road to doubletrack.
Season: Spring and fall, also winter when snow level allows.
Facilities: Water, parking, restrooms and shade at Millpond Park. All amenities in Bishop. None along the route. Take all the water you need—minimum of 3-4 pints. Treat *all* water from local sources.
Features: Spring wildflowers, a tungsten mine, the Buttermilk Boulders and great views of Owens Valley.
Access: Take Highway 395 about 3 1/2 miles north of Bishop. Turn west on Ed Powers Road and take the first right toward Millpond Park. Park by the baseball fields. Many equestrians, motorcyclists, and four-wheel drive enthusiasts use this area, a popular spot with Bishop locals. Please extend appropriate courtesies and respect to these users.

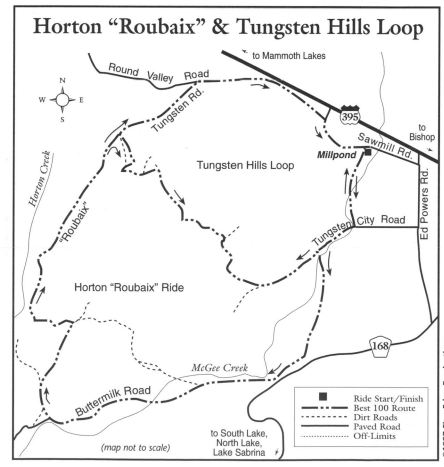

Horton "Roubaix" & Tungsten Hills Loop

Caution: Since equestrians frequently use the lower part of this route; please give them full right of way and show common courtesy.

Start from the three-way junction at Millpond entrance. Take the middle road past the ball fields to the log arch, bear right, and pass through the campground toward the Tungsten Hills. At the back of the campground (western side), pass through the gate and continue up a jeep road parallel to McGee Creek. At a Y-junction, bear left close to the creek. This road ends at Tungsten City Road,

Cycle west on Tungsten City Road, a well-graded dirt road which heads toward the old mining town site. At mile 1.6, just past the entrance to Deep Canyon, a prominent notch in the hills, you take a left branch downhill and cross McGee Creek. The road now climbs for 2 miles to meet the intersection of Highway 168 and Buttermilk Road at mile 3.6. From this intersection take Buttermilk Road—wide, graded, often "washboardy" and sandy—and head west toward the Sierra Crest.

At mile 7.2, you cross a cattle guard and turn right on the next doubletrack, ungraded road, heading north. You are now at the high point of the ride, elevation 6,450 feet, and you pass the Peabody Boulders rock climbing area on the right.

Half a mile later you reach a Y-intersection at mile 7.7. Take the right branch (the left branch heads toward two tall, free-standing boulders). After a mile of gentle terrain, you make a hard left and head due west. In a half-mile you come to the edge of the drop-off to Horton Creek, elevation 6,120 feet.

The doubletrack now drops steeply down to a water course that parallels—and is east of—Horton Creek. The next section is the Horton Roubaix, named by locals after France's Paris-Roubaix Race whose route traverses some formidable cobblestone roads. The Horton Roubaix twists around doubletrack of firmly packed cobbles, a few larger rocks and thickets of willows on its gentle downhill run.

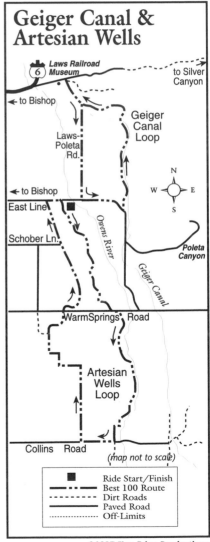

Geiger Canal & Artesian Wells

Laws Railroad Museum
to Silver Canyon
to Bishop
Geiger Canal Loop
Laws-Poleta Rd.
to Bishop
East Line
N W E S
Schober Ln.
Owens River
Poleta Canyon
Geiger Canal
WarmSprings Road
Artesian Wells Loop
Collins Road
(map not to scale)

■ Ride Start/Finish
▬▬▬ Best 100 Route
- - - - - Dirt Roads
▬▬▬ Paved Road
·········· Off-Limits

This fun section ends at mile 10.5, where the track leaves the drainage course and continues down the alluvial fan. In 2 miles you have to make a decision: continue the full route or take a short cut.

[**Option:** If you have had enough climbing or your time and/or energy are short, continue on this road until it intersects with paved South Round Valley Road. Turn right. Go to Sawmill Road, turn right and head to Ed Powers Road. Turn right again and proceed to the starting point ahead on your right.]

To continue the full loop: at the T-junction at 15.4 miles, go right and head down past Tungsten Blue Mine, where the road becomes Tungsten City Road. You soon reach the point where—at the start of your trip—you left Tungsten City Road to cross McGee Creek. In another 1.6 miles you return to your original starting point.

5 Geiger Canal Loop

Distance: 6.8 miles.
Difficulty: Easy.
Elevation: Mostly level at about 4,100'.
Type: Loop ride on dirt roads and along two canals.
Season: Year-round.
Facilities: Water and picnic tables at the White Mountain Research Center. All amenities are available in Bishop.
Features: Ride alongside an historic irrigation ditch and an extension of the Carson & Colorado narrow gauge railroad grade. A few foundations and an irrigation ditch are all that's left of Poleta, once a station on the railroad. Geiger Canal, a major irrigation ditch, carried water from the Owens River to Bishop area farms and ranches. There are fantastic views of the Sierra.
Access: From the junction of Highway 395 and East Line Street in Bishop (first traffic light at south end of town), go east 3.5 miles to the Owens River bridge. Park off the road west of the bridge.

Start at the Owens River Bridge and head east toward the White Mountains. (East Line Street becomes Poleta Road at the bridge). On the left, you pass the Laws-Poleta Road—a wide gravel road—then the White Mountain Research Station on your right. Just past the research station, you cross the railroad grade.

[**Side trip:** To the left (north) of the road are some cottonwoods; take a side trip there to find the remains of Poleta and the old Carson & Colorado Station.]

Continue on the paved road toward the White Mountains. At the first curve, go left and up the hill to Geiger Canal, a large irrigation ditch. Cross the canal and go left, heading north.

Follow the canal north along the base of the White Mountains. At a large square cluster of trees is an old ranch site, two smaller irrigation ditches, and a lovely view of the Owens River, Bishop, and the Sierra.

At a junction at 3.5 miles, go left and head west along a small ditch leading toward the Owens River.

Cross the grassland toward a cluster of trees. At a road to the right, there is a running ditch, and to the left, a well with electric lines running to it. Keep straight 100 yards to a big green gate.

Go through the gate and turn left (south) on Laws-Poleta Road. Within a mile, you come to a corral, site of an old ranch. Look carefully. The elevated gravel bed of the historic Carson & Colorado narrow-gauge crossed here. Follow the straight, wide, level road south to a T-junction (6.4 miles) with the Poleta-East Line road. Go right toward the Owens River and your starting point.

6 Artesian Wells Loop

Distance: 16.5 miles.
Difficulty: Moderate.
Elevation: Mostly level at about 4,000'.
Type: Loop ride along the Owens River on paved and jeep roads.
Season: Year-round.
Facilities: None. All amenities available in Bishop.
Features: This is a pleasant ride featuring two historic canals and five artesian springs. Ride beside the Owens River with its lush foliage and abundant wildlife—especially birds.
Access: From the junction of Highway 395 and East Line Street in Bishop (first traffic light at south end of town), go east 3.5 miles to the Owens River bridge. Park off the road west of the bridge.

Just west of the Owens River bridge you will find the first artesian spring, a small gurgle of warm water from a corrugated pipe. Head south on the road beside the river, ignoring several spurs.

At 0.75 mile, go left at a Y-junction and continue along the base of a small bluff. The second artesian spring is at the end of a spur near the river; bird life is abundant here. Pass two cement silos by a big cottonwood.

At 1.5 miles you pass the third artesian spring, visible to the left. The road runs along the base of a small bluff and there are dense cottonwoods and willows along the river.

At 2.6 miles, go left at a junction and up a short, sandy hill. The fourth artesian well is in a cluster of trees. Continue south on the curving road parallel to the Owens River until you come to a T-junction with Warm Springs Road. Take a left toward the Owens River for 0.25 mile, then a right onto the wide, sandy road that parallels Owens River. After one mile, some cottonwoods appear and the road becomes hard-packed.

At 4.8 miles you come to the last artesian spring; this one offers an inviting shower. Continue south on the wide road along the winding Owens River.

At a three-way junction, go right through a gooseneck curve along the Big Pine Canal. Follow it 0.5 mile to a four-way junction. Go right and head west on Collins Road.

At 7.7 miles, take a right onto a narrow dirt road. The line of green on the right is the Owens River. Head toward a line of trees. Keep a sharp

Owens River, White Mountains in background

lookout for many species of hawk and golden eagles—this is a prime hunting ground.

In about a mile you pass the foundation of an old ranch. Follow the road, which now deteriorates to a jeep road, toward White Mountain.

At a Y-junction, go left and follow the curving jeep road along a shallow ditch. At the next Y go right onto the better road that begins to follow Rawson Canal. After numerous zigzags and curves, you return to Warm Springs Road.

At 11.7 miles, cross the road and continue along the canal on well maintained gravel. You pass two small ponds, home to riparian life—a jungle in contrast to the desert vegetation. From this point on, you follow Rawson Canal. As you continue north along the ditch, watch for ducks and other waterfowl among the tall grasses, willows, and cattails.

Continue along this dirt road around a long, wide curve. In one mile, at a junction by a big cottonwood, stay along Rawson Canal and ride past several more ponds, also rich in waterfowl. Cross the canal and bear right at a cluster of cottonwoods. At East Line Street, the paved road, go right to Owens River bridge and your car.

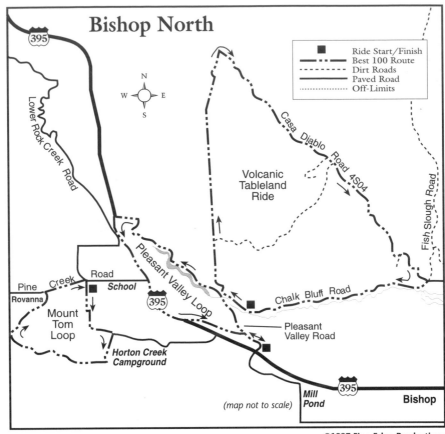

©1997 Fine Edge Productions

CHAPTER 7

Bishop North

Rivers of molten lava, ice, and water have sculpted the land at the north end of Owens Valley. Evidence of volcanic activity can be found in the massive lava flow called the Volcanic Tableland that extends almost to Crowley Lake. This table-land, formed about 700,000 years ago when the Long Valley caldera erupted, created the basin that holds Crowley Lake. The explosion, 2,000 times greater than that of Mount St. Helens in 1980, sent ash as far east as Nebraska, cover-ing over 500 square miles north of present-day Bishop with 500 feet of pumice that eventually welded itself into the pinkish rock known as Bishop tuff. Ancestors of the Paiute Indians once roamed this area leaving their traces in the form of petroglyphs on desert-varnished rocks.

Owens Valley is a big "trench," almost 100 miles long, that is sinking between two uplifting mountain ranges. In places, it is almost two vertical miles from the valley to the peaks—one of the most dramatic mountain scarps in the world—and has earned its other name, Deepest Valley.

Note: While visiting petroglyph sites, please do not touch or walk on these sensitive traces of the past. Remember, archeological and cultural resources are a non-renewable resource. Once disturbed or removed, they are gone forever.

1 Pleasant Valley Loop

Distance: 14 miles.
Difficulty: Moderate.
Elevation: Starting point: 4,100'; highest point: 4,600'.
Type: Loop ride on paved road, dirt road, and jeep road.
Season: Year-round.
Facilities: Water and toilets at Pleasant Valley Campground; gas and store at Mill Creek Station. All amenities available in Bishop.
Features: Travel through cool, pleasant riparian habitat rich with bird life; admire the Owens River Gorge with its dramatic, sheer rock faces that rise to the blue desert sky.
Access: Drive seven miles north of Bishop on Highway 395, turn right (east) onto Pleasant Valley Road and park off the road.

Pleasant Valley Campground, Mount Tom in background

Ride northeast on Pleasant Valley Road across a big meadow. The white bluff ahead is Chalk Bluff, the edge of the Volcanic Tableland. Cross Mill Creek and climb to a low saddle. Below you can see Pleasant Valley and the Owens River running through it. Lush marshlands occupy the bottom and cottonwoods and willows line the river. Hawks and eagles are common here. In the summer, it is cooler here near the river, and the tall green grasses and trees contrast with the surrounding high desert.

Follow the road as it dips down and then continues up the canyon past Pleasant Valley Campground and across Owens River.

You come to a gate across the road with a sign warning of falling rock and rising water. This is Los Angeles Department of Water and Power land. Bikers and pedestrians are welcome to use DWP roads and trails for day-use recreation. But, enter at your own risk. No camping or fires are permitted.

Go around the gate and up to the crest of the dam. Stay on the trail along the reservoir. About halfway up the reservoir there is a single tree and a boat ramp. This is an excellent rest spot, a Pleasant Valley indeed!

As the reservoir continues, it gradually narrows to a river. Cottonwood, willow, and aspen trees grow along its bank and grasses, cat-tails, and brush create a dense jungle appreciated by the numerous birds that visit the area.

At 5.4 miles you cross a small bridge by a DWP power plant—one of four along the Owens River Gorge. From here most of the river flows into the huge penstock, or conduit. Bear left around the building and then right, uphill along the tuff.

As you ascend to the crest, the Sierra comes into full view. Mount Tom is the magnificent triangular peak across Round Valley with Pine Creek Canyon cutting along its northern base. Wheeler Crest is the long granite crown to the north of

Mount Tom; the low desert hills to the south of Mount Tom are the Tungsten Hills.

Follow the paved road to an intersection by the giant water pipe, take a left, and go downhill. Cross Highway 395 and continue a short distance to the road's end at the old highway (Lower Rock Creek Road).

Turn left, paralleling 395 and head south. Large cottonwoods line the irrigation ditches and creeks and there are ruins of old ranches amid the trees. Low stone fences, visible in several places, are remains of the historic Sherwin Toll Road. Follow Lower Rock Creek Road for 2 miles to its end at Pine Creek Road.

(9.4 miles). Take a left and cross Highway 395 to Mill Creek Road, once the historic stage route, following it south to Mill Creek Station Store. Just north of the store, you can see a couple of old stone buildings that once served as the stage station.

Past the store, continue south on the paved road paralleling the main highway, then continue straight on the old road which first becomes broken pavement, then dirt. Follow the base of the bluff, parallel to Mill Creek, still on the historic stage route to Mammoth Lakes.

Along the way you can find petroglyphs if you look carefully. *Admire, but do not touch.* This rock art is fragile and irreplaceable.

Continue along Mill Creek below the cliffs, cross under some power lines and pass through a gate. The road, now almost a trail, passes through dense willows. Cross under three more power lines and keep heading straight along the base of the cliff.

At 13.5 miles, the dirt road ends at Pleasant Valley Road. Go right, cross a broad meadow, and head toward Highway 395 and your vehicle.

2 Volcanic Tableland Loop

Distance: 21.6 miles.
Difficulty: Moderate and non-technical.
Elevation: Lowest point: 4,000'; highest point: 5,000'.
Type: Loop ride on dirt roads and utility roads.
Season: Year-round.
Facilities: Water and restrooms at Pleasant Valley Campground; gas and store at Mill Creek Station. All amenities available in Bishop.
Features: Ride across the volcanic landscape that runs from Crowley Lake nearly to Bishop; excellent views of the Owens Valley and surrounding mountains.
Access: Take Highway 395 north of Bishop for 7 miles, turn east on Pleasant Valley Road. Just past the Pleasant Valley Campground, park off road at the junction with Chalk Bluff Road.

From the junction with Chalk Bluff Road, go left and curve northward on the road that ascends a rocky grade toward three big power lines. At the top, take a short detour to the left for a great view down to Pleasant Valley, then go right along the triple power line and across the Volcanic Tableland, an area of weathered, pink volcanic rock covered with sparse high-desert vegetation. The road is rough, solid rock with occasional sand.

The long, gradual climb culminates in two shelves. The buff-colored rock is Bishop tuff. Sage, rabbit brush, and some cactus grow in little pockets of soil in this rocky desert terrain. The road climbs to a panoramic vista, then descends toward Casa Diablo.

At 7.5 miles there is an intersection with 4S04, the Casa Diablo Road. Take the road right and downhill toward Owens Valley. Cross the Volcanic Tableland and several small ridges that are earthquake faults. Pass a quarry where bricks were once cut from the pink Bishop tuff, and continue your long gradual downhill.

At 16 miles you come to a five-way junction. There is a small parking area with a kiosk here. Stop to read the information about the area's natural history and the BLM's philosophy of semi-primitive management which seeks to maintain the area in its most natural state.

Take the road to the right that hugs the base of the Chalk Bluff cliffs and parallels the river for about five miles. The road passes a double canal with thickets of willow and cottonwood along the river. You pass a corral on the left; go through two boulders in a narrow slot, then past a field of boulders and Pleasant Valley Campground to your starting point at the junction of Pleasant Valley and Chalk Bluff roads.

2 Mount Tom Loop

Distance: 9.3 miles.
Difficulty: Moderate with some technical jeep road.
Elevation: Starting point: 4,500'; high point: 5,400'.
Type: Loop ride on pavement, dirt road, and jeep road.
Season: Year-round.
Facilities: Restrooms at Horton Creek Campground. Gas and store at Mill Creek Station. All amenities in Bishop.
Features: Views of Round Valley, the Volcanic Tableland, and the White Mountains from the base of Mount Tom.
Access: Take Highway 395 north of Bishop for 9 miles to Rovana-Pine Creek Road (signed only as Rovana on Highway 395). Go west 1.7 miles to the intersection with Round Valley Road. Park off the road near Round Valley School.

Head south on Round Valley Road toward the Tungsten Hills. This green farming land has been used for ranching for over a century and you pass several ranches. The road is lined with cottonwoods and small irrigation ditches.

Continue south on Round Valley Road as it zigs and zags, following old irrigation ditches at the base of Mount Tom. At the junction to Horton Creek Campground, go right (west) and uphill toward the Buttermilk Basin on a narrow paved road parallel to Horton Creek. The road leads steeply up the alluvial fan to Horton Creek BLM Campground, goosenecks past a bulletin board, and through the campground.

At 3.0 miles you take a right onto the power line road and head north toward Mount Tom. As it traverses the vast alluvial fan across the base of the mountain, the road is rugged and

Pleasant Valley Reservoir

technical. Your reward is a magnificent view of Round Valley, Rock Creek Canyon, the Volcanic Tableland, and the White Mountains.

For one mile, the road descends across stony wasteland. Cross a small creek that drains the flank of Mount Tom and climb a rocky route toward the lateral moraine of Pine Creek Canyon—the most difficult part of the ride. This area was burned in a 1996 wildfire so the rocky slope is barren.

At 5.9 miles, you come to an intersection. Take the right and head downhill on a sandy section. The road splits twice, coming together again. Near the bottom of the moraine you pass a gravel pit. Here the road turns to pavement, curves around the end of the moraine, and comes to a T-junction.

Go right and downhill. Take the first left through the trailer park to a second T-junction with Pine Creek Road. Go right and downhill to your starting point.

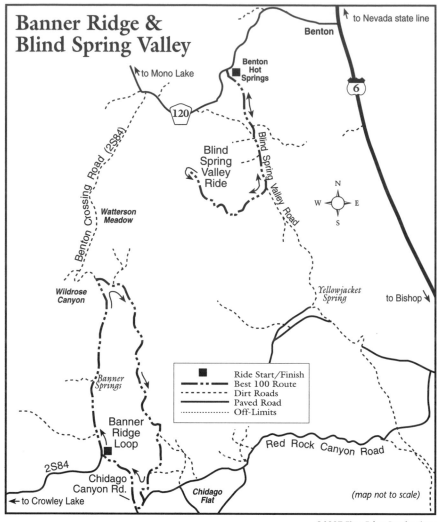

**Banner Ridge &
Blind Spring Valley**

to Nevada state line

Benton

to Mono Lake

Benton Hot Springs

120

6

Blind Spring Valley Ride

Blind Spring Valley Road

Benton Crossing Road (2S84)

Watterson Meadow

N
W   E
S

Wildrose Canyon

Yellowjacket Spring

to Bishop

Banner Springs

■ Ride Start/Finish
—·—·— Best 100 Route
- - - - - Dirt Roads
———— Paved Road
········· Off-Limits

Banner Ridge Loop

Red Rock Canyon Road

2S84

Chidago Canyon Rd.

Chidago Flat

to Crowley Lake

(map not to scale)

©1997 Fine Edge Productions

CHAPTER 8

Benton

In the 19th century, Benton was an important crossroads. Yellow Jacket Road (marked Blind Spring Valley on most maps) was the stage road to Bishop, and Benton Crossing Road served as the freight road to Mammoth Lakes. Highway 120 follows what was once the wagon road to Bodie. During the mining boom in the late 1800s, Benton and Bodie were contemporary settlements. The area's Blind Spring Mining District produced millions of dollars in silver from 1864 to the 1880s. The third Fremont-Carson party camped here and soaked in the Benton Hot Springs. From Benton, half of the party continued southward, "discovering" Owens Valley and naming it for their cartographer.

A few buildings still stand in Benton as a reminder of the once-thriving community. One, a cut-stone building, now a store and gas station, was a Wells Fargo station back in the 1870s. An extensive collection of wagons and farm implements are located uphill behind the building. Across the street is a white wooden building—the new focus of Benton—a privately-owned bed & breakfast and hot springs. Several redwood hot tubs are open to the public for a fee.

1 Banner Ridge Loop

Distance: 14 miles.
Difficulty: Moderate, with some technical sections.
Elevation: Starting point: 6,900'; highest point: 8,500'.
Type: Loop ride on pavement, dirt road, and jeep road.
Season: Spring, summer, and fall.
Facilities: None. Be prepared with snacks and plenty of water—a minimum of 3-4 pints.
Features: Excellent views of the White Mountains and surrounding area, with scattered small ranches and mines; a combination of high desert, mountain meadows and forests of pinyon pines.
Access: From Mammoth Lakes, at the junction of Highways 395 and 203, drive south 6 miles on Highway 395 to Benton Crossing Road at the green church. Go east around Lake Crowley for 19 miles. Park near a corral and windmill, just south of the junction of Benton Crossing Road (2S84) and Chidago Canyon Road (4S34).

Go north on Benton Crossing Road (2S84), cross under the power lines, and head toward a low saddle. Glass Mountain Ridge lies ahead.

Pass over the saddle and follow the pavement 4.5 miles to dirt road (3S50) where you turn right, cross a basin of sagebrush, and pass a junction to the left. Continue straight toward a saddle along the side of Banner Ridge.

At 6.0 miles you reach the saddle. Both basins are covered in rabbit brush and sage, and pinyon pine grows along the ridge. Continue down the far side of the saddle toward the White Mountains, passing the Gold Crown Mine (6.5 miles) at the bottom of this bowl. Blind Spring Hill is to the east.

Continue straight to a second saddle where you have a view of the Sierra from the crest. Banner Ridge is to the west, Blind Spring Hill and the White Mountains to the east. The meadow here is covered with colorful

wildflowers in the spring.

The graded road ends at 8.4 miles. A sign warns that the road is not maintained and—it's a rocky road! Climb the hill into the pinyon forest and, at the crest, pass a road leading off to the left. Go straight down the ridge for a short but very steep section through the pinyons toward Casa Diablo Mountain, visible to the south.

Cross under a triple power line. Just past the power line, go right on a jeep road. It is a steep descent across a dry drainage and down to Chidago Canyon whose walls are sheer and black. After a mile, the primitive jeep road ends at a wide graded road (3S53). Take a right and go downhill to a junction with Chidago Canyon Road (4S34). Take another right here, and head uphill toward a narrow gap.

Pass over the slit in the ridge into a wide bowl and ride around the meadow to your starting point at the junction of Chidago Canyon Road and paved Benton Crossing Road.

Glass Mountains from Banner Ridge

2 Red Rock Canyon Ride

Distance: 16.5 miles with shuttle.
Difficulty: Moderate.
Elevation: Starting point: 6,900'; finish: 4,100' (2,800' of downhill with one 300-foot climb).
Type: A downhill delight for most of its 16 miles with either a shuttle or a sag.
Season: Spring, summer, and fall. Avoid the ride in unsettled weather.
Facilities: None. Store, gas and water in Benton. No water along the route; carry at least 2 quarts.
Features: This rides goes through Chidago (pronounced Shi-day-go) and Red Rock Canyons, two scenic, strikingly different canyons. Petroglyphs can be seen in Red Rock Canyon and near the finish of your ride.
Access/Shuttle: From Mammoth Lakes, at the junction of Highways 395 and 203, drive south 6 miles on Highway 395 to Benton Crossing Road at the green church. Go left (east) around Lake Crowley for 19 miles to the junction of Benton Crossing Road (2S84) and Chidago Canyon Road (4S34). Park off the road near a corral and windmill.
To set up a shuttle, continue on Benton Crossing Road to its end at Highway 120. Go right (east) to Highway 6 at Benton. Turn right (south) for about 14 miles to White Mountain Ranch Road. Park one car here on the west side of Highway 6 and drive your other vehicle back to start of the ride.

It's more convenient to have a sag vehicle that can follow you down Red Rock Canyon. However, a small four-wheel drive is required to negotiate the narrow canyon.

Take the Chidago Canyon Road (signed) south and follow it around a meadow, passing through a narrow gap. On the far side of the gap, you pass through a flat-bottomed valley covered with sagebrush and pinyon. The road descends Chidago Canyon, a deep trench cut through the lava.

At a Y-junction, go right. Pass a mill site at Antelope Spring and continue past a ranch. Follow the road down the valley toward the White Mountains. At 4.5 miles there is another junction. Go left and out of the canyon toward the crest of a low saddle, ignoring another road to the

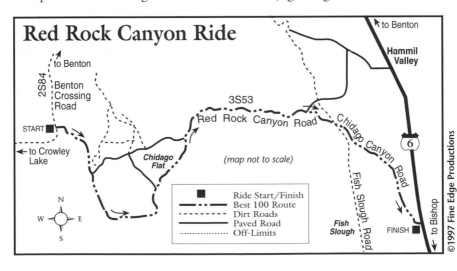

Red Rock Canyon—the long descent

left. Stay right toward the low saddle. At the crest of the saddle there are wonderful views of both the White Mountains and the Sierra.

The road now descends a long, wide basin. Ignore several dirt roads on your left and keep going straight, down-canyon.

At 7.2 miles take the road down-canyon under the power lines and through a narrow slit hundreds of feet deep. The canyon widens as you descend eastward toward the White Mountains.

At 9 miles, you come to the beginning of Red Rock Canyon with its eroded red sandstone and fantastically sculpted rocks full of holes and bowls—there are no sharp angles here, just curves. Look carefully for petroglyphs near the top of the canyon.

This part of the road through the narrow, sandy wash is too narrow for all but four-wheel drive vehicles. *It is not the place to be caught in a thunderstorm, when flash-floods can occur.*

At a little over 10 miles you can see the bas-relief of a miner on a rocky face. Continue 0.5 mile through this unique canyon until it opens up onto a huge shelf directly below the

Old wagons and farm machinery, Benton

White Mountains. As the road descends toward Hammil Valley across wide open desert, ignore the wide road to the left.

Continue east and downhill, crossing 3V01 (Fish Slough Road), and then down Chidago Canyon Road to a large irrigated field and along the base of the cliff at the south edge of the field. The road makes a sharp left toward Highway 6 where your ride ends. If you're not in too much of a hurry, you may discover more petroglyphs on your downhill ride.

3 Blind Spring Valley Ride

Distance: 13 miles.
Difficulty: Moderate with technical sections.
Elevation: 5,400' to 6,850'.
Type: Out-and-back on dirt road.
Season: Year-round.
Facilities: A store, gas and hot spring resort in Benton. Carry a minimum of 3-4 pints of water.
Features: Visit Old Benton and see fantastic views of the White Mountains.
Access: From the junction of Highways 395 and 203, drive south 6 miles on Highway 395 to Benton Crossing Road at the green church. Go east on Benton Crossing Road around Crowley Lake, over Glass Mountain Ridge, and down to Highway 120. Go right on Highway 120 over a summit and down to Benton, a total of about 29 miles.

Blind Spring Hill, White Mountains from Banner Ridge

Former Wells Fargo Office, Benton Hot Springs

Start by the small cut-stone building at the corner of Highway 120 and Yellow Jacket Road (signed)—the old stage road to Bishop. Go south on Yellow Jacket Road, paved at first. Follow it past three ponds and through the Paiute Indian Reservation. To your left is Blind Spring Hill, the site of extensive silver mines in the 1860s where you can still see the remains.

The pavement ends in a little over a mile and the road continues toward a gap. Banner Ridge is to the right. Pass a road on the left that climbs Blind Spring Hill, pass several pit mines, and continue on the road to the saddle.

At the crest there is a cattle guard and a fence line (3.5 miles). The power lines are very close to the road. Take the road to the right after passing the fence and follow the single power line toward Banner Ridge. The steep and stony road leads toward a small canyon and levels out after a good climb. It then continues uphill and turns north across a sandy wash. The climb along the side of Banner Ridge is on a steep, technical jeep road. Follow the single wooden power poles.

At a crest, you can see the Radio Relay ahead. Cross a bowl and climb to the small ridge with a level pad. Stay outside the fenced area. There are fantastic views of the Glass Mountains, Blind Spring Valley and, across Blind Spring Hill, the face of the White Mountains. White Mountain is the tallest, over 14,200 feet high.

Return the way you came. Follow the single power line across the bowl, down the ridge, and across the gully. Go left down to the big power lines and the wide road, and left again down Yellow Jacket Road to Benton and your vehicle.

CHAPTER 9

Rock Creek

Upper Rock Creek Canyon, which extends high into the Sierra from Toms Place, was formed by the uplifting of the Sierra Nevada. Lower Rock Creek Canyon, which drops from Toms Place toward Bishop, on the other hand, was carved by water flowing through volcanic lava. Upper Rock Creek Canyon offers spectacular alpine vistas of meadows, lakes, and peaks. Lower Rock Creek has cut a stunning gorge through the Bishop tuff where, in some places, columnar formations resemble those of Devils Postpile. It is hard to believe two such different canyons share one creek. Rock Creek itself once flowed directly into Owens River in Long Valley, but uplifting of the earth at the outlet of the upper canyon moved it to its present course.

The road in Upper Rock Creek Canyon is the highest paved road in the Sierra; Lower Rock Creek Canyon road, the early Highway 395, closely parallels the historic toll road between Bishop and Mammoth Lakes, and the trail takes you, literally, to Paradise!

Lower Rock Creek Canyon

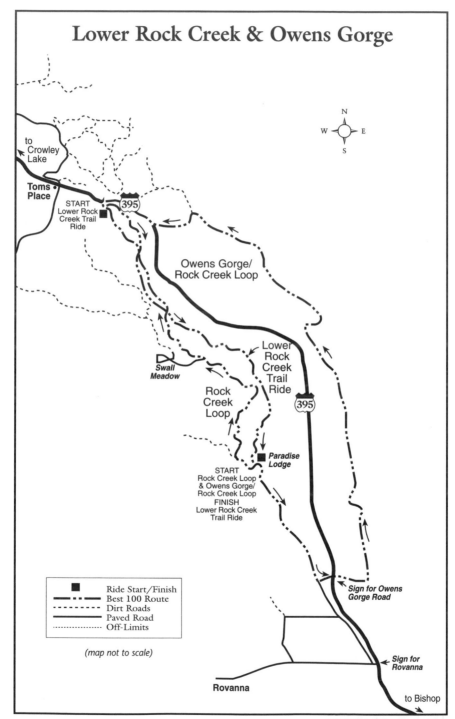

Lower Rock Creek & Owens Gorge

to Crowley Lake

Toms Place

START
Lower Rock
Creek Trail
Ride

Owens Gorge/
Rock Creek Loop

Lower
Rock
Creek
Trail
Ride

Swall
Meadow

Rock
Creek
Loop

Paradise
Lodge

START
Rock Creek Loop
& Owens Gorge/
Rock Creek Loop
FINISH
Lower Rock Creek
Trail Ride

Sign for Owens
Gorge Road

Sign for
Rovanna

Rovanna

to Bishop

Legend

■　Ride Start/Finish
—··—··—　Best 100 Route
---------　Dirt Roads
————　Paved Road
················　Off-Limits

(map not to scale)

©1997 Fine Edge Productions

1 Lower Rock Creek Trail Ride

Distance: 7.9 miles with shuttle.
Difficulty: Moderate at first; technical in the third section.
Elevation: From 7,000' to 5,000'.
Type: Downhill on singletrack with shuttle.
Season: Spring, summer, and fall.
Facilities: Toilets, cafe and store at Toms Place. Dinner restaurant at Paradise Lodge. (Soft drinks, candy bars, and ice available at Paradise Lodge office.)
Features: A challenging singletrack with interesting geology and cool, creek-side habitat. One of the finest mountain bike trails in the Eastern Sierra, Lower Rock Creek Trail is maintained by local riders, the Forest Service, and the Bureau of Land Management. Abusive riding could lead to its being closed to bikers, so please be courteous. Respect other users, pass with consideration, and control your bicycle. Excess speed leads to dragging your brakes, causing washboard and ruts. Enjoy it—don't destroy it!
Access/Shuttle: To leave your shuttle vehicle, exit Highway 395 at Rovana-Pine Creek Road (signed *Rovana* on 395), 9 miles north of Bishop. Cross the southbound lane of the highway, and turn right almost immediately, paralleling Highway 395. Drive about 5 miles north to Paradise Lodge. For the shuttle, leave a vehicle here across the road from the lodge and continue 7.9 miles up Lower Rock Creek Road, passing Swall Meadow Road, almost to the junction with Highway 395. Park at a small parking area across the road from the creek at the start of the trail.

Note: The lower end of the trail passes through Paradise Lodge private property. While to date the lodge has allowed mountain bikers to cross this property, a single mishap could change this situation and close the trail permanently.

The entire Rock Creek Trail is used by hikers and fishermen. Please be cautious and courteous at all times.

SECTION ONE: Begin between two rocks on the east side of the road across from the small parking area. Immediately below the rocks, you see a sign, *Lower Rock Creek Mountain Bike Trail*, and a register; please sign in. Go down the trail through tall grasses, sage, and willows, cross a culvert over the creek and follow the rolling dips of the sandy trail along Rock Creek. Aspen and Jeffrey pine line the trail, while pinyon, sage, and rabbit brush cover the slopes of the canyon.

A small stone causeway leads across a wet area where it can be a little tricky. The trail continues through

rolls and dips very near the creek. The next technical spot is between two small boulders. Then an aspen tunnel leads down a short, sandy hill back to the Rock Creek Road—the end of section one at 2.2 miles.

[**Option:** From here, a short loop back on the road to the start is an easy-ride possibility.]

SECTION TWO: To continue, turn right on the pavement, across the bridge, and left into a small parking area.

From this turnout the trail continues along the creek like a twisting roller-coaster, somewhat technical, yet not really difficult, and a whole lot of fun. There are some off-camber turns and tricky gullies.

You cross a small bridge; farther down at a boulder, you are forced to dismount. The second section (3.3 miles) ends at a parking area beside a second bridge. This is where the road climbs out of the gorge.

SECTION THREE: Only experienced cyclists should continue on this section. The third downhill section begins across the road by a sign. From this point on, the trail is highly technical and there are no bail-out points. The first half-mile runs along a shelf above the creek, below Rock Creek Road, where you pass a vintage car circa 1930. The trail gets more challenging as it drops off the shelf, winding through brush and tall pines to the first bridge. There is a boulder and several wrecks by the first bridge.

At 4.2 miles, where a huge fallen tree was sawed through to clear the trail for passage, for fun you can count its rings to determine its age. At 4.4 miles the trail is blocked by a boulder half the size of a Volkswagen. At 4.9 miles you pass a downed 6-foot-diameter "grandfather" tree and a cabin-sized boulder. There's a nice picnicking area along this particular stretch of the creek. Look up and examine the basaltic columnar rock formations here similar to those of Devils Postpile.

Next, the trail curves up a scree and talus slope away from the creek for 100 miserable yards; then at 5.3 miles you return to the creek.

At a bridge (5.8 miles), there are dense willow thickets along the creek and the trail is loose gravel with tight rolling turns and some rooted sections. Two rock culverts drain the springs. There is one dismount by a waterfall.

After crossing a third bridge at 6.0 miles, the trail widens. A fourth bridge comes up soon as the canyon widens. The fifth bridge crosses the creek to a wider trail, an easy section in a sunnier part of the canyon. At 6.9 miles there is a 4-foot diameter rock in the center of the high-speed part of the trail.

Cross one more bridge (7.0 miles) to a wide, well-built section of trail. Soon, on the right, are a sign board and a register. Again, please sign in; let the BLM know that mountain bikers use and enjoy their efforts.

The trail becomes a road and follows the creek to the last bridge. There are cabins and cottonwoods along the remainder of the short downhill to Paradise, mile 7.9, and your shuttle car.

2 Rock Creek Loop

Distance: 15.5 miles.
Difficulty: Advanced ride with a strenuous uphill and technical singletrack downhill.
Elevation: From 5,000' to 7,000'.
Type: Loop ride on paved road and singletrack.
Season: Spring, summer, and fall.
Facilities: Store and cafe at Toms Place. All amenities available in Bishop. Be sure to carry plenty of water. Treat any water taken from local sources.
Features: This challenging loop, for advanced riders only, includes the singletrack to Paradise. At the beginning of the ride, you have panoramic views encompassing Wheeler Crest, Swall and Sky meadows, Lower Rock Creek Canyon, the Volcanic Tableland, Highway 395, Casa Diablo, and the White Mountains beyond.
Access: Exit Highway 395 at Rovana-Pine Creek Road (signed *Rovana* on 395), 9 miles north of Bishop. Cross the southbound lane of the highway, and turn right almost immediately, paralleling Highway 395. Drive about 5 miles north to Paradise Lodge. Park across the road from the lodge.

Rock Creek Lake

Note: The lower end of the trail passes through Paradise Lodge private property. While to date the lodge has allowed mountain bikers to cross this property, a single mishap could change this situation and close the trail permanently.

Start at Paradise Lodge and ride up paved Lower Rock Creek Road through Paradise Estates, past a fire station, and uphill past an old corral. Along the side of the road you can still see traces of the historic Sherwin Grade wagon trail that led to Mammoth.

Continue up through a set of steep 'S' curves where the view of Owens Valley and Bishop opens up. At the curve with a white wooden guard rail (2.3 miles), take a break and look down into Rock Creek Canyon where you can see the volcanic rock walls and the creek.

At 3.7 miles, you pass Swall Meadow Road. To the left there are wagon tracks in the rock—the old toll road. Continue riding to the crest of the road past a small parking area to the left, then drop into Rock Creek Canyon.

At the canyon bottom, where the creek goes under the road (5.1 miles), you begin another uphill grind.

After you cross a second bridge the road is less steep, and you eventually round a big curve into sight of Highway 395 at 7.9 miles.

The entrance to Lower Rock Creek Trail is across the road from a small parking area just before you reach Highway 395.

For the rest of the ride, please refer to the Lower Rock Creek Trail Ride. Remember to sign the register and to ride lightly on this magical trail. Avoid abusive riding.

3 Owens Gorge/ Rock Creek Loop

Distance: 24.2 miles.
Difficulty: Advanced ride with strenuous climb and a technical downhill singletrack
Elevation: Start: 4,900' to 7,000' to 4,900'.
Type: Loop ride on secondary pavement and dirt road along the rim of Owens River Gorge and down the Lower Rock Creek Trail.
Season: Spring, summer, and fall.
Facilities: There is a cafe and store at Toms Place. All amenities available in Bishop. Carry at least 4 pints of water. Treat water from local sources. *Note:* The lower end of the trail passes through Paradise Lodge private property. While to date the lodge has allowed mountain bikers to cross this property, a single mishap could change this situation and close the trail permanently. All amenities available in Bishop.
Features: The uphill parallels the Owens River Gorge and the Los Angeles Aqueduct, passing several hydroelectric plants. You return along the magnificent Lower Rock Creek Trail.
Access: Exit Highway 395 at Rovana-Pine Creek Road (signed Rovana on 395), 9 miles north of Bishop. Cross the southbound lane of the highway, and turn right almost immediately, paralleling Highway 395. Drive about 5 miles north to Paradise Lodge. Park across the road from the lodge.

From Paradise Lodge, head south on Lower Rock Creek Road for 3 miles. Turn left (east) at the T-junction of Gorge Road and Lower Rock Creek Road. Cross Highway 395 and head east toward the White Mountains until you reach a T-junction.

At 3.9 miles, go left and uphill parallel to the power lines and the pipeline—part of the DWP hydroelectric power system. Keep heading uphill with Casa Diablo Mountain in view to the north. Near the crest is a white cement tank.

There are dramatic views of Owens Valley, Mount Tom and Wheeler Crest along this section.

After crossing a big dip, the road continues its ascent. At 7.3 miles you pass a junction that leads to Owens River Gorge. Continue straight up the paved road. You can see the point at which the pipeline drops into the gorge ahead.

At a junction (9.3 miles),there are a cement water tank and a tailing pile. Continue up the paved utility road. Owens River Gorge is visible with the White Mountains beyond.

The road climbs up the volcanic slope and across a narrow cut (probably a volcanic cooling fissure). The next road to the right leads into the gorge to Power Station 2. Stay left.

At 11.2 miles go left at a Y-junction onto broken pavement. This leads through pinyon forest to another junction and cement tank where the pavement ends. The right fork leads to an overlook. Take the left and head uphill through a gate, into and across a bowl surrounded by volcanic buttes.

There is a three-way junction on the far side of the bowl. Take the road to the left toward Wheeler Crest and Highway 395. At the highway, turn right and head north for one mile. Look for Lower Rock Creek Road on the left at 16.2 miles. This is the beginning of Lower Rock Creek Canyon. Cross the highway, and ride down the road 0.1 mile to a small parking area. Across the road, between two rocks, the Lower Rock Creek Canyon Trail begins.

From the beginning of the singletrack, follow the route of the *Lower Rock Creek Trail Ride.*

4 Sky Meadow Loop

Distance: 10.5 miles.
Difficulty: Strenuous and technical.
Elevation: Highest point: 7,100'; lowest point: 6,400'; frequent 500' gain/loss.
Type: Loop ride on dirt road, pavement, and singletrack.
Season: Late spring, summer, and fall.
Facilities: Cafe and store at Toms Place. All amenities in Bishop or Mammoth Lakes.
Features: There is fantastic scenery and interesting geology. Travel the upper part of Lower Rock Creek Canyon.
Access: From Bishop, take Highway 395 north 22.1 miles. Turn left onto Lower Rock Creek Road to a small parking area by the Lower Rock Creek sign. There is additional parking just down the road.

The ride starts at the top of the Lower Rock Creek Trail. Go back uphill to Highway 395, turn left, staying on the west side of the freeway. Turn left on the second dirt road (power line road). At a Y-junction go left toward the pinyon-covered ridge. Follow the power line road to the second left where it improves, still following the power line. At the next junction, go left up a switchback on the ridge. At the crest you have great views of Glass Mountain Ridge, Long Valley, part of Crowley Lake, and the Eastern Sierra.

The road drops and then ascends a second ridge. At a junction near the top, go left to a water tank.

Follow the road along the power line as it drops into a gully, around a curve, and down the drainage. The road, stony, sandy, and steep, ends in a small bowl above the canyon before it veers right, up and out of the bowl, traversing the side of Rock Creek

Views of Mount Tom/Owens Valley from Witcher Creek

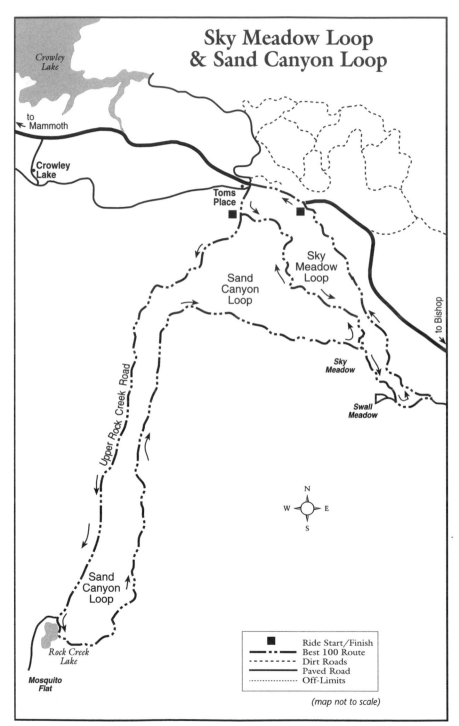

Sky Meadow Loop
& Sand Canyon Loop

Crowley
Lake

to
Mammoth

Crowley
Lake

Toms
Place

Sky
Meadow
Loop

Sand
Canyon
Loop

to Bishop

Sky
Meadow

Swall
Meadow

Upper Rock Creek Road

N
W ◆ E
S

Sand
Canyon
Loop

Rock Creek
Lake

Mosquito
Flat

■   Ride Start/Finish
—··—   Best 100 Route
--------   Dirt Roads
———   Paved Road
·········· Off-Limits

(map not to scale)

Canyon. The creek and the road are below. Cross a crest, descend to Birch Creek, cross it, and climb another ridge.

At 4.3 miles you come to the junction by Witcher Creek, the scenic high-point of the ride. (The dirt road heading west leads to Sand Canyon— see next ride.)

Cross Witcher Creek and follow the road for a half-mile, crossing sev-

eral seasonal creek beds. At the last creek drainage, you curve up toward Wheeler Crest and pass a quarry before coming to the junction of Sky Meadow Road. Take a left and head down Sky Meadow Road to the junction of Swall Meadow Road where you go left again and downhill to Rock Creek Road. Turn left and cycle 4.2 miles to your starting point.

5 Sand Canyon Loop

Distance: 24.7 miles.
Difficulty: A very strenuous and technical loop.
Elevation: 7,100' to 10,200' and return.
Type: Loop ride on pavement, jeep road, and singletrack.
Season: Summer and fall.
Facilities: There is a store at Rock Creek Lodge, a store and cafe at Rock Creek Lake Resort, and a store and cafe at Toms Place. Carry a minimum of 3 to 4 pints of water.
Features: One of the highest Sierra mountain biking trails, reaching 10,200 feet in elevation. Travel through Upper Rock Creek Canyon—one of the few north/south-facing canyons in the Eastern Sierra—along an outstanding high alpine traverse, pine forests and alpine meadows, and back along Sand Canyon Trail with stunning vistas.
Access: Exit Highway 395 at Toms Place (Upper Rock Creek Road), 16 miles south of Mammoth Lakes Junction or 24 miles north of Bishop. Turn left (south) onto the spur road and park at the side of the road. (Toms Place is 100 yards to the north.)

Begin riding uphill on Upper Rock Creek Road, passing the entrance station and two campgrounds. Enter the canyon—a slit in the debris of two moraines— and cross a bridge. This is a steep climb. The canyon widens at the second bridge. At 3.4 miles you pass Aspen Campground, and the first views of the incredible Sierra Crest appear as your unrelenting ascent continues.

The next landmark is Big Meadow Campground. East Fork Camp is a mile farther up the canyon. Wheeler Crest rises above the lateral moraine. The road climbs into the basin where Rock Creek Lodge is located. The upper basins of Rock

Creek are still ahead. Continue cranking in your granny gear to just past Rock Creek Lake Resort at 8.2 miles.

Turn left and head to the end of the road at Rock Creek Lake Campground on the east side of the lake. From here, you pick up a dirt service road for the summer cabins on the slopes a little farther south. Watch for and take the trail that leads sharply northeast (left) and contours up across an open rock face. Across the face, the trail turns more easterly and climbs up a small shallow canyon. At 10.3 miles you come to Kenneth Lake Trail, the high point of the ride at 10,200 feet and the Wilderness Boundary trailhead *(no bikes allowed)*. At the sign—*Sand*

Canyon Mountain Bike Trail—follow the singletrack until you pick up a jeep road that starts its long 3,000-foot descent along the bench, all the way back out of the canyon. This is a beautiful high area and is seldom visited. *Use caution befitting remote areas and do not be tempted to enter the John Muir Wilderness Area.*

Six miles north of Rock Creek Lake, the road reaches the northern extreme of Wheeler Ridge, veers sharply east and drops steeply down Sand Canyon. *Caution:* It is difficult to maintain bike control if you are tired. Walk your bike down the one mile stretch if necessary. The road is also badly rutted by 4WD vehicles which adds to the downhill excitement!

After climbing out of Sand Canyon, you pass through a fine old forest of Jeffrey pine, and once again drop down a gnarly path that chal-

lenges the best. As you come out into the open along Witcher Creek, at about 6,700 feet elevation, take the power line road 4S54 left (north). This road winds its way to just below the Holiday Group Campground. At the campground entrance, turn right onto Upper Rock Creek Road and return to your starting point at Toms Place.

Note: This route may get early snow. At any time you're travelling the backcountry of the High Sierra, keep one eye out for abrupt weather changes.

Caution: This route crosses the Sherwin Deer Migration path. In both fall and spring, 2,000 or more deer travel through these slopes. Needless to say, people feel strongly that these "natives" deserve the right-of-way and cyclists should be careful not to offend or molest these gentle creatures.

Autumn cycling near Sand Canyon

CHAPTER 10

Crowley Lake

Crowley Lake, the large reservoir in Long Valley, was created in 1941 when Los Angeles Department of Water and Power built a dam across the Owens River. Although there was a lake here in the Pleistocene era, Native Peoples, and more recent settlers, saw only the Owens River meandering through the caldera. The caldera is a long basin formed by a tremendous volcanic explosion over 700,000 years ago. The blast spread ash as far east as Nebraska and Kansas. Volcanic ash and debris carpeted the entire area and evolved into the characteristic pink or orange Bishop tuff. Examples of tuff can be seen throughout the area, notably in the Volcanic Tableland, Owens River Gorge, and the Aeolian Buttes south of Mono Lake.

The remains of the vast caldera's rim are the Glass Mountain Ridge on the east, and the Sherwins, Mammoth Mountain, and San Joaquin Ridge on the west. Active steam vents, hot springs, and even hot creeks are found through-out the area. Geothermal power plants tap into the plentiful hot water.

The Long Valley Caldera and surrounding mountainous terrain boast many great rides, all with spectacular scenery.

Crowley Lake lies in the Long Valley Caldera

109

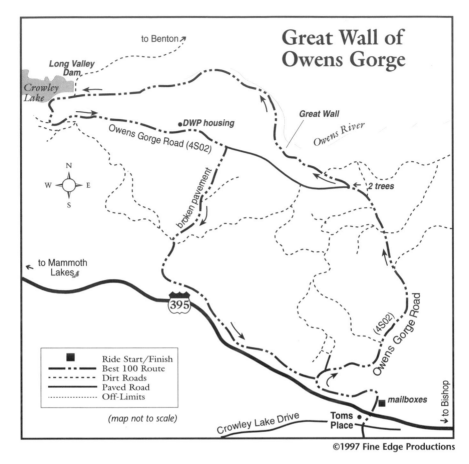

©1997 Fine Edge Productions

1 The Great Wall of Owens Gorge Ride

Distance: 7.5 miles.
Difficulty: Moderate.
Elevation: 7,000' with about 300' of loss and gain.
Type: Loop ride on pavement, singletrack, and dirt road.
Season: Spring, summer, and fall.
Facilities: Store and a cafe at Toms Place. No water along the route. Carry a minimum of 2 pints.
Features: The stone walls seen in the early part of the ride were built by hand without mortar. The craftmanship resembles that of the early Chinese laborers who worked on the Transcontinental Railroad, giving rise to its local name, "Great Wall of China." Who made the rock wall with such careful craftsmanship, what its purpose was, and when it was built no one knows for sure.
Access: 16 miles south of Mammoth Lakes Junction or 24 miles north of Bishop, turn east off Highway 395 at the Toms Place/Owens Gorge Road exit. Park by the mailboxes at the T-intersection.

From the mailboxes, go left at the T-intersection on Owens Gorge Road (4S02), pass several cabins, loop across a meadow, and through the center of the Sunny Slopes subdivision.

Follow 4S02 (about 1.8 miles) past a summit where it turns left (north) toward Crowley Lake. Turn right by two pine trees and take this sandy road across the flats toward the edge of Owens River Gorge. Cross the jeep road and take a faint single-track that leads left and downhill into the gorge. Be cautious on your downhill—there may be hikers or other cyclists on the trail.

The singletrack follows the old road bed a little more than a mile to the bottom of the gorge. Toward the bottom of this trail, look below you to the right to see the "great wall." The fine rock work has withstood numerous earthquakes and kept this old trail from washing out. Perhaps someday the story behind the wall will be uncovered. From a vantage point just above the wall, you can often see red-tailed hawks, golden eagles, gulls and herons, as well as deer, rabbits and coyotes. During the winter, you may spot a bald eagle or two.

When you reach the canyon floor, your loop route goes left on the graded dirt road, following the stream up-canyon to the top of Long Valley Dam (at the south end of Crowley). [**Side trip:** Turn right and head downstream to the end of the dirt road. The vegetation, birdlife and the view into Owens River Gorge are worth the extra time.]

Resuming your loop route, curve left on 4S02 and climb steeply to the top of the rough pavement through a rock wonderland covered with juniper and Jeffrey pines, and passing the Los Angeles DWP housing. At the crest (5.3 miles), go right onto a closed road with broken pavement.

Cross the basin and go straight at the junction. Soon the road drops steeply to the base of the pink cliffs. Follow the fringe of wet meadow that parallels Highway 395.

The dirt road ends in Sunny Slopes at Owens Gorge Road (4S02). Go right onto the pavement and follow this road back to your start.

2 Crowley Lake Loop

Distance: 38 miles.
Difficulty: Difficult due to long distance; the roads and terrain are moderate.
Elevation: Starting point: 6,900'; highest point: 7,400'.
Type: Loop ride on good dirt road, pavement, and jeep road.
Season: Spring, summer, and fall; sometimes winter.
Facilities: Store in Crowley Lake; store and cafe at Toms Place; Brown's Owens River Campground on Benton Crossing Road (open in summer only). Restrooms and water available at the Whitmore baseball fields. All other amenities available in Mammoth Lakes.
Features: This is a long, scenic loop around Crowley Lake. Vantage points highlight the geology of the Long Valley Caldera.
Access: From Mammoth Lakes Junction, go south 12 miles on Highway 395 to Crowley Lake exit. Drive southwest past the store to a stop sign at Crowley Lake Drive and park along the side of the road.

From the stop sign, go southeast and uphill on paved Crowley Lake Drive to a gap in the tuff. Behind you, you can see blue Crowley Lake, with Glass Mountain Ridge and the White Mountains rising behind it. Downhill you can see Aspen Springs in a wide meadow-covered bowl.

Drop into Aspen Springs and traverse the bowl past ranches and houses. Along this section, you can see Highway 395 to your left. Climb out of the bowl over a low saddle, past Rainbow Tarns Road, and then on to Toms Place and Lower Rock Creek Road (4.0 miles).

Go left on Lower Rock Creek Road, crossing Highway 395 carefully. As you pass a long line of mailboxes, go left and follow Owens Gorge

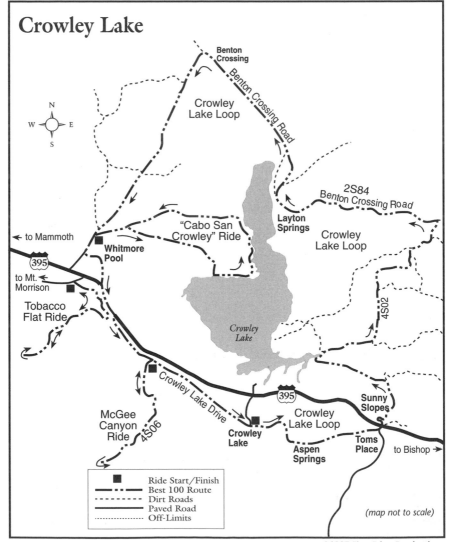

Crowley Lake

(map not to scale)

©1997 Fine Edge Productions

Road (4S02) through Sunny Slopes subdivision. The beautiful pink weathered rock you see in this area is Bishop tuff. Continue riding on the pavement up the hill to a crest where you can see Lower Owens River Gorge.

The paved road now curves north toward Crowley Lake and drops into the gorge, and at 8.3 miles, you cross Long Valley Dam. Down-canyon from the dam, you can see examples of different lava flows that were cut by the river. The ride then climbs out of the gorge onto dirt road (still 4S02) and continues across a high desert of sage and rabbit brush.

At the junction of 4S02 and 4S03, you go left, still on 4S02, and enter the zone of pinyon pines.

At 14.4 miles, you come to Benton Crossing Road (2S84), an historic road that connected the mines in Mammoth Lakes with the Benton mines in the 1870s.

Go left (west) on Benton Crossing Road—four fast miles on pavement to the bottom of a dry drainage. Just before 2S84 makes a sharp right, turn left off Benton Crossing Road at the sign for Layton Springs. Turn right again on the faint jeep road that parallels the lake. The route is dotted with meadows and beaches as it follows the lake shore across the Long Valley Caldera.

There are many jeep roads along the lake shore and riverbank, but it is best to remain on the route in the meadow, paralleling the lake and river. Past a whitish knoll, the road again meets Benton Crossing Road where you turn left.

At 24.5 miles you come to Brown's Owens River Store and Campground (open in summer and early fall). Cross the Owens River bridge and head southwest toward Mount Morrison over a small rise past two alkali ponds, some hot springs and steam vents. Continue on Benton Crossing Road past Whitmore Pool and the baseball fields.

Entrance to McGee Canyon

At 30.9 miles (about a quarter-mile before the green church) go left onto a dirt road signed *City of Los Angeles DWP Day Use Only.* The road divides immediately; go left parallel to the fence and, at a three-way junction, go right over or under the green gate. Immediately go right again, cross the creek, and follow the base of a hill. This road crosses a flat and comes to a gate near Highway 395. "Jump" the gate, cross the highway, and go left down the hill along the shoulder of the highway. At 33.3 miles turn right (west) onto Crowley Lake Drive. You now have a great 5-mile stretch where you can shift into your highest gear. Drink in the views of Crowley Lake and McGee Canyon as you fly along. At 36.8 miles, you reach the fire station. A wide bike lane leads you through the village of Crowley Lake and back to your start.

3 McGee Canyon Ride

Distance: 6.6 miles.
Difficulty: Moderate.
Elevation: Starting point: 6,900'; highest point: 8,300'.
Type: Out-and-back on paved and gravel roads.
Season: Spring, summer, and fall.
Facilities: Restrooms at McGee Creek Campground; restrooms and picnic tables at the trailhead. (Both areas are seasonal.) All other amenities available in Mammoth Lakes.
Features: See well-preserved glacial moraines, an earthquake fault scarp, and lovely alpine scenery.
Access: From Mammoth Lakes Junction, head south 9 miles on Highway 395 to the McGee Creek exit. Go west across Crowley Lake Drive to the four-way stop and park off the road.

Start at the stop sign and ride up the paved road (4S06) toward McGee Canyon. The road climbs for a mile across a terminal moraine, makes a big S-turn and follows McGee Creek which flows between two major lateral moraines. As you climb, you have a magnificent view of McGee Mountain. If you dare look behind you, the views are equally stunning.

The road enters a narrow canyon where you can look up and see evidence of the glacier-carved, U-shaped canyon, including glacial erratics—rocks brought down by glacial action.

At 1.6 miles, you enter a bowl and pass McGee Campground. Here you see a blend of sagebrush, alpine grasses and flowers. Alpine willow and birch line the creek. Steep and dramatic reddish mountains rise on three sides. Ahead, the line of rocks you see could easily be mistaken for a terminal moraine but it is actually a fault scarp. At its crest, a solar panel and instrument hut monitor the activity of this fault.

The pavement ends as you approach McGee Creek Pack Station. Continue up the road along the creek to its end at a parking area. There are restrooms, picnic tables, and a kiosk here. The trail from this point enters Wilderness. *No bikes are allowed.* Reverse your route to return to your starting point. Be careful to guard against excessive speed on your downhill run.

Tobacco Flat jeep trail

4 Tobacco Flat Ride

Distance: 7.4 miles.
Difficulty: Moderate with a strenuous climb.
Elevation: Starting point: 7,000'; highest point: 8,000'.
Type: Out-and-back on dirt roads.
Season: Late spring, summer, and fall.
Facilities: None. All amenities available in Mammoth Lakes.
Features: Pass through high-desert and alpine landscapes with views of Convict Lake and breathtaking Mt. Morrison with its striking vertical face of red and gray rock.
Access: From Mammoth Lakes Junction, go south 6 miles on Highway 395. Turn right onto Mt. Morrison Road (about a quarter-mile south of Benton Crossing Road). Go west for 0.4 mile and park by a cemetery.

Take the road to the left side of the cemetery to a green metal building. Go left and follow the power lines. Climb a ridge, then continue down the other side to a three-way junction where you go right on 4S47 (0.9 mile) and up the drainage. The road climbs the gully, opening up into a wide valley at 1.8 miles. Mount Morrison with its almost vertical face towers high above.

As the road goes up and across the basin, you continue to a four-way junc-tion below a series of switchbacks (2.7 miles). Turn right and up through the basin, passing a boulder and a road to the left. Climb to a flat area with a water tank, contour to the right down the center of the valley, then climb to the top of the lateral moraine at 3.9 miles, your turn-around point. Take time to enjoy the view down into Convict Lake before you begin your descent!

Retrace your route to Mt. Morrison Road. Use caution on your descent!

5 "Cabo San Crowley" Ride

Distance: 9.3 miles.
Difficulty: Easy.
Elevation: 6,900'.
Type: Loop ride on dirt roads.
Season: Spring, summer, and fall.
Facilities: None. Water at Whitmore Pool during summer only.
Features: This ride gives you beautiful scenery, a chance to swim, and one of the flattest rides in the Mammoth Lakes area.
Access: From Mammoth Lakes Junction, go south 6 miles on Highway 395. Turn left (east) by the green church on Benton Crossing Road. Continue past the ballfields and park to the side of the first dirt road past Whitmore Pool.

Start at the first dirt road east of Whitmore Pool and ride toward Crowley Lake, passing two posts. After 0.5 mile, ignore a road to the right and continue straight across a cattle guard toward Crowley Lake.

At the second right turn and gradually descend to a dry ditch—part of an abandoned irrigation system. This is Department of Water and Power (DWP) land; day use is allowed, but fires or camping are not permitted.

Cross a second ditch by a gate and remain on the road that heads toward the lake through a grassy meadow. Continue downhill to another junction by a gate. Pass the end corner of the fence by a second ditch.

At a junction at 3.5 miles you can turn right to Crowley Lake to take advantage of a white sandy beach and a swimming spot, but your route goes left (north) and parallels the shore. Ignore several jeep roads leading to the lake and continue toward Glass Mountain Ridge and a spit called North Landing where you can see a pond. At North Landing, go left (west), past a series of low, white cliffs that resemble the beaches of Cabo San Lucas in Baja California—thus the local nickname, Cabo San Crowley.

At an intersection of four roads, go right and follow the shoreline. Pass another cove with a beach and climb a second bluff. Follow the shore to another cove and onto a third bluff.

At 6.0 miles, take a left at the junction, heading west and uphill away from the lake. At the T-junction by the fence, go left and follow the fence on a straight road heading toward Mammoth Mountain.

The first curve in the road coincides with a junction on the right near a gate. Bear left around a curve toward Doe Ridge—the ridge just behind Whitmore Pool—and pass the junction on the left. Keep straight, ignoring the next left as well. Continue to Benton Crossing Road and your vehicle.

CHAPTER 11

Mammoth Lakes

With its proximity to the Wilderness and to Devils Postpile and Reds Meadow, the Mammoth District of Inyo National Forest is one of the most popular recreation areas in California. The Mammoth Lakes area offers fantastic scenery, cool summer weather, and clean air. There are alpine lakes and streams, meadows, forests, high desert and volcanic terrain, with interesting history, geology, and ecology. The Mammoth Lakes basin, which lies immediately south of Mammoth Mountain, contains five major lakes—Twin Lakes, Lake Mary, Lake Mamie, Lake George, and Horseshoe Lake—which range in elevation from 8,540 to 9,008 feet. With its broad beaches and no outlet, Horseshoe Lake is the best of these for swimming.

The area, originally settled by miners in the late 1870s, takes its name from

Cyclists gather below Brass Mammoth, Mammoth Mountain Bike Park

Cycling in pure mountain air, solitude, and natural beauty

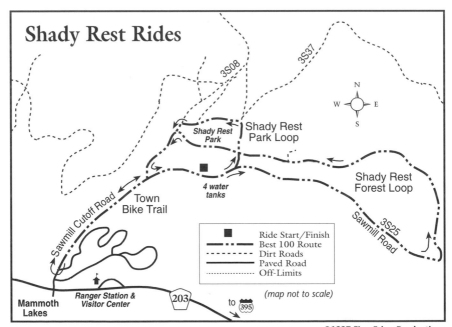

Mammoth Mine on Red Mountain. (There is no Mammoth Lake.) The first settlements, established to service the mining operations, were short-lived and abandoned by the early 1880s. In the early Twentieth Century, the area began to draw summer tourists for fishing, hiking and swimming. By the late 1930s, skiing operations were drawing winter visitors as well.

Mammoth Mountain, which receives more snow than any spot in the Sierra, soon became a premier ski resort for Californians.

The Mammoth Lakes area is the heartland of mountain biking in the Eastern Sierra. There are many rides in and around the town, including the town's Bike Trails System, as well as some singletrack, and many dirt and paved roads. Topping it all off is Mammoth Mountain Bike Park.

We have divided the rides into seven convenient staging areas around Mammoth Lakes—Shady Rest, North Village, Mammoth Creek Park, Lakes Basin, Mammoth Mountain Bike Park, Geothermal, and Smokey Bear Flat.

A. SHADY REST STAGING AREA

Season: Mid-spring, summer, and fall.
Facilities: All amenities available in Mammoth Lakes. Carry water on all rides.
Access: As you enter Mammoth Lakes on Highway 203, the Sawmill Cutoff Road is on the right directly across the highway from McDonald's, two blocks before the first traffic light. A hundred yards down Sawmill Cutoff Road and on the right is a sign for the start of the paved Shady Rest bike trail. A mile down Sawmill Cutoff Road you come to the park. The bike trail crosses just at the entrance to the parking area by four tall water tanks. This end of the paved bike trail, 0.7 mile past New Shady Rest Campground, is the starting point for several rides in this staging area.

Shady Rest Park is the result of a partnership between the town of Mammoth Lakes and the Inyo National Forest, and the paved trail is part of Mammoth's Bike Trails System, which is being expanded annually. The Bike Trail is a safe alternative to the road.

Shady Rest is indeed shady and there is plenty of parking for your vehicle. Restrooms and water are available.

1 Town Bike Path

Distance: 0.8 mile one way; 1.6 miles round trip.
Difficulty: Easy.
Elevation: 7,800'.
Type: Paved bike trail, ridden either as an out-and-back or access trail.
Features: This ride—the shortest in the Mammoth Lakes area—goes through woods and past the campground.

This paved bike trail, which is only 0.8 mile long, accesses the park and has only 80 feet of elevation gain and loss as it winds through the forest at the edge of the campground. This is the safest access to the park.

2 Shady Rest Park Loop

Distance: 2 miles.
Difficulty: Easy.
Elevation: 7,800'.
Type: Loop ride on singletrack, dirt road, and paved bike trail.
Features: An easy ride around Shady Rest Park.

This easy loop begins at the paved bike trail near the entrance to the park. Head toward town and take an immediate left onto a dirt singletrack. This dirt trail goes around the edge of the park, crosses two dirt roads and ends at a third behind the ballfield.

From this point, follow the power lines across the back of Shady Rest Park for 0.5 mile to a singletrack on the left under the power line.

Soon you go left again on a better singletrack trail and follow the blue diamonds 0.7 mile to its end at a sign with a map for the Knolls Ride. Go left across Sawmill Cutoff Road and left again on the paved trail and downhill back to your starting point.

3 Shady Rest Forest Loop

Distance: 4 miles.
Difficulty: Easy.
Elevation: 7,800' with 200' gain and loss.
Type: Loop ride on singletrack, dirt roads, and paved bike trail.
Features: A fun ride through Shady Rest Park and forest.

Start at the bike trail near the entrance to Shady Rest Park. Take an immediate left on the singletrack and go 0.3 mile to the first road crossing. Go right on Sawmill Cutoff Road.

Climb over a slight rise, and go downhill into open sageland with terrific views of the Sherwins. At 1.4 miles, there is a signed junction, but the little brown carsonite sign on the right is difficult to see.

Go left for 100 yards, then left again along the power line. The road runs along the base of a large hill.

Continue uphill on the utility road into the forest.

At 2.8 miles, take the singletrack on the right for one hundred yards, then follow the power lines for 0.5 mile across the back side of Shady Rest Park.

At 3.3 miles, turn onto a singletrack under the power line. You soon go left again onto a better trail signed by blue diamonds. Follow this trail to its end by a sign for the Knolls Ride. Go left across Sawmill Cutoff Road and left again downhill on the paved bike trail to your starting point.

4 Knolls Loop

Distance: 11 miles.
Difficulty: Moderate, non-technical; one big climb.
Elevation: Starting point: 7,800'; highest point: 8,300'.
Type: Loop ride on paved bike trail, singletrack, and dirt roads.
Features: An up-and-down ride, with wide vistas from Obsidian Knoll and other spots.

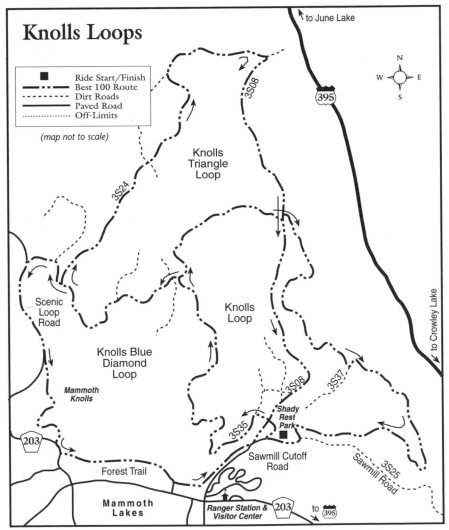

Knolls Loops

to June Lake

■	Ride Start/Finish
—··—··—	Best 100 Route
– – – –	Dirt Roads
————	Paved Road
············	Off-Limits

(map not to scale)

3S08

395

N
W — E
S

Knolls
Triangle
Loop

3S24

Scenic
Loop
Road

Knolls
Loop

to Crowley Lake

Knolls Blue
Diamond
Loop

*Mammoth
Knolls*

3S08
3S37

203

3S35

**Shady
Rest
Park** ■

Sawmill Cutoff
Road

3S25
Sawmill Road

Forest Trail

**Mammoth
Lakes**

*Ranger Station &
Visitor Center* 203 to 395

©1997 Fine Edge Productions

Lakes Basin from Mammoth Mountain

Start at the bike trail near the entrance to Shady Rest Park, head toward town, and up a small hill for 0.4 mile. Go right, across Sawmill Cutoff Road, near a sign and map of the Knolls Loop. Take the singletrack marked with blue diamonds and follow it to its end at a dirt road.

At one mile, go left on a dirt road for 100 yards, then left again on a better dirt road. The blue diamonds mark both of these turns. Follow this road uphill around several curves. At 2.3 miles, you come to the crest in a right-hand turn.

[**Side trip:** On the left, there is a trail, marked by blue diamonds, 0.2-mile long, that leads to a great view of Mammoth Lakes.]

Continue to the right on the Knolls Loop, go down through the forest and climb a steep sandy section which may require walking.

At 3.2 miles the road ends at another road. Go right and climb 0.4 mile to a five-way junction known as the Hub. Take a right at the Hub, leaving the blue diamonds, and proceed along a ridge, around curves and dips, and down toward a saddle.

At 5.1 miles, you reach a junction in a saddle. Cross the Sawmill Cutoff Road (3S08) and follow the jeep road, up over rolling hills. A pull-out on the right offers good views of the Shady Rest Park area. The road you are following ends at a T-junction. Go right downhill about a 100 yards to another junction where you take a left. This portion of the loop contours across a ridge with great views.

At 7.0 miles you come to an intersection. Go left and climb toward Obsidian Knoll. At the summit, you have views of Long Valley to your left.

[**Side trip:** At the summit, take the road to the right that leads to Obsidian Dome and a panoramic view—the finest overlook on the ride. You can see from Mount Morrison to Mammoth Mountain, and the town looks like a textured map.]

Continuing the Knolls Loop, go right and down Cardiac Hill. One mile down, the road veers right. At 8.8 miles, the road joins a utility road. Take a right and follow it along the base of the ridge. About a mile up this road, go right for about 100 yards on a singletrack which ends at a T-junction. Follow the road straight ahead that runs behind Shady Rest Park to another singletrack under the power line and turn left.

You soon go left again onto a better singletrack marked with the blue diamonds. This is the same trail on which you started your loop. It ends by the map of the Knolls Loop. Go left across Sawmill Cutoff Road and left again on the paved bike trail to your starting point.

5 Knolls Blue Diamond Loop

Distance: 9.8 miles.
Difficulty: Moderate, non-technical—one hard climb.
Elevation: Starting point: 7,800'; highest point: 8,300'.
Type: Loop ride on paved bike trail, singletrack, dirt roads and pavement.
Features: There is an excellent view of Mammoth Lakes and a pleasant ride through pine forest.

Start at the bike trail near the entrance to Shady Rest Park, head toward town, and up a small hill for 0.4 mile. Go right, across Sawmill Cutoff Road, near a sign and map of the Knolls Loop. Take the singletrack marked with blue diamonds and follow it to its end at a dirt road.

At one mile, go left on a dirt road for 100 yards, then left again on a better dirt road. The blue diamonds mark both of these turns. Follow this road uphill around several curves. At 2.3 miles, crest the climb in a right-hand turn.

Continue to the right on the Knolls Loop, go down through forest and climb a steep sandy section which may require walking. At 3.2 miles the road ends at another road. Go right and climb 0.4 mile to a five-way junction known as the Hub.

Continue straight across the Hub, still following the blue diamonds, and up a small hill along the crest of the knolls. At the first junction, go right and continue on the main road to the Scenic Loop Road at 5.7 miles.

Take a left on a singletrack parallel to the Scenic Loop Road. Follow the trail, which becomes a jeep road, along the back side of the Knolls subdivision to the Water District's cement block pumphouse.

At 7.2 miles, pass the pumphouse and go straight ahead on Knolls Drive to a stop sign. Take a right and go two blocks to Highway 203. Go left, ride one block, and go left again on Forest Trail. Follow Forest Trail downhill for about one mile. Look for the trail just past the last house on the left. (If you get to the fire station, you have gone too far.)

This trail follows phone lines to the start of the Blue Diamond Singletrack, where a map is displayed. Cross Sawmill Cutoff Road and go left on the paved bike trail to your starting point.

6 Knolls Triangle Loop

Distance: 12.5 miles.
Difficulty: Moderate with one hard and one moderate climb.
Elevation: Starting point: 7,800'; highest point: 8,300'.
Type: Loop ride on paved bike trail, singletrack, and dirt roads.
Features: See the town of Mammoth Lakes from an overlook, then ride through forests of red fir and Jeffrey pine. Watch for wildlife—small mammals and birds.

Start at the bike trail near the entrance to Shady Rest Park, head toward town, and up a small hill for 0.4 mile. Go right, across Sawmill Cutoff Road, near a sign and map of the Knolls Loop. Take the singletrack marked with blue diamonds and follow it to its end at a dirt road.

At one mile, go left on a dirt road for 100 yards, then left again onto a better dirt road. Blue diamonds mark both of these turns. Follow this road uphill around several curves. At 2.3

miles, crest the climb in a right-hand turn.

Continue to the right on the Knolls Loop, go down through forest and climb a steep sandy section which may require walking. At 3.2 miles the road ends at another road. Go right and climb 0.4 mile to a five-way junction known as the Hub.

Go straight across the Hub, still following the blue diamonds, and up a small hill along the crest of the Knolls. At the first junction, go right.

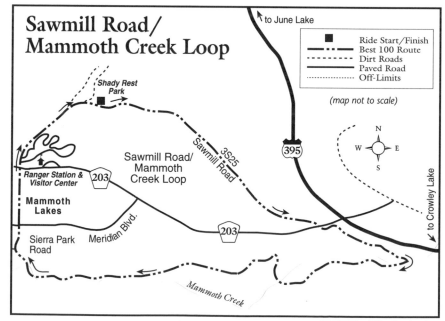

©1997 Fine Edge Productions

In a quarter-mile you come to a sandy turn at 5.2 miles. Go right, here, onto 3S24 high along the crest of the Knolls. Descend for over 3 miles through red fir, then Jeffrey pine. Ignore all roads to your left and right.

At 8.5 miles, 3S24 ends at the Sawmill Cutoff Road (3S08). Go right and head uphill and in 1.5 miles you come to a saddle where the Knolls Loop crosses the Sawmill Cutoff Road.

The last leg is a fast downhill on Sawmill Cutoff Road; at the stop sign turn left to Shady Rest Park and your starting point.

5 Sawmill Road/ Mammoth Creek Loop

Distance: 8.2 miles.
Difficulty: Moderate.
Elevation: Starting point: 7,800'; with about 500' loss and gain.
Type: Loop ride on dirt roads, singletrack, and paved bike trail.
Features: Outstanding vistas of the Sherwins and Mammoth Mountain. There is a natural park near Mammoth Creek.

Start at the paved bike path and take an immediate left onto the single-track that leads around the edge of Shady Rest Park for 0.3 mile to Sawmill Road (3S25). Go right and ride through the forest and over a mild rise before dropping to a sage-brush plain. The view of the Sherwin Range and Mammoth Mountain is breathtaking.

At a junction (1.4 miles) Shady Rest Loop goes left. Continue straight downhill until you reach pavement at Highway 203 at 2.0 miles.

Cross Highway 203 and pick up the road on the far side which swings around a right curve where the pavement ends. The next quarter-mile runs along Mammoth Creek. This is a good place for a picnic—a natural park with grasses and flowers all around, groves of aspen for shade, and birds everywhere.

At the next right curve, the climb begins. Climb three curves to a cattle guard where pine trees obscure the view and offer shade. When you break into the open, you are reward-ed with a view of Mammoth Mountain, the Sherwins, Long Valley Caldera, and Crowley Lake.

At 5 miles, cross the paved bike trail. Go right onto dirt singletrack between two rocks. Follow this trail behind the Southern California Edison building. The trail crests behind the Sierra Center Mall and drops to Meridian Boulevard. (The high school is across the road.)

Cross Meridian to Sierra Park Road and ride to Highway 203. McDonald's is on the left at this intersection, directly across from Sawmill Cutoff Road.

Cross the highway, go down Sawmill Cutoff Road 50 yards, and take the paved bike trail on the right to your starting point.

B. NORTH VILLAGE STAGING AREA

Season: Late spring, summer, and fall.
Facilities: All amenities are available in town. Restrooms and parking at the Earthquake Fault area; restrooms at Minaret Vista. No water along the routes; be sure to fill up before you start any of the rides.
Features: The Earthquake Fault Interpretive Area is located on the north side of Highway 203, 1.7 miles above North Village. Take time to visit this geologic site and learn how the long fracture in the earth was formed. The site, which is the trailhead for the Mountain View Trail, has parking and restrooms. (Access to the Downtown/Uptown Trail is located across Highway 203 from the entrance to the interpretive area.) Minaret Vista offers incredible views of the San Joaquin River Canyon, the Minarets, and Mounts Banner and Ritter.
Access: From the stoplight at Old Mammoth Road and Highway 203, go uphill on Highway 203 for one mile to the junction of Lake Mary Road (traffic light). Turn right and park near the bus stop. This section of Mammoth Lakes is known as North Village.

Caution: Above its junction with Lake Mary Road, Highway 203 becomes two-lane; it has a high volume of traffic all year. Watch for oncoming cars and guard against excessive downhill speed.

1 Uptown/Downtown Singletrack Loop

Distance: 5.6 miles.
Difficulty: Moderate.
Elevation: Starting point: 8,200'. Negligible gain and loss.
Type: Loop ride on singletrack.
Features: Singletrack ride through a mature red fir forest.

From the bus stop, follow Highway 203 uphill toward Mammoth Mountain Ski Area. The trails start at the edge of town. Take the Uptown Trail on the right side of 203 that leads into red fir forest paralleling Highway 203. (The trail to the left is Downtown Trail, your return route.) The trail climbs gradually past the Scenic Loop Road, becoming steeper, and passing through wide-open forest, a sign of mature growth. Soon you skirt the edge of the earthquake fault.

At 2.7 miles, you come to a sign and a junction. Go left on a short spur, then left again onto the Downtown Trail. Now the downhill fun begins! The trail sweeps through red fir forest in curves wide enough for passing in most places. Be cautious of loose sand and pumice.

A little farther down, just above some condominiums, there are two sharp corners. The trail steepens around several wide curves, and dozens of more curves keep it interesting.

After you pass a second set of condominiums, the trail levels out. The last section becomes almost a tunnel through small trees before it emerges by the road on the edge of town. Be careful of the deep pumice by the edge of the road. Turn right and return to your starting point.

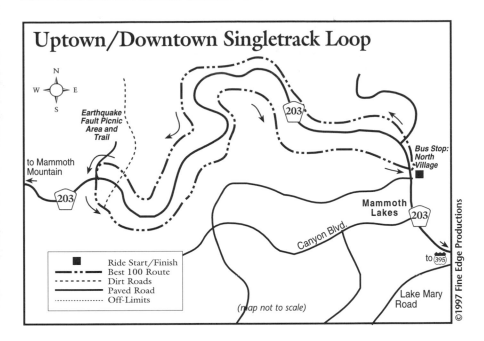

Uptown/Downtown Singletrack Loop

Earthquake Fault Picnic Area and Trail

to Mammoth Mountain

203

203

Bus Stop:
North Village

Mammoth Lakes 203

Canyon Blvd.

to 395

Lake Mary Road

■   Ride Start/Finish
—··— Best 100 Route
·········· Dirt Roads
——— Paved Road
············ Off-Limits

(map not to scale)

©1997 Fine Edge Productions

2 Mountain View Ride

Distance: 11.2 miles.
Difficulty: Moderate; somewhat technical.
Elevation: Starting point: 8,300'; highest point: 9,200'.
Type: Out-and-back on singletrack and jeep road.
Features: A fun, rolling ride through transitional forests consisting of old-growth red fir, Jeffrey pine, lodgepole pine, whitebark pine and juniper.
Access: On Highway 203, go 1.5 miles past North Village to the Earthquake Fault area and park.

Starting at the Earthquake Fault parking area, head back toward Highway 203 and go right on a jeep road marked with blue diamonds (the diamonds, mounted high in the tree, mark winter cross-country ski trails).

Follow this trail uphill through tall red fir toward a set of cliffs where the road curves left to a T-junction with another jeep road. Turn right and through a gap and continue to another junction where you turn left. The Inyo Craters come into view

where the road crests the hill. The road becomes singletrack then climbs to a wide, graded road. Turn right at this graded road and head downhill, still following the blue diamonds.

At a wide curve (2.0 miles), another section of singletrack heads left. Take this trail to the left, crossing the creek. If you miss this junction, you are off to the Inyo Craters!

This excellent trail crosses two bridges and winds through rolling Jeffrey pine forest. The singletrack ends at a road where you go right for a few yards, then bear left onto the first jeep road. Brown paddles mark the route. The trail leads through lodgepole pine with several good views of Mammoth Mountain.

At 3.2 miles you come to a junction of jeep roads. Take the one on the right. (The one to the left leads to Mammoth Mountain Inn.) At this point the trees are larger and the tread gets firmer.

You begin another singletrack section at 4.2 miles, heading up a steep hill, rolling over dips and gullies and crossing a small creek among white-

bark pines. After climbing two switchbacks, the trail turns into a jeep road.

The road crosses the slope, then winds up a shallow gully where stunted trees grow near the summit. The route ends at a dirt parking area at 5.6 miles, your turnaround point. Go left, uphill and right, onto the pavement for a spectacular view from the Minaret Vista Overlook. (Hard Core Trail, described below, is the jeep road leading north along San Joaquin Ridge.) Go back to Highway 203 and reverse your route to return to your starting point.

3 Minaret Vista Ride

Distance: 11.4 miles.
Difficulty: Strenuous, but not technical.
Elevation: Starting point: 8,200'; highest point: 9,200'.
Type: Out-and-back on paved road.
Season: Summer and fall. (The road beyond the Main Lodge is closed until the end of ski season.)

Time for a rest!

Courtesy Mammoth Mountain Bike Park

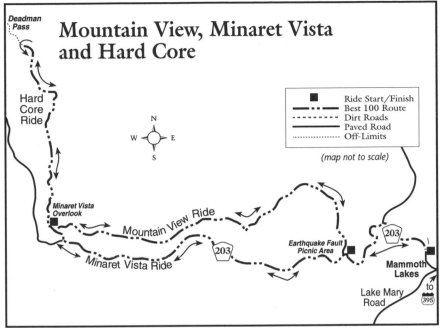

Mountain View, Minaret Vista and Hard Core

Deadman Pass

Hard Core Ride

Ride Start/Finish
Best 100 Route
Dirt Roads
Paved Road
Off-Limits

N
W   E
S

(map not to scale)

Minaret Vista Overlook

Mountain View Ride

203

Earthquake Fault Picnic Area

203

Minaret Vista Ride

Mammoth Lakes

Lake Mary Road

to 395

©1997 Fine Edge Productions

From the parking area in North Village, follow Highway 203 uphill toward Mammoth Mountain, through mature red fir forest. Within a mile, you pass the Scenic Loop Road; at 1.7 miles, you pass the turnoff to the Earthquake Fault interpretive area on your right.

Continue on Highway 203. At 2.1 miles, the entrance to Mammoth Mountain's garage is on the left. A hundred yards beyond that, on the right, you pass a dirt road leading to a power substation and the Inyo Craters Road.

You pass over a crest and come to Chair 2 parking lot. Continue up the road to the Main Lodge (4.1 miles) parking area at the brass statue of a mammoth.

Follow Highway 203 across the parking lot and climb past the 9,000-foot elevation marker. After a short dip in the road, you being your final climb to the entrance station at the summit.

The road continues to Devils Postpile, Reds Meadow, and Rainbow Falls, but you go right 0.4 mile to the Minaret Vista Overlook for truly outstanding views. The Minarets, Mount Ritter, Mount Banner, and the San Joaquin River Canyon are to the west; San Joaquin Ridge heads north; Mammoth Mountain to the south. This is where you'll find some of the best sunsets in the Eastern Sierra.

Return to 203 and turn left, reversing your route. Be cautious of cars and speed.

[**Option:** Ride up the road and return by the Mountain View Trail.]

4 Hard Core Ride (San Joaquin Ridge)

Distance: 5 miles.
Difficulty: A difficult, challenging, and technical ride at high elevation.
Elevation: Starting point: 9,200'; high point: 10,700'. [**Option** starting point: 8,200'.]
Type: Out-and-back.
Season: Midsummer through fall. Be prepared for sudden weather changes in the mountains. Take plenty of water drinking water, some snacks, and extra clothes.
Features: Outstanding views of the San Joaquin River Canyon, the Sierra, Mono Craters and Mono Lake. San Joaquin Ridge, an ancient volcanic ridge, is slowly being uplifted by the massive block of granite on which it sits.
Access: From North Village, drive up Highway 203, past the Mammoth Mountain Inn to Minaret Summit. Go right at the Minaret Vista Overlook and park.

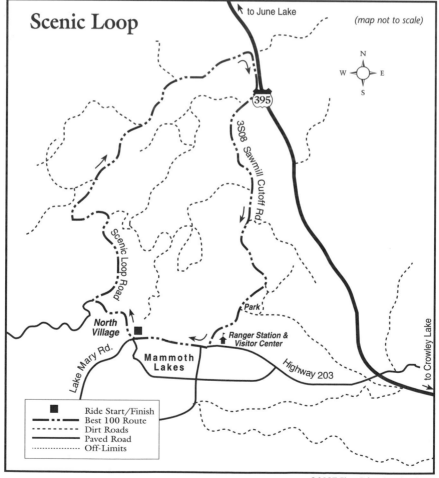

©1997 Fine Edge Productions

At the Minaret Summit entrance station, take the paved road to the right and another right into a small dirt parking area. Bear left on a jeep road—the Hard Core Ride. This jeep road follows San Joaquin Ridge through stunted juniper forest, and views are outstanding from the beginning. As the jeep road crosses the crest, the San Joaquin River Canyon and the Minarets come into view.

You enter a forest of small whitebark pine and bear right up a short, steep section into a wide bowl and across it. Tight clusters of stunted forest line the ridge.

On the north side of the bowl, the road becomes quite steep and loose before reaching its final hump at the top of San Joaquin Ridge—the end of your route. *Bicycles are not allowed beyond this point.*

Take time to sit down, have a snack, and admire the views—they don't get much better than this! To the west across San Joaquin River canyon are the Minarets, Mount Ritter, and Mount Banner; to the north, San Joaquin Ridge stretching toward June Lake; to the northeast, Mono Craters and Mono Lake; and to the east Glass Mountain Ridge. There was once a fire lookout here; you can see why.

To return to your starting point, the descent takes less work than the climb, but it is tricky. Walk down the steep pitches. Mammoth Mountain now dominates your view as you head back along the jeep road to the parking area at Minaret Vista Overlook.

[**Option:** Make an epic ride by biking up Highway 203 from North Village to Minaret Summit, then doing Hard Core out and back, and taking Mountain View and Downtown trails to North Village. This option is 19.3 miles with an additional 1,000 feet of elevation gain and loss.]

5 Scenic Loop Ride

Distance: 12.0 miles.
Difficulty: Moderate.
Elevation: Starting point: 8,200'; highest point 8,400'; lowest point: 7,600'.
Type: Loop ride on paved and dirt roads.
Season: Spring, summer, fall.
Features: Forested ride leading to fantastic views of Sherwin Ridge, Mammoth Mountain.

From the parking area in North Village, head uphill on Highway 203 for one mile, and turn right at the Scenic Loop Road.

Ski trails on both sides of Scenic Loop Road near the crest are marked by blue diamonds (the left leads to Inyo Craters, the right to the ranger station). Beyond the high point, the road drops through young forest, along the fringe of one the largest contiguous Jeffrey pine forests in the West—home to hundreds of deer.

At 3.7 miles, you pass the main turnoff to Inyo Craters (3S30) on the left. Continue east on Scenic Loop Road down three distinct terraces to Highway 395 at 6.5 miles where you turn south onto a wide bike lane. In 0.4 mile go right onto Sawmill Cutoff Road and follow the signs back to New Shady Rest Campground. From there, return to Highway 203, turn right and uphill to your starting point in North Village.

6 Inyo Craters Loop

Distance: 10.5 miles.
Difficulty: Moderate, somewhat technical.
Elevation: Starting point: 8,100'; low point: 7,600'.
Type: Loop on dirt roads.
Season: June through October.
Features: The route circles the two lake-studded Inyo Craters, formed from a volcanic explosion approximately 1,500 years ago, part of a chain of volcanic formations stretching from Mammoth Mountain north to Mono Lake. To visit the craters, you can leave your bike in the parking lot and walk the short trail uphill.
Access: From North Village, head up Highway 203 for one mile to the turnoff for Scenic Loop Road. Turn right and take Scenic Loop Road 2.7 miles to the signed Inyo Craters turnoff (3S30). Go left and continue one mile to the parking lot at the craters' trailhead and park.

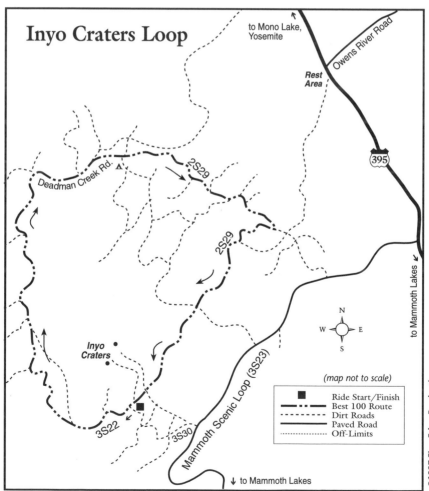

[**Side trip:** Before you start your ride, leave your bike in the parking lot and take the self-guided tour to the craters. Both have small lakes several hundred feet down from the rim, an unusual feature since most of the craters in this region are dry. A sign explains: *These craters are one of the youngest features, probably less than 1500 years old, on a belt of old volcanoes, extending from Mono Lake to Mammoth Mountain. They were formed by violent explosions of volcanic gas that hurled more than five million tons of rock and debris into the surrounding terrain . . .*]

From the parking area, ride back on 3S30 toward Scenic Loop Road. Go 0.1 mile and turn right onto 3S22. Begin following the signs along this road through Crater Flats. The road divides at 1.1 miles. Stay right along the edge of the crater. (The left takes you through lodgepole pine forest.)

At 2.1 miles the roads rejoin. Head steeply downhill, and through the trees. At 2.6 miles, go right. At 3.0 miles the roadbed gets bumpy and gravelly, so slow down. Notice the lava flow to your right and the Sierra Crest to your left.

Cross an unnamed creek at 3.4 miles and keep left. Cross Deadman Creek (which can be deep and hazardous) at mile 4.0 and turn right onto Deadman Creek Road.

Head downstream on the road, passing a dome to your left. The road widens at 4.5 miles and is well graded. Continue straight ahead to a major intersection at 5.0 miles. (The road north leads to Obsidian Flat, a group campground; Deadman Campground is to your right, south). Stay on the 30-foot-wide road until mile 5.8. Then take a right, ride 100 yards and bear left. Pass another jeep trail to the left at 7.5 miles. Bear right on the more frequently traveled road. At 7.6 miles continue straight ahead and pass the road on your left at 8.1 miles. Just after you cross a stream, you rejoin 3S22 and head back to the parking area.

C. MAMMOTH CREEK PARK STAGING AREA

Season: Spring, summer, and fall.

Facilities: Parking, restrooms, and water at Mammoth Creek Park.

Access: To reach the park from the junction of Highways 203 and 395, go west on 203 to Old Mammoth Road (traffic light). Turn left and go one mile to the far end of the shopping area. Mammoth Creek Park is on the right just before the road crosses Mammoth Creek. The parking lot and paved bike path are the starting point for these rides. There are restrooms and drinking water here.

The paved bike path goes upstream a short distance, crosses a bridge, and becomes a bike lane on the shoulder of Old Mammoth Road. In the opposite direction, the bike path passes under Old Mammoth Road and back along the creek toward Highway 395.

1 Town Bike Trail Loop

Distance: 3.2 miles.
Difficulty: Easy.
Elevation: 7,800'.
Type: Paved bike trail and singletrack.
Features: Historic Hayden Cabin, the local museum, is in Mammoth Creek Park. Travel along Mammoth Creek and up to one of the best panoramic views available.

From the parking lot, take the spur trail past the restrooms and go left on the main bike path through the tunnel under Old Mammoth Road. The trail runs along Mammoth Creek for 0.5 mile, then crosses Mammoth Creek Road and leads up a little hill across an open area covered with sage.

[**Side trips:** At 0.2 mile, cross the foot bridge and go left 100 yards to the historic Hayden Cabin (open in summer). At 0.9 mile, there is another short side trip to a spectacular 360-degree panoramic view of the surrounding mountains.]

Return to the main path and go right down a hill, around a couple of curves to Meridian Boulevard. (The Business Park is on the west side of Meridian.)

Cross the boulevard and go left on the bike path uphill toward town on a curving trail through sagebrush and pine. Be careful at the intersections on your way back into town. The third road crossing is just above the elementary school.

The bike path ends at the corner of Meridian Boulevard and Sierra Park Road. Cross Meridian and take a wide dirt trail that climbs a small hill behind Minaret Village Mall. The roughest part is the crest. The path ends at Mammoth Creek Road by the paved bike trail where you go right to return to the park.

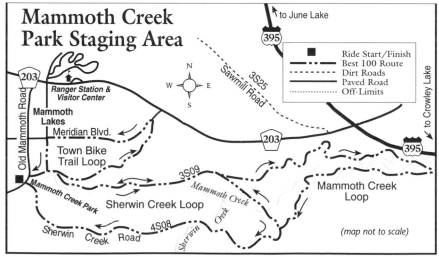

©1997 Fine Edge Productions

2 Mammoth Creek Loop

Distance: 8.5 miles.
Difficulty: Moderate.
Elevation: 7,800'.
Type: Loop ride on paved bike trail, dirt roads, and singletrack.
Features: A lovely ride along Mammoth Creek offering bird-watching opportunities and pleasant sites for a picnic.

From the parking lot, take the spur trail past the restrooms and go left on the main bike path through the tunnel under Old Mammoth Road. The trail runs along Mammoth Creek for 0.5 mile.

At 3S09, turn right and head downhill. The road follows the creek with great views of the Glass and White mountains.

At 1.7 miles, go right onto a dirt road down the hill toward Mammoth Creek. At first the road is gradual and open, but it soon enters trees for a short, steep descent.

Take the footbridge across the creek, climb a small hill and follow the road through the forest. At 2.5 miles, take the second road on the left, just before Sherwin Creek Road. It drops down two terraces and then approaches Mammoth Creek. Parallel the creek until you see a singletrack by a metal-framed sign at 4.3 miles.

Go left onto the singletrack that leads to the creek and an old wooden bridge. This is a great spot for a break.

Nearby are formations of black rock and old lava flows; bird-watching is prime here.

The singletrack bears left along the creek, a fun, winding section. All too soon you come to a jeep road that leads to a curve at 3S09.

Go left on 3S09 and parallel the creek. This natural "park" of grass and aspens is a good spot for a picnic.

At the end of the level creek area, the main road leads to the right uphill through several S-curves. The grade tapers off as it enters the trees. When you come into the open again, Mammoth Mountain is straight ahead and remains in view the rest of the ride.

Pass the junction you turned on earlier in the ride and keep heading straight up 3S09 toward Mammoth Mountain. Eventually you come to the paved bike trail where you turn left and go under Old Mammoth Road to the start of your ride.

[**Options:** This ride can be extended by combining it with the Town Bike Trail or the Sherwin Creek Ride.]

3 Sherwin Creek Loop

Distance: 5.5 miles.
Difficulty: Easy.
Elevation: 7,800'.
Type: Loop ride on paved bike trail and dirt roads.
Features: Historic Hayden Cabin, the local museum, is in Mammoth Creek Park. You will have excellent views of Mammoth Mountain and Mammoth Lakes.

From the parking lot, take the spur trail past the restrooms and go left on the main bike path through the tunnel under Old Mammoth Road. The trail runs along Mammoth Creek for 0.5 mile. At 3S09, turn right and head downhill. The road follows the creek with great views of the Glass and White mountains.

At 1.7 miles, go right onto a dirt road down the hill toward Mammoth Creek. At first the road is gradual and open, but it soon enters trees for a short, steep descent. Take the footbridge across the creek, climb a small hill and follow the road through the forest until its end at Sherwin Creek Road. Go right and up the hill.

Pass the Sherwin Creek Campground, cross Sherwin Creek, and pass the Sherwin Creek Day Use Area.

Continue up Sherwin Creek Road toward town. As you break into the open, you can see Mammoth Mountain. At the crest of the hill, the town comes into view.

Near town, pass between two stables. Be sure to yield to any horses in this area. Sherwin Creek Road ends at the corner of Old Mammoth Road. Go right, cross the bridge, and make a quick left turn into Mammoth Creek Park.

[**Option:** Follow directions for this ride to Sherwin Creek Road and go left. At its end, cross Highway 395, continue on the Sheriffs Substation Road to the geothermal plant, go left under Highway 395, and take an immediate left on 3S09 directly back to Mammoth Creek Park for a trip of 12 miles.]

4 Laurel Canyon Ride

Distance: 17.6 miles.
Difficulty: Very difficult, even brutal.
Elevation: Lowest point: 7,400'; highest point: 10,000'. Climbs 2,600 feet in 4.5 miles up Laurel Canyon.
Type: Out-and-back on dirt roads and steep jeep road.
Season: Summer and fall.
Facilities: Parking, restrooms, and water at Mammoth Creek Park. Take plenty of water with you.
Features: Travel past aspen-lined creeks to an alpine retreat at Laurel Lakes. This ride takes you to nearly 10,000 feet where the views are as breath-taking as the climb.

From the parking lot, take the spur trail past the restrooms and go left on the main bike path through the tunnel under Old Mammoth Road. The trail runs along Mammoth Creek for 0.5 mile. At 3S09, turn right and head downhill. The road follows the creek with great views of the Glass and White mountains.

At 1.7 miles, go right onto a dirt road and downhill toward Mammoth

Creek. At first the road is gradual and open, but it soon enters trees for a short, steep descent to a footbridge. Use caution here; there may be fishermen. Take the footbridge across the creek, climb a small hill and follow the road through the forest to its end at Sherwin Creek Road (4S08). Go left and ride past the YMCA camp to an open area edged with aspen. Pass a small ranch by Laurel

Creek. Aspens line the face of the terminal moraine.

At 4.0 miles you come to Laurel Canyon Road (4S86), and your ride really begins. For a half-mile, it is very steep and sandy. After the first curve, it becomes rocky as it winds around several ascending curves; this part is difficult due to loose rock and uneven road. Meanwhile, elevation and steepness start to take their toll. You will probably need periodic rests; you may even want to walk!

At 5.2 miles, there's a small shack containing a laser that monitors changes in the Long Valley Caldera. Keep pedaling in your granny gear and eventually you reach the crest of the terminal moraine. You can see the first hanging valley of Laurel Canyon and a notch cut by the creek.

Drop into the aspens by the creek. Pass through a gate (please keep it closed) and travel up through a canopy of aspens to a long meadow along the side of a lateral moraine.

At 6.5 miles, you enter the second hanging valley where there's a meadow and an aspen-lined creek. The valley displays the classic U-shape of a glacial canyon. The road steepens drastically just past a jeep road; the steepness and loose shale make things difficult.

Next you climb two switchbacks. Just past the second switchback is a wide pullout under a saddle where a hiking trail—*Closed to bikes!*—leads to Convict Canyon. The last leg of the road, lined with miniature trees, is not bad in comparison to what you've been through—8.5 miles to this point. You can see Laurel Lakes below you in the third hanging valley. Above is Red Slate Peak, and down-canyon on the right is Laurel Mountain; you are at almost the same level as the peak (about 10,000

feet). At the north end of the hanging canyon, you'll find a nice stand of gnarled aspen carved with initials and dates from the early 1900s. (These carvings are called "arborglyphs.")

The return ride is technically challenging. Stop to rest your hands and allow your brakes to cool. Take your time; it would be a crime to waste this fantastic scenery.

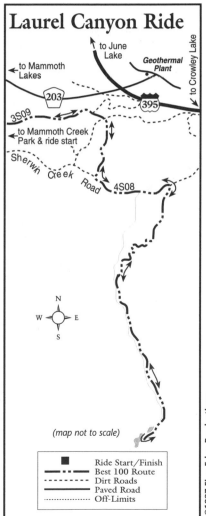

Laurel Canyon Ride

to June Lake
to Mammoth Lakes
Geothermal Plant
to Crowley Lake
203
395
3S09
to Mammoth Creek Park & ride start
Sherwin Creek Road
4S08

N
W — E
S

(map not to scale)

■ Ride Start/Finish
━━━ Best 100 Route
------ Dirt Roads
━━━ Paved Road
·········· Off-Limits

©1997 Fine Edge Productions

5 Old Mammoth Road Ride

Distance: 8 miles round trip.
Difficulty: Moderate.
Elevation: 7,800'.
Type: Out-and-back.
Season: Opens in late spring; possible closure by early fall.
Features: Visit the remains of Mill City where an old stamp mill, powered by water from Twin Lakes, crushed ore from the Mammoth mines. Its half-mile flume is still intact. Uphill from the mill is the site of Mammoth Mine and Mammoth City. The Mammoth gold strike of 1877 was substantial, but costs such as the mill, flume, and rails ate up profits causing the operations to fold by 1880.

Take the spur around the restrooms and go right on the paved bike path along Mammoth Creek. Cross the bridge onto a wide bike lane on Old Mammoth Road. Views of Mammoth Mountain and the Sherwins from here are superb. Pass the driving range and golf course. Near the entrance to Snow Creek there is an old metal water wheel from Mill City. The bike lane ends here.

Continue along paved Old Mammoth Road, around a curve, and out of the meadow. Be cautious along the next mile because the road is narrow and winding, heavily used, and has no shoulders.

At 2.0 miles, you pass Red Fir Road and leave the subdivisions. Forests grow more dense as the road gets steeper and turns to dirt; this can be quite a washboard. Watch carefully for downhill vehicles.

At 2.3 miles, a road on the right with several cabins is the site of Mill City, the site of an old stamp mill. Continue up Old Mammoth Road about a quarter-mile to a gravesite with a cement block house across from it.

[**Side trip:** A trail starts on the right behind the cement block house. Hike a quarter-mile along the trail to a 16-ton flywheel and the foundation of the stamp mill. If you hike uphill following the race you will find the flume; this water trail is still intact after over 130 years.]

Continuing from the grave site, bike uphill around several curves to a wide pullout with an excellent view down to Mammoth Lakes, the Long Valley Caldera, and Glass and White mountains. Look carefully at the side of Panorama Dome where you can see the historic flume. A bike trail starts from this point and traverses the side of Panorama Dome below the flume.

Head uphill toward the Mammoth mines on the side of Red Mountain. Within 200 yards, there is a flat graded area to the right, where ore carts once dumped their contents. Farther up to the left near the mines are an interpretive sign and the foundations of many cabins, stores, and saloons that dotted the hillsides in the 1870s. In the "mammoth" winter of 1879-80, when snow and avalanches crushed many of the buildings, most of the miners left.

You can turn around here or continue uphill to Lake Mary Road for your turnaround point.

[**Options:** If you continue to Lake Mary Road, you can return down Lake Mary Road for a loop with breath-taking scenery. You can also access rides in the Lakes Basin, connecting with the Vista Trail, Lake Mary Loop, and Horseshoe Lake Trail.]

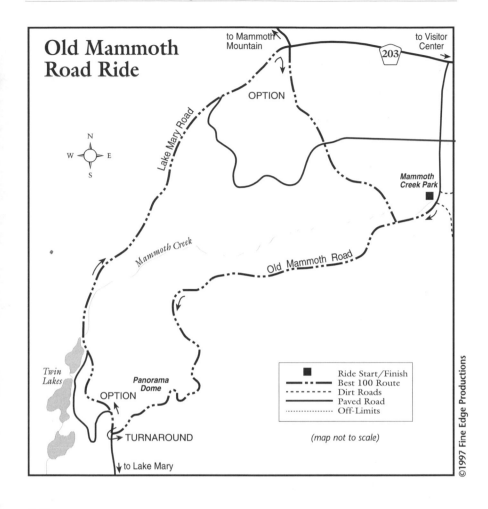

D. LAKES BASIN STAGING AREA

Season: Summer and fall.

There are numerous roads open to mountain bikes in the Lakes Basin area. However, due to conflict between horse packers and inconsiderate bicyclists, most of the extensive singletrack is now off-limits. Please be responsible and observe these closures. Ignoring regulations hurts all cyclists. If you have constructive comments for this area, write to the Inyo National Forest.

1 Panorama Dome Loops

Distance: 3.9 miles.
Difficulty: Easy.
Elevation: Starting point: 8,500' with about 300' of gain and loss.
Type: A figure-eight loop ride on singletrack, dirt road, and pavement.
Facilities: Limited parking.
Features: Easy singletrack with expansive views. The historic Water Flume and the site of the original settlement of Mammoth.
Access: From the stoplight at Highway 203 and Lake Mary Road (by Whiskey Creek Restaurant), head up Lake Mary Road, through the tunnel, and across the bridge at Twin Lakes. Two hundred yards past the bridge on the left is a small parking area.

Begin this ride from the sign marked for Panorama Dome. Follow the overgrown jeep road along the ski trail blue diamonds. Go right at a split in the road. In 0.4 mile, there is a trail to the right. Note this junction, but continue left on the blue diamond trail which leads uphill through lodgepole pine

Courtesy Mammoth Mountain Bike Park

and aspen. At one clearing on the hillside, you can see Lincoln Mountain above and Mammoth Creek below. The trail then drops to Lake Mary Road just below where you started.

Follow the trail a second time to the junction at 1.3 miles where the new trail cuts to the right. Take the other trail this time which immediately crosses a wide ditch—the historic flume that carried water from Twin Lakes to Mammoth City and powered the stamp mill in Mill City.

The trail traverses the side of Panorama Dome for almost a mile through red fir forest. There are several excellent views of the town of Mammoth and the Long Valley Caldera with Lake Crowley. The trail ends at the Old Mammoth Road Overlook.

Take a right and head uphill on Old Mammoth Road. Keep a sharp lookout on the right, and you can see the grade of the old ore track. Farther up to the left are the foundations of two log cabins and part of the old mill. On the side of Red Mountain, ahead, are several of the old mines. A historic marker tells the story of the original Mammoth City.

Climb Old Mammoth Road to its end at Lake Mary Road. Go right and downhill past the art gallery to your starting point.

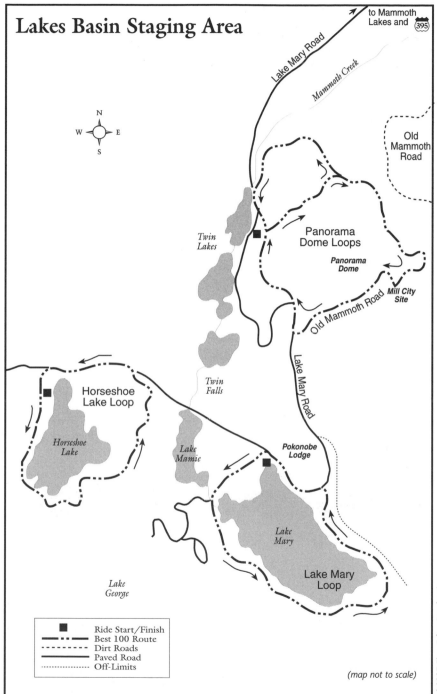

Lakes Basin Staging Area

to Mammoth Lakes and 395

Lake Mary Road

Mammoth Creek

Old Mammoth Road

Twin Lakes

Panorama Dome Loops

Panorama Dome

Mill City Site

Old Mammoth Road

Lake Mary Road

Horseshoe Lake Loop

Twin Falls

Horseshoe Lake

Lake Mamie

Pokonobe Lodge

Lake Mary

Lake Mary Loop

Lake George

Legend:
- ■ Ride Start/Finish
- –·–·– Best 100 Route
- - - - - - Dirt Roads
- ——— Paved Road
- ·········· Off-Limits

©1997 Fine Edge Productions

(map not to scale)

2 Lake Mary Loop

Distance: 2.4 miles.
Difficulty: Easy.
Elevation: 8,800'.
Type: Loop ride on paved roads.
Season: Late spring, summer, and fall.
Facilities: Parking, water, restrooms, cafe, and store at Pokonobe Lodge; a store, cafe and restrooms at Barrett's Landing Marina.
Features: Fabulous views from the trail around Lake Mary. There are optional side trips to Lake George or the Mammoth Mine area.
Access: From the stoplight at Highway 203 and Lake Mary Road (by Whiskey Creek Restaurant), head up Lake Mary Road, through the tunnel, and across the bridge at Twin Lakes, continuing to Pokonobe Lodge at 4.2 miles. Park close to the road in the dirt lot; avoid blocking access to the lodge.

Starting from the parking area, head south on the paved road. Pass over a small rise with campgrounds on both sides and drop down to a small bridge at the outlet of Lake Mary, the biggest lake in the basin. Across the lake, the view of the Red Mountain Ridge is excellent. At the stop sign, go left.

[**Side trip:** To the right is a steep, short road to Lake George, a 1.7 mile option with 200 feet of climbing.]

Continue along the southwest shore of Lake Mary, with its mild curves and dips. On the right side of the road are cabins and, a little farther along to the left, Barrett's Landing Marina and Store. From the boat dock, check the view of the seldom-seen south side of Mammoth Mountain.

Farther on, to the right is Coldwater

A hidden lake near Mammoth Muntain Bike Park

Campground. [**Side trip:** At the top of Coldwater Campground, near the end of the parking loop, is a trail to Mammoth Consolidated Mine. This turn-of-the-century mining camp is well preserved and historically interesting. An interpretive sign explains the story behind the buildings. This is a popular horse trail, and *bikes are not allowed.*]

Continue your ride north through forests along the lake. Watch for cars; visibility is poor at this point, and drivers may be admiring the scenery, not watching for cyclists!

At 2.0 miles, you reach Lake Mary Road again and a stop sign. Go left and ride along the eastern shore of Lake Mary back to Pokonobe Lodge.

Let's meet at the Mammoth Mountain Bike Park

3 Horseshoe Lake Loop

Distance: 1.7 miles.
Difficulty: Easy.
Elevation: 8,400'.
Type: Loop ride on singletrack, closed dirt roads, and pavement.
Facilities: Parking and restrooms at Horseshoe Lake Group Campground.
Features: Easy, pleasant ride through forests and by a mountain lake.
Access: From the stoplight at Highway 203 and Lake Mary Road (by Whiskey Creek Restaurant), head up Lake Mary Road, through the tunnel, across the bridge at Twin Lakes, to the end of the road. Park in the Horseshoe Lake parking lot.

From the back side of the parking lot by a kiosk that displays a map of the trail, follow the road about 200 yards. The singletrack starts on the left side just before the end of the road. This singletrack dips in and out of two creeks. Walk these dips if you're in doubt—it's quite sandy.

Along the backside of the lake are foundations of a camp that once existed here. From this point the trail becomes jeep road; follow it around to a junction and go left. Follow the jeep road around Horseshoe Lake through lodgepole forest.

In 0.5 mile you emerge from the forest onto Lake Mary Road. Across the road there is a great view of the Lower Lakes Basin. Go left and follow the road back to the parking area.

[**Option 1:** Ride up Lake Mary Road from town. **Option 2:** Add the Lake Mary Loop to the Horseshoe Loop.]

E. MAMMOTH MOUNTAIN BIKE PARK

Distance: Varied; combining trails is easy and optional, and downhill rides can easily be made by using the shuttle service from town and the gondola on the upper mountain. Access to trails and roads outside the Park expands the opportunities.

Difficulty: Moderate to very technical; for riders of all levels. Helmets are mandatory.

Elevation: Varied (North Village 8,000'; Main Lodge about 9,000'; Mid-Chalet 10,400'; summit for Mammoth Mountain 11,053'). All Park rides are on Mammoth Mountain.

Type: Interconnecting singletrack trail system, primarily downhill, with steeper rides on the upper mountain reached by gondola. Fee for use of the Park.

Season: Summer—post-ski season.

Facilities: Water and restrooms in all public buildings, several food service operations, shuttle service and gondola; Bike Center with full-service bike shop, rentals and high-end demos, maps; two sport shops; day care available; guides available.

Features: Well-maintained and well-marked trails, all offering spectacular scenery, alpine forests, and fresh air. There are benches, picnic tables, and water stops throughout the Park. Guided rides depart the Bike Center twice a day. There is a Bike Patrol on the paths to offer assistance and directions. The IMBA Rules of the Trail apply.

Access: Take Highway 203 west through Mammoth Lakes, turn right at the junction of Lake Mary Road and 203 (traffic light) and continue uphill to Mammoth Mountain Ski Area. The Bike Center is located at the far end of the main lodge.

Mammoth Mountain has had an outstanding place in the short history of mountain biking. The first "Kamikaze" downhill—the fastest race course in America, with speeds exceeding 60 miles per hour—was held here in 1985. The annual Mammoth Mountain Bike Race, the largest in North America, receives intensive media coverage. The "dual slalom" and "eliminator" race formats were introduced here. Three early world mountain bicycling championships were held in Mammoth, and the Mountain has also hosted three national championships. The gondola was the first in the nation to carry bikes to the summit of a ski slope.

The facilities of the Mountain are converted to a bike park in the summer. The Main Lodge is the center of operations. The Bike Center, eating places, Adventure Connection, the gondola, restrooms—all are in or near the Main Lodge. The wide lawn across from the lodge, behind the brass woolly mammoth statue, is a good place for regrouping or resting.

Gondola rides (with your bike if you wish) to the top of 11,053-foot

Mammoth Mountain, hiking, including walks guided by volunteers, and a climbing wall and ropes course are also available.

The Reds Meadow Shuttle (tickets available at Mammoth Mountain Inn front desk) provides access to Devils Postpile and Reds Meadow Resort. You can ride your bike to Reds Meadow and catch the shuttle back to the Mountain. There is excellent fishing in the San Joaquin River. Bikes must stay on roads throughout this San Joaquin River Valley.

Mammoth Mountain Bike Park is for riders of all levels. Stay on the trails and do not cut across switchbacks. Practice consideration and control, and be realistic about your abilities. Follow the IMBA Rules of the Trail.

For information call The Adventure Connection, 760-934-0606, or write to Box 353, Mammoth Lakes, CA 93546.

Carry your bike to the top of Mammoth Mountain

Courtesy Mammoth Mountain Bike Park

F. GEOTHERMAL STAGING AREA

Season: Spring, summer, and fall.
Facilities: Restrooms at Hot Creek Day Use Area. No water, so carry plenty with you. All amenities available in Mammoth Lakes.
Access: From Highways 203 and 395 cross to the east side of 395, pass the cattle guard and turn left on Substation Road, which becomes Antelope Springs Road (3S05), the first left just past the north ramp to Highway 395. Park off the road. You can see two geothermal power plants nearby.

1 Geothermal Loop

Distance: 21.2 miles.
Difficulty: Moderate, long.
Elevation: Starting point: 7,280'; highest points: 7,600'-7,700'.
Type: Loop ride on dirt road, jeep road, and pavement.
Features: Excellent vistas of mountains and volcanic landscape, including hot springs and creeks, mud pots, geysers and steam vents. You can visit the Hot Creek Fish Hatchery.

Take Substation-Antelope Springs Road (3S05) over a rise and down to the end of the pavement where the road turns right, crosses the flat and takes a second sharp right climbing the hill. There are a few steep ups and downs for 2.5 miles when the road crests near the junction with 3S13.

Stay on Antelope Springs Road as it rolls up and down along the ridge. At 3.3 miles, you pass 3S59 on the left, part of Big Smokey Loop which leads to the geothermal hill. Continue right, still on Antelope Springs Road. As you traverse a ridge, the view stretches from Wheeler Crest to the Sherwins.

At 4.8 miles the road bears left and drops down toward Little Antelope Valley. At a junction at 5.5 miles, stay on the main road as it curves right and crosses Little Antelope Valley. On the far side, just before the main road climbs out of the basin, there is a jeep road on the left (3S06). Turn left onto this road and follow it down the drainage of a dry basin.

At 7.8 miles you pass a chalk mine. A little farther along there is a junction. Take the right-hand road down the drainage, down a narrow canyon, make a sharp left, and continue

Geothermal area

around the edge of the meadow. After a couple of curves and some rocky road, you come to a fenced area, the Little Hot Creek source, with over two dozen bubbling hot springs.

The entire flow is very hot and the ground in the area is fragile. Stay out of the fenced area. Several structures can be seen along the creek where devices measure the temperatures and flow of the hot spring.

Proceed along the fence, past the small reservoir for 2 miles toward Glass Mountain Ridge.

At 11.4 miles, the jeep road ends at Owens River Road (2S07), which is wide and well maintained; go right, south, and cross the meadow. Over a small rise, at the junction with 3S05, there is a corral. Continue south on the Owens River Road—the bridge over Hot Creek gives you an excellent view of Mount Morrison and Laurel Mountain.

At the top of a small hill, the road reaches a T-junction where Owens River Road goes left. You go right toward Doe Ridge. Up the hill 0.5 mile, the road (3S45) forks. Take another right toward the nearby ridge. [**Side Trip:** Hot Creek Day Use Area is at 15 miles. For details, please see the Hot Creek Ride. Side trip mileage is not included.]

Continue on Hot Creek Fish Hatchery Road (3S45) and ride over a crest and down toward the airport. Just past Hot Creek Ranch, the road splits. Take the paved road to the right with Mammoth Mountain ahead. On your right is the Hot Creek Fish Hatchery that uses water from the hot springs to raise trout year-round. Beyond the fish hatchery, at the base of a ridge, you can see steam rising from a large hot spring known as Mammoth Pool.

At 18.2 miles, Fish Hatchery Road ends at a paved road by the old school. Directly across it is a utility road. Take this road and cross the wide open flat toward Mammoth Mountain. The road is primitive, but distinct, a rocky ride over an old lava flow, leading 2 miles across the flat. Stay on the jeep road to the left of the fences; eventually it emerges onto a paved road by a ranch. Go north on the Sheriffs Substation Road over Mammoth Creek and uphill to Antelope Springs Road and your vehicle.

2 Hot Creek Ride

Distance: 10 miles.
Difficulty: Easy.
Elevation: Starting point: 7,280' with little gain and loss.
Type: Out-and-back ride on paved road, jeep road, and dirt road.
Season: Year-round.
Facilities: Restrooms at Hot Creek Day Use Area. No water. Carry 3–4 pints minimum. All amenities available in Mammoth Lakes.
Features: Visit the Hot Creek area where cold water blends with hot springs, creating a pleasant temperature. A sign warns about hazards. People have died here, so exercise caution. The area inside the fences is unstable and dangerous and entry is prohibited. There are steam vents and a couple of hot springs up the creek. Downstream are pools on both sides of Hot Creek. *Please do not ride the fragile trails upstream from the footbridge.*

Ride down Sheriffs Substation Road and go right at a sharp corner. Cross Mammoth Creek and continue past the substation to the dead-end of the pavement at 1.6 miles.

A jeep road continues almost straight ahead. As you ride it, stay to the right of the fences past some corrals. (The ranch is private property; please respect it.) The jeep road is faint and rocky over a black lava flow. To your right are the Sherwins, Laurel Mountain and Mount Morrison; Mammoth Mountain is over your shoulder.

At 2.7 miles, the jeep road ends by the old school. Go straight across

the junction on Hot Creek Fish Hatchery Road (3S45), and past Hot Creek Fish Hatchery to the end of the pavement.

At a junction by Hot Creek Ranch, turn left up the hill toward the Glass Mountains. To your right is Doe Ridge. 0.8 mile up the hill, you crest the saddle and go downhill to the Hot Creek Geologic Site at 5.5 miles.

From the Hot Creek overlook you may see people wading in the creek. The Forest Service recommends not entering the water. Note the warning sign. Avoid the area inside the fences that is unstable and

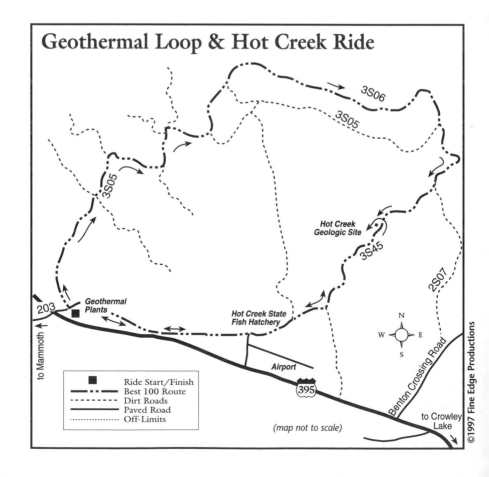

Geothermal Loop & Hot Creek Ride

3S06

3S05

3S05

Hot Creek Geologic Site

3S45

2S07

203

Geothermal Plants

Hot Creek State Fish Hatchery

to Mammoth

N
W   E
S

Airport

395

■   Ride Start/Finish
—··—   Best 100 Route
·······   Dirt Roads
——   Paved Road
··········   Off-Limits

Benton Crossing Road

to Crowley Lake

(map not to scale)

©1997 Fine Edge Productions

dangerous as well as the nearby boiling springs. The area below the bridge is the favored spot. There are pools downstream on both sides of Hot Creek. The cold water blends with hot springs, creating a pleasant temperature. The flow of hot water changes frequently; at times there have been geysers here.

Leave your bike and walk down the paved path to the footbridge. *Please do not ride the fragile trails upstream from the footbridge.* This is the local beach if you want to soak; it is usually crowded.

To return, retrace your route.

G. SMOKEY BEAR FLAT STAGING AREA

Season: Spring, summer, and fall.
Facilities: None. All amenities available in Mammoth Lakes. Carry a minimum of 3-4 pints of water.
Access: From the junction of Highway 203, drive north on Highway 395 for 4 miles. Turn right onto a dirt road to the kiosk and park.

This takes the prize for the most scenic staging area. Views of the Sherwins are excellent. There are options to combine two or more of the three rides in this section.

1 Little Smokey Loop

Distance: 6.1 miles.
Difficulty: Easy.
Elevation: Starting point: 7,500' with little gain and loss.
Type: Loop ride on dirt roads.
Features: Incredible panoramic views.

Start by the sign at the junction of road 3S04 and the power line road. Head toward the base of the hill, go left and ascend the primary dirt road.

At 1.2 miles is a triangle intersection. Brown carsonite paddles mark Big Smokey and Little Smokey. Go right onto 3S13. Views of San Joaquin Ridge, the Minarets, Mount Ritter and Banner Peak, Mammoth Mountain, and the Sherwin Range open before you for two miles. Keep your eyes peeled for birds; eagles and hawks are common.

At 3.6 miles, turn right and downhill along the double-pole power line. Follow the signs and go right. Two sweeping turns lead down to Smokey Bear Flat. Ride across the wide open flat for 1.7 miles. The soft pumice can be difficult. The start and kiosk are on the far side.

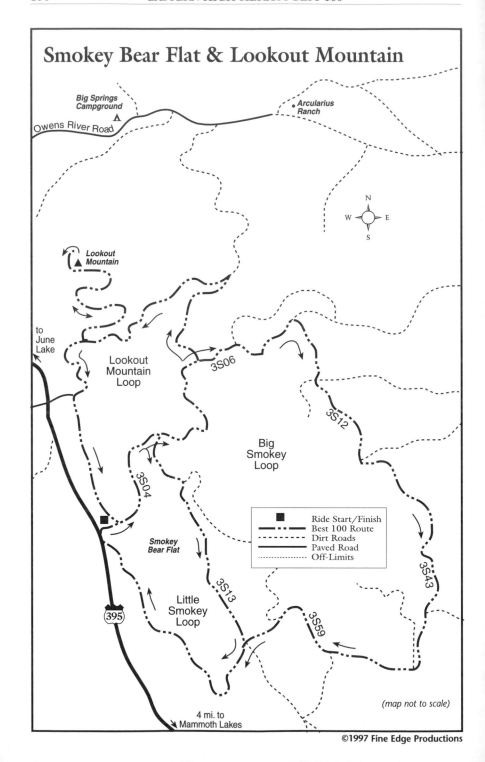

Smokey Bear Flat & Lookout Mountain

Big Springs
Campground

Owens River Road

Arcularius
Ranch

N
W — E
S

Lookout
Mountain

to
June
Lake

Lookout
Mountain
Loop

3S06

3S12

Big
Smokey
Loop

3S04

Smokey
Bear Flat

■ Ride Start/Finish
—··— Best 100 Route
········ Dirt Roads
——— Paved Road
········· Off-Limits

3S13

Little
Smokey
Loop

395

3S59

3S43

4 mi. to
Mammoth Lakes

(map not to scale)

2 Big Smokey Loop

Distance: 13 miles.
Difficulty: Moderate, with some climbs.
Elevation: Starting point: 7,500' with ups and downs for gain of no more than 600'.
Type: Loop ride on dirt roads.
Features: You pass the world's deepest geothermal well where drilling is being carried on in an effort to reach liquid magma; incredible views.

Big Smokey starts at the junction of 3S04 and the power line road. Head toward the circular track and bear left up the main dirt road (3S04). At 1.2 miles there is a triangle junction. Bear left on 3S04 over a rise and down to Lower Dry Creek Flat. After 1.5 miles you come to a junction, go right on 3S06, and climb uphill. In about one mile is a split in the road. Go right on 3S12. Views of Bald Mountain and the Upper Owens River Valley open up as you continue south on a roller coaster ride, gradually losing elevation.

At a steeper downhill, there are great view of the Sherwins straight ahead. Then take a sharp right and follow a new road to two higher bowls toward the ridge where you have views of Antelope and the Glass Mountains.

At Antelope Springs Road, turn right. The big white area below is a chalk mine. Cross the saddle to the west. A fantastic view opens of the Sherwins, Laurel Mountain, Mount Morrison, and McGee Mountain. The road crests and then drops into the forest.

At 9.2 miles, Antelope Springs Road meets with 3S59 in a curve. Take a right on 3S59 and climb a quarter-mile to a drilling platform. This is the world's deepest well—an experiment to drill until molten rock is found. At a junction just past the well, go right to a crest and follow the double-pole power line toward Mammoth Mountain.

At 10.5 miles, you rejoin Little Smokey at 3S13. Go straight along the power lines. At a double sign go right and downhill and cross Smokey Bear Flat to your starting point.

[**Option:** Combine Big and Little Smokey for a 19-mile-long ride.]

3 Lookout Mountain Loop

Distance: 12.3 miles.
Difficulty: Moderate with one strenuous climb.
Elevation: Start: 7,600'; Lookout Mountain: 8,350'.
Type: Loop ride with an out-and-back on Lookout Mountain.
Features: From Lookout Mountain, there is a panoramic view around the rim of the Long Valley Caldera which includes Wheeler Crest near Rock Creek Canyon to Mount Dana near Tioga Pass; Mammoth Mountain, the Ritter Range and the San Joaquin Ridge; June Mountain, Reversed Peak, and Mount Dana; Deadman Summit; the Glass Mountains from Bald Mountain to Glass Mountain Peak; the Upper Owens River drainage; McGee Mountain, Mt. Morrison, Laurel Mountain, and the Sherwins.

Start by the kiosk under the power line and head east on 3S04 toward the base of the hill, bearing left on the main dirt road. At the triangle junction (1.2 miles) go left, still on 3S04, over a gap and down to Lower Dry Creek Flat. At 3.7 miles, the road ends at 3S06. Go left there across Lower Dry Creek Flat toward Lookout Mountain. At a T-junction, go left and climb to a saddle with views of Bald Mountain.

At 5.4 miles there is a road (2S02) on the right and a sign for Lookout Mountain on the left. Go right, climb steeply to the first left curve, ride through forest, and then break out into the open. Make a sharp curve to the right and enter the forest again. Ascend two broad curves and into the open for a last switchback to the loop at the top.

Lookout Mountain once had a lookout but now all that remains is a foundation. An Inyo National Forest sign greets you. Bring your Eastern Sierra Recreation Topo Map and have fun locating points of interest. Notice all the obsidian chips lying around.

The return begins with a fast, fun 2.2-mile downhill. Keep in mind the three sharp corners on the way down. At the junction with 3S06, take a right and then, a few yards down the road, a left still on 3S06. This leads over a rise and down to a double tree near Highway 395.

At 10.8 miles, take the first left and follow the power line road over a rise, into a dip, and past an underpass. Climb another rise and descend to the starting point in Smokey Bear Flat.

[**Options:** Combine Big Smokey and Lookout Mountain for a total of 25 miles. Combine Little Smokey and Big Smokey together with Lookout Mountain for a 31-mile ride.]

CHAPTER 12

Glass Mountain Ridge

The western slopes of Glass Mountain Ridge, east of Mammoth, are sheer and barren, giving no hint of the extensive forests and meadows, canyons and springs found on its eastern slopes. The ridge is volcanic rock and, along with Bald Mountain on the west, forms the north "wall" of the Long Valley Caldera. On these eastern slopes, aspen groves provide shade from the summer sun; in the fall their leaves paint flames of orange and gold along ridges and streams. This remote area is a land of contrasts and awe-inspiring vistas, a magical and enchanting part of Mono County.

Since the early 1900s, Basque sheepherders have brought their sheep from the summer-scorched valleys of Nevada to graze on the grasses of Glass Mountain Ridge. These lonely men, along with an occasional miner or soldier, carved not only names and dates, but drawings of women and self-portraits into the soft white aspen bark. An "arborglyph" is preserved in the bark of a tree only

Glass Mountain and Sawmill Meadow

as long as the tree lives—sixty to eighty years— or until it is cut down or damaged by storms. Fragile and transient, these carvings provide an insight into a little known part of American history. Watch for them.

Easily accessible from Mammoth Lakes, this is a great place for overnight "bikepacking" trips, and extensive jeep roads provide unlimited possibilities for bicycling and camping.

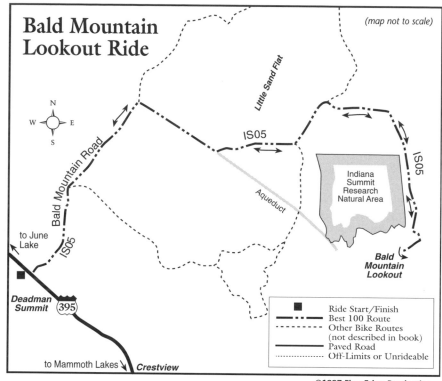

©1997 Fine Edge Productions

1 Bald Mountain Lookout Ride

Distance: 23 miles.
Difficulty: Moderate, but long.
Elevation: Start: 7,800'; Bald Mountain Lookout: 9,104'.
Type: Out-and-back on gravel road.
Season: Spring, summer, and fall.
Facilities: Restrooms at Bald Mountain Lookout. All amenities available in Mammoth Lakes. Carry drinking water with you.
Features: Pass through old-growth Jeffrey pine forest to Bald Mountain Lookout for fantastic 360-degree views.
Access: From the junction of Highway 203 and Highway 395, drive north 11.5 miles. Just past Deadman Summit, there is a parking area and kiosk on the left (west) side of the highway. Park here.

Bald Mountain Lookout

To start your ride, cross to the east side of Highway 395, passing a sign for Bald Mountain Lookout. The wide gravel road, 1S05, leads to Bald Mountain Lookout. Although some transitions of this road are confusing, it is well signed.

At first the road follows the edge of a pumice flat, a sparse meadow surrounded by huge Jeffrey pines. There are panoramic views of Mammoth Mountain, the Sherwins, and Laurel Mountain; and you frequently see eagles in these high meadows.

At the far end of the pumice flat, continue straight on 1S05, passing the junction with 2S42. Ignore several other junctions on the long gradual climb.

At the junction of two wide roads (3.6 miles), a sign points left to Highway 120 (1S06). Go right, remaining on 1S05 up a mild grade. The road climbs through Jeffrey forest and past several small, sparse meadows.

You pass a junction at 5.3 miles, where road 2S09 leads southeast to Alpers Canyon. Go left toward Bald Mountain, pass the junction of 1S88 (on your left), and continue straight on 1S05.

At the next major junction (2S04) there are two signs. Go left on 1S05 toward Bald Mountain and Indiana Summit. [**Side trip:** Just up the road you pass 1S47, signed *Indiana Summit Research Natural Area*. This is an area where old-growth Jeffrey pine have been preserved. No bikes are allowed within this research area, but you can leave your bike at the boundary and walk into the forest.]

Continuing your ride, stay on 1S05, ignoring 1S13 to the left. At the next intersection, take 1S05—the narrower road to the right (east)—uphill toward Bald Mountain Lookout which you can see through the trees.

At 10 miles, the road reaches a saddle. Take 1S05 to the right to Bald Mountain Lookout, visible at this point. Climb to a green closure gate, go around it and up a steeper hill through the sagebrush meadow of Bald Mountain. Ascend the ridge toward the summit, ignoring a road on the left that leads to a lower sub-peak. Keep right toward the Lookout.

The Lookout, a two-storied unmanned structure, has a spectacular view from its deck. There is a small log cabin to the right, and an outhouse to the left.

To the south are the sub-peak and a partial view of Glass Mountain Peak. Upper Owens River and Crowley Lake are laid out before you; Casa Diablo is south of Crowley, and

you can see the White Mountains and the Sierra from the Palisades to Yosemite. Also visible are Mammoth Mountain and the Minarets, with Ritter and Banner the highlights of this view. To the west are Glass Flow Ridge and Wilson Butte; to the north are the Mono Craters, Mono Lake, and the Bodie Hills beyond the lake. Around you is an unlikely mixture of sagebrush and alpine flowers.

After you have had your fill of the fantastic views, return the way you came, following 1S05 to your starting point.

2 Sagehen Summit Loop

Distance: 20 miles.
Difficulty: Moderate. Fairly strenuous.
Elevation: Sagehen Summit: 8,000'; highest point: 9,000'.
Type: Loop ride on dirt road, jeep roads, and pavement.
Season: Late spring, summer, and fall. Fall colors are outstanding.
Facilities: None. Amenities are available in Lee Vining, Mammoth Lakes or June Lake Junction. Carry drinking water with you—a minimum of 2 quarts.
Features: This is a remote and scenic ride through Jeffrey pine forest and alpine meadows.
Access: From Highway 395, 5 miles south of Lee Vining, drive east on Highway 120 to the signed Sagehen Meadow Summit. Park off the highway along 1N02.

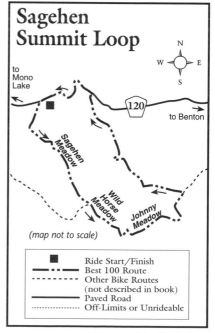

Sagehen Summit Loop

to Mono Lake

120

to Benton

Sagehen Meadow

Wild Horse Meadow

Johnny Meadow

(map not to scale)

■ Ride Start/Finish
▬▬ Best 100 Route
---- Other Bike Routes (not described in book)
▬▬ Paved Road
········· Off-Limits or Unrideable

©1997 Fine Edge Productions

Head south on the wide sandy road (1N02). The road winds around a big hill, gradually ascending through Jeffrey pine to Sagehen Meadow—a pumice flat covered by sparse grasses and alpine flowers. The road then veers toward Sagehen Peak, across a wide open ridge ascending to an aspen grove near the summit above Wild Horse Meadow (4.4 miles).

There are marvelous views of Adobe Valley and the canyons on the east side of Glass Mountain Ridge.

Sagehen Peak

Descend through Wild Horse Meadow, a long alpine meadow lined with aspen. The road leads along a shelf then drops toward Dexter Canyon. You join Dexter Canyon Road and turn left along the shelf, still on 1N02. The road then crosses the shelf and enters the trees.

At 8.6 miles there is an intersection with Johnny Meadows Road (signed). You continue straight toward a distinctive red rock outcropping. Turn left on a jeep road (29E03) by the outcropping, into the trees, and over the ridge. Follow the road across a dry drainage, cross an intersection, and keep straight across a shelf to an old mine site from where the road drops to North Canyon Creek.

Cross North Canyon Creek, turn west on 1S15A which leads out of the drainage and climbs an open ridge to a corral at Baxter Spring. Bear left (north) on 1S15 to Highway 120.

Go left at Highway 120 and follow it uphill around a curve and through a gap to Sagehen Summit. There is an animal watering trough on the left. From the gap, it is an easy downhill to your vehicle.

3 Sawmill Meadow Ride

Distance: 22 miles round trip.
Difficulty: Strenuous and extended ride in a remote area.
Elevation: 3,200-foot gain and loss to Sawmill Meadow at 9,500'.
Type: Out-and-back on good dirt and gravel roads.
Season: Late spring, summer, and fall.
Facilities: There are toilets, picnic tables, and a primitive camp at Sawmill Meadow. Store and campground at Owens River Campground on Benton Crossing Road, open only in summer. Restrooms and water available at the Whitmore baseball fields. Carry an adequate supply of water. Due to cattle and sheep, any water from springs may be contaminated. *Water must be treated.*
Features: This is a ride from desert to alpine meadow with fascinating views along the way. Sawmill Meadow is a fantastic camping area and a good overnight; there is a cabin and old mines. A hiking-only trail leads to the summit of Glass Mountain from near Sawmill Meadow. Wildflowers are excellent in early summer.
Access: From Mammoth Junction, go south on Highway 395 for 6 miles to Benton Crossing Road. Turn left (northeast) by the green church. Take this road 30 miles to its end at Highway 120. Go west on Highway 120, about 6 miles, to Black Canyon turnoff. Park off the highway.

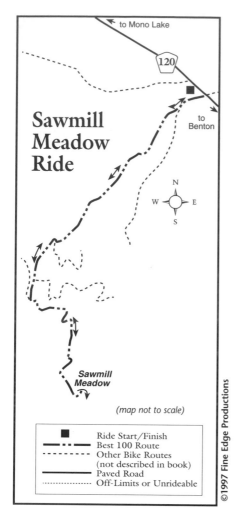

Sawmill Meadow Ride

to Mono Lake

120

to Benton

N
W ← ◇ → E
S

Sawmill Meadow

(map not to scale)

■   Ride Start/Finish
▪-▪- Best 100 Route
------ Other Bike Routes
        (not described in book)
——— Paved Road
············ Off-Limits or Unrideable

©1997 Fine Edge Productions

The ridge levels out where the pinyon becomes a thin forest. Views north include Taylor and McGee Canyons and Sagehen Summit. Adobe Valley lies behind you. As the ridge widens, Jeffrey pine appear. The bowls and meadows of Glass Mountain Ridge come into better view as you climb higher.

At 7 miles is a junction with a wide road (1S16). Go left uphill (still on 1S01) and over a low ridge. From the crest, you drop into a bowl of meadow and aspen and bear right up the drainage. You cross the creek and climb to the next ridge where you drop into another, larger bowl. There is a good primitive campsite here among the aspen. Follow the road up the drainage and up a third ridge covered with whitebark pine. This third basin is larger still, and the meadow mostly grass and flowers. Climb to a fourth ridge into the forest of whitebark pine. At the crest of this ridge, you pass a road leading left to Black Canyon Cow Camp. Stay right on the wide graded road and around a point of rock to the ridge.

At 10.6 miles there is a junction. [**Side trip:** Straight ahead at this junction, you find the trailhead to the summit of Glass Mountain. Lock your bike and hike to the top. *Bikes are not allowed on the trail.*]

To continue your ride, stay left, cross the cattle guard, and go through a forest. You can see Sawmill Meadow between the trees. You come to a cabin and a primitive camp site on the edge of the meadow where there are an outhouse and three tables with fire rings. This is Sawmill Meadow.

The ring of mountains above and around the meadow are impressive. Glass Mountain, the highest peak in the area (11,123 feet), stands on the easternmost edge of the Long Valley Caldera. Return the way you came.

Follow the wide gravel road (1S01) uphill into Black Canyon through open sage and rabbit brush. In less than a mile, 1S01 turns right and climbs out of the canyon.

You continue up the ridge toward Glass Mountain, a long, steady climb. Views down into Black Canyon and to the mountains above are tremendous. You can see the basin of Sawmill Meadow on the east side of Glass Mountain. Higher up, desert plants mingle with pinyon.

4 Glass Mountain Ridge Ride

Distance: 11.2 miles.
Difficulty: Moderately strenuous. Non-technical.
Elevation: Start: 7,514'; highest point: 9'500'.
Type: Out-and-back on dirt roads.
Season: Spring, summer, and fall.
Facilities: None. Store and campground at Owens River Campground on Benton Crossing Road, open only in summer. Restrooms and water available at the Whitmore baseball fields. Carry plenty of water with you. Treat *all* water from local sources.
Features: From Third Knoll, there is a panoramic view of Glass Mountain Ridge and Glass Mountain stretching to Bald Mountain to the west; Banner Ridge and the White Mountains to the east; Casa Diablo and the Volcanic Tableland to the south, as well as the Sierra Crest for over 100 miles. You can see the shape of the Long Valley Caldera.
Access: From Mammoth Junction, take Highway 395 south 6 miles to Benton Crossing Road at the green church. Go left and follow this road 15 miles to its crest by the Owens Gorge Road (4S02). Park here, off the road.

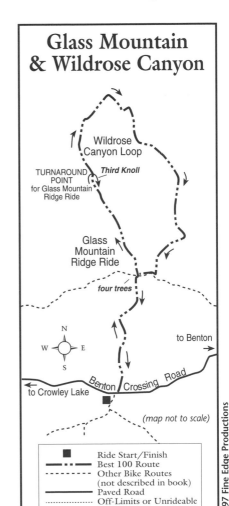

Glass Mountain & Wildrose Canyon

Wildrose Canyon Loop

TURNAROUND POINT *Third Knoll*
for Glass Mountain
Ridge Ride

Glass Mountain Ridge Ride

four trees

N
W — E
S

to Benton →

Benton Crossing Road

← to Crowley Lake

(map not to scale)

■ Ride Start/Finish
━ ·━ Best 100 Route
- - - - Other Bike Routes
      (not described in book)
━━━ Paved Road
·········· Off-Limits or Unrideable

©1997 Fine Edge Productions

From the intersection of 4S02 and Benton Crossing Road (2S84), head due north on a jeep road (not shown on the USFS map) toward four trees on a knoll visible about 3 miles ahead. Head along a low ridge with views in both directions. In a quarter-mile, the road bears right and drops to a saddle.

At a Y-junction, go left into a bowl from where you have good views of Crowley Lake and the Sierra; on the far side is a small meadow.

Your road climbs the far side of the meadow in a series of five terraces covered with sparse sage and pinyon. From the fifth terrace, you can see your road leading to a bald knoll with four trees; you can also see along Glass Mountain Ridge to Glass Mountain, a vast open sweep.

Continue along the crest of a ridge to the knoll with the four trees; you can see Crowley Lake and over 100 miles of the Sierra Nevada.

You drop off the knoll into a gap, go left along the power line road for twenty yards, then take a right onto the jeep road north toward Glass Mountain Ridge. The open, high desert becomes more alpine as you climb; in the spring there are great displays of wildflowers.

At 4.0 miles, the road curves to the right. Look back behind you—the Inyo Mountains and Owens Valley are visible and Casa Diablo Mountain is below. The road continues up the fantastic ridge—a ride to the sky. A triple knoll is ahead and the road gets steeper.

At the first knoll, go right to the saddle on the far side and climb to the second knoll. At the top you can see the Radio-Microwave Satellite Uplink. The road now heads for Third Knoll, and becomes steeper than the last two pitches as it climbs toward Glass Mountain.

At 5.6 miles you reach the crest of Third Knoll, above a vast meadow of sage, alpine grasses and flowers. From here you have a spectacular panoramic view of over half the area covered in this book.

Return the way you came—an almost 2,000-foot descent in 5.6 miles with excellent views.

5 Wildrose Canyon Loop

Distance: 19.6 miles.
Difficulty: Difficult because of distance, elevation, and technical sections.
Elevation: Start: 7,500'; highest point: 9,700'.
Type: Loop ride on jeep roads.
Season: Spring, summer, and fall.
Facilities: None. Store and campground at Owens River Campground on Benton Crossing Road, open only in summer. Restrooms and water available at the Whitmore baseball fields. Amenities available in Mammoth Lakes. No drinking water along the route; carry at least 2 quarts of water.
Features: This is a challenging ride from high desert to alpine meadows with outstanding views of the region.
Access: From Mammoth Junction, take Highway 395 south 6 miles to Benton Crossing Road. Go left (east) by the green church and follow the road 15 miles to the crest by the Owens Gorge Road (4S02). Park here, off the road.

Follow the directions for the Glass Mountain Ridge Ride to Third Knoll. Enjoy the magnificent views. An unnamed peak (elevation 10,148 feet), known locally as Squaw's Teat, rises to the northeast, east of Wilfred Canyon.

Continue over Third Knoll and take a right in the saddle that leads toward an electronics site. Please do not touch any of the sensitive equipment.

The road climbs to the crest in the trees, bears left, and runs along the crest of the ridge. Go right at a junction and drop to a big bowl at the base of "Squaw's Teat".

Follow a poor jeep road across the bowl and begin an uphill traverse across the alpine meadows covering the northern slopes of the unnamed peak. At 8.3 miles, the jeep road ends and intersects with a better jeep road.

[Side trip: To the right is an optional ride to the top of "Squaw's Teat," about 0.25 mile to the

Panoramic view looking toward Mammoth

10,148-foot summit where views of the White Mountains, Owens Valley, and Sierra Crest are incredible.]

To continue, go left from the junction and cross the ridge toward a lower saddle. At a split in the road, go right down a drainage of alpine meadow. Head east, ignoring a jeep road to the left, and continue down the meadow.

At 9.0 miles, a junction to the left leads to Kelty Meadows. You continue right and begin a high traverse along the south edge of Glass Mountain Ridge with exceptional views eastward across Banner Ridge and Hammil Valley to the White Mountains.

Climb to a crest between bowls and continue the traverse, descending to a saddle. Go one mile to the edge of Wildrose Canyon where the road descends to a second saddle.

At a junction in a gap, go right on 3S01B. The road south drops steeply into Clover Patch, a long valley filled with grasses, flowers, and clover. This is a good area to spot red-tailed hawks that thrive on mice and pikas. You may also see deer and antelope, coyotes and rabbits.

At the valley bottom, stay on 3S01B, ignoring the side roads, to 3S01 (at 15.5 miles), the wide graded road that runs along the power lines. Go right on 3S01toward the knoll with 4 trees. Go left and south on the same road you took on the first leg of the ride, back to your starting point at paved Benton Crossing Road (refer to Glass Mountain Ridge Ride).

Reaching a peak on a summer's evening

CHAPTER 13

June Lakes Basin

The June Lakes basin, where Mono Basin's high desert meets the alpine terrain of the Sierra Nevada, is surrounded by high granite peaks. Four lakes—June, Gull, Grant, and Silver—nestle among the basin's dark pines and restless aspen. Glaciers were the prime movers in shaping June Lakes basin, while volcanoes formed much of southern Mono Basin.

In winter, dramatic, snow-covered peaks remind visitors of the European Alps. In spring and early summer, crystalline waterfalls tumble down granite faces, surrounded by a profusion of wildflowers. In fall, the aspen leaves turn to gold, creating a striking contrast with the blue lakes.

The area provided its original settlers, the Paiutes, with water, plentiful fish and game, wood for fires and shelter, and obsidian that was traded to other tribes.

June Lake Loop, Highway 158, circles Reversed Peak, passing through the village of June Lake and skirting the four lakes. June Lake village is a small, friendly place with many amenities, including several resorts along Highway 158. Downhill and cross-country skiing, fishing, hiking, pack rides, and camping are all available here. For hiking enthusiasts, many trails lead into the Ansel Adams Wilderness from the June Lakes Basin.

In places, the line between alpine and desert climates is thin, crossing back and forth from desert to temperate forest—the rides in this chapter do the same.

1 Glass Flow Ridge Loop

Distance: 7 miles.
Difficulty: Moderate with two short technical sections.
Elevation: Starting point: 8,000'; highest point: 8,500'.
Type: Loop ride on dirt road and jeep road.
Season: Late spring, summer, and fall.
Facilities: None. Gas, toilets, and store at June Lake Junction. Crestview Roadside Rest Area, a few miles south of your starting point, has restrooms and drinking water. No water along the route—be sure to carry a minimum of 3-4 pints.
Features: Travel through lush forest and see Glass Flow Ridge, a huge ridge of black obsidian over a mile long and up to 300 feet high.
Access: From the junction of Highways 158 and 395, go south on 395 to a parking area on the west side of the highway, just 0.3 mile short of Deadman Summit. Park near the small kiosk.

Start at the parking area and head west on the wide graded road, 2S10, across a pumice flat toward Glass Flow Ridge—a barren ridge of black obsidian. Climb into a dense forest and, in about a mile, you come to the junction of Hartley Springs Campground. Stay left on the wide curve and climb to a gap. At the crest are a parking area and an interpretive display that explains the formation of Glass Flow Ridge. A quarter-mile past the display you come to a closed road. [**Side trip:** At the gated road, you can hike to the top of Obsidian Dome for a panoramic vista.]

Continuing your route, follow the road (2S79) down to Glass Creek, crossing an avalanche path and entering pine forest. The ridge across the way is also a glass flow.

At a triangle junction near Glass Creek, go left, following a shelf along the base of Glass Flow Ridge. There are views of Deadman Flat and Bald Mountain from here.

At this point the road deteriorates, becoming a poor jeep road that heads downhill, and is very sandy and pitted. Walk it if in doubt; it is a short stretch. Cross the lower shelf above Glass Creek and ascend a steep rugged climb to a high shelf.

At the top, continue around Glass Flow Ridge through meadows and forest. Follow the sandy road to a junction and take a right, away from the base of the ridge, that leads into the forest along the crest of the ridge. Take another right at the second junction. At the next two junctions go left, following the orange diamonds.

You reach a point overlooking Highway 395 at Deadman Summit. Go downhill to a pumice basin and parallel the highway to the power lines. At the junction near the highway, follow the power lines up a long valley through a sparse meadow. You pass two cliffs along here which are popular for rock climbing.

At the head of this valley, the road climbs left to a long narrow trench on the next level, and again to a higher shelf.

The road ends at 2S10 near the junction to Hartley Springs Campground. Retrace your route downhill to the right for about a mile, your starting point at Highway 395.

Glass Creek, Glass Flow Ridge

Looking toward Mono Lake from Hartley Springs ride

2 Hartley Springs Loop

Distance: 9.3 miles.
Difficulty: Moderate.
Elevation: Starting point: 7,900'; highest point: 8,800'.
Type: Loop ride through forest and along the ridge.
Season: Late spring, summer, and fall.
Facilities: Pit toilets in Hartley Springs Campground. Gas, water, and store at June Lake Junction. Some amenities available at June Lake Village. Carry all drinking water.
Features: Take a ride through pine forests to high crests; exciting views and a few steep downhills. This USFS-designated route is signed at all junctions.
Access: From Highway 395 and June Lake Junction (Highway 158), go south 0.5 mile. On the west side of Highway 395 there is a parking area (difficult to see) and a sign with a map. (This is directly across Highway 395 from Pumice Mine Road.) Park here.

From the parking area, ride west across the pumice flat and, at the first junction, go right uphill toward Oh! Ridge. Ascend through the pine forest to a second junction and go left up a drainage. The road tops out on a shelf where there are views of Devils Punchbowl.

At the junction on the shelf, go right along the ridge, a lateral moraine of June Lake Canyon. The road climbs through the trees with limited views of Mono Basin.

At 2.1 miles, a flat pad on the right has the best view of the ride: June Lake, Reversed Peak, and Carson Peak to the west; Mono Lake to the north with the Bodie Hills beyond it; Mono Craters and Aeolian Buttes to the east.

Go left and uphill through forest on road 2S10 to a basin. There is a short climb out of this basin to a saddle at the crest of the climb from where you can see Bald Mountain Lookout.

Your route now makes a long, gradual descent through red fir forest with occasional views of Highway 395 to the east. The road rolls and dips along the ridge.

[**Side trip:** A road up the hill to the right is open to mountain bikes; it leads to a meadow on the crest of Hartley Springs Ridge.]

At 5.2 miles, take a sharp left down-hill to a lower shelf. At a wide dirt road, go left on 2S48 and uphill through old growth forest to the entrance of Hartley Springs Campground. Keep to the left around the edge of the camp; frequent signs guide you through this area. On the far side of the camp-ground, the signs at a junction direct you to the right for a long downhill. Follow the signs, taking three lefts and

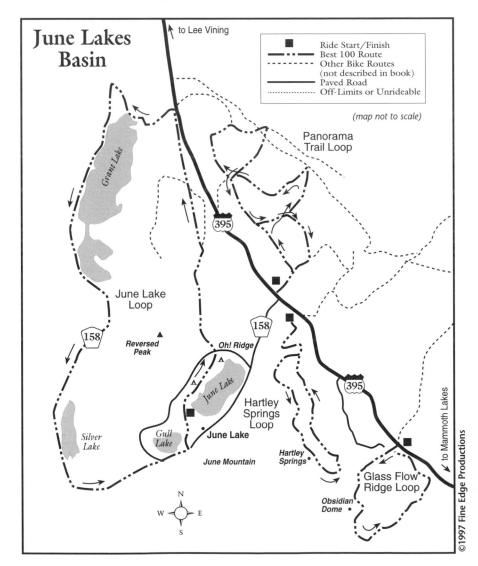

June Lakes Basin

to Lee Vining

Legend:
- ■ Ride Start/Finish
- Best 100 Route
- Other Bike Routes (not described in book)
- Paved Road
- Off-Limits or Unrideable

(map not to scale)

Panorama Trail Loop

Grant Lake

June Lake Loop

395

158

Reversed Peak

Oh! Ridge

158

June Lake

Hartley Springs Loop

Gull Lake

June Lake

Silver Lake

June Mountain

Hartley Springs

395

Glass Flow Ridge Loop

Obsidian Dome

to Mammoth Lakes

N W E S

©1997 Fine Edge Productions

descending toward Highway 395.

At road end, turn left on the road parallel to Highway 395 and follow the orange diamonds. In a half-mile, there is a sharp left leading steeply uphill to a saddle, with a steep descent on the other side, still following the orange diamonds.

At the next junction, go left through the forest to the first junction of the ride and go right across the pumice flat to your starting point.

3 June Lake Loop

Distance: 21 miles.
Difficulty: Moderate, but extended, with no big hills.
Elevation: 7,700' with small ups and downs.
Type: Loop ride on dirt road and highway.
Season: Late spring, summer, and fall.
Facilities (Seasonal): Parking, restrooms, and water at Gull Lake Park. Resorts and campgrounds along the way have water and restrooms. Some amenities are available in June Lake Village.
Features: Spectacular views of the Sierra Nevada and the Mono Basin. There are many examples of glacial and volcanic geology.
Access: From the junction of Highways 395 and 158 (June Lake Junction), go west on 158 to the Village of June Lake. Go right onto Gull Lake Drive and left on Granite Avenue for 2 blocks to Gull Lake Park. Park in the parking lot.

June Lake Village

June and Gull lakes, Mono Lake in distance

From the park, take the first left, behind the community center, and go left again, traversing the hill above Gull Lake below several houses. Continue to the baseball fields where you will find the Winter Access Road (under construction as we go to press). Go right onto the new road, traverse two high shelves above June Lake, following the power line east along the back edge of a campground.

When the road emerges into a wide pumice basin, look for a pair of parallel jeep roads, and take either one. (They both cross the meadow and rejoin on its far side.) After the roads rejoin, climb to a low saddle beside a large boulder and cross a small basin to a higher saddle. Here you have your first view of the Mono Craters, a series of volcanic vents in the Mono Basin.

Keep June Lake on your right and continue straight downhill through a junction and down a dry drainage to another basin at a power line where you take a sharp left and follow the power line uphill. Reversed

Peak is to the north and west. A long descent dips and rolls across the plain toward Mono Lake.

At the bottom, you come to a junction with a wide, graded road and go left. Here the aqueduct enters a tunnel that runs underground to the Owens River.

Cross the flat and climb the moraine. At the top is an incredible view of Mono Lake. Climb over a second ridge from where you can see Grant Lake. Descend past a cement tower across the dam, and go right downhill. At the bottom, go left across the one-lane bridge over the spillway and continue downhill on the dirt road.

At 9.3 miles, this road ends at Highway 158, the June Lake Loop. Go left onto the paved road and up to where you can see Grant Lake again. The road heads south along the Grant Lake shore. Sage and rabbit brush cover the slopes of the moraine and the creeks are lined with aspen. At the far side of the lake you come to Grant Lake Marina.

Continue along the lake shore past a Day Use Parking area and into Reversed Creek Canyon. Reversed Creek gets its name from the fact that it once flowed west, but the lifting of the Sierra reversed its flow east into Mono Basin. At the end of the canyon, the landscape opens into meadow. There are tremendous granite walls in this section and aspen and pine line the creek.

You continue past the Silver Lake Resort where there is a campground, store, marina, restaurant, and cabins. Meadows line the shores of the lake and you can see Reversed Peak across the water. There are large stands of aspen, spectacular in the fall. The road continues steeply up the canyon in a series of curves through a dense mixed forest and past glacier carved granite domes.

At 20 miles you come to June Mountain Ski Area. The new Winter Access Highway is across the road. Go left, climb the Access Road back to the baseball fields, and take a right back toward June Lake village. Two quick right turns at the bottom of the hill lead you to your starting point at Gull Lake Park.

4 Panorama Trail Loop

Distance: 10.5 miles.
Difficulty: Moderate with some sandy sections.
Elevation: Starting point: 7,684' with moderate ups and downs.
Type: An overlapping triple loop.
Season: Late spring, summer, and fall.
Facilities: None. A store, restrooms, and water at June Lake Junction. Some amenities are available in June Lake Village. No water available on the loop—carry 3-4 pints minimum.
Features: Panorama Trail offers outstanding views of Mono Basin, taking you to Mono Craters, a line of volcanic cones, and the Aeolian Buttes. This USFS-designated route is well signed.
Access: From Highway 158 (June Lake Junction) go north for 0.1 mile on Highway 395. Go right on 1S35 for about 30 yards and park near the sign *Panorama Mountain Bike Trail*.

Start at the sign (there is a trail map on a board here) and go north toward a ridge where there are several junctions, each signed. Go right at the first junction, straight at the second, then left twice. Climb to a shelf, then to the crest of the forested ridge.

Take two quick rights. There are good views of June Mountain and the Sierra here. Follow the road along the crest of the ridge. At a double sign, go left along the crest of the ridge. (You will return to this junction a second time and go right.)

[**Side trip:** At the next junction on the crest, you can take a road to the left leading to a high rocky point with a breathtaking view of Mono Craters, Mono Lake, and the Bodie Hills.]

You continue east along the ridge, pass between two boulders, and descend to the base of Mono Craters. The road ends at a wide graded road (1S37) where you turn left in a short distance, and take a second left on an unlikely-looking jeep track. There is a sign at the junction and another a few yards down the road. The road leads past a corral, heading toward the Sierra. At a T-junction with another

Mono Craters, Panorama Trail

wide well-graded road, go left and up-hill. (This section will be overlapped at the end of the second loop.) At the next intersection are three signs: one says *Panorama Trail*, one points straight ahead, and another points to the left. For the first loop, go straight, and circle Aeolian Buttes. When you return to the three signs, go left. Got it?

[**Option:** You can shorten the ride by omitting the Aeolian Buttes circle.]

Continue straight up the hill. At 4.5 miles, take the road on the right, and follow the trusty signs. This new road leads along the crest of the Aeolian Buttes, site of the most recent volanic activity in this area. There are tremendous views of Reversed Peak and the Sierra on the left, Mono Craters on the right, and Mono Lake directly ahead.

The road drops to a gap and a junction by some mushroom-shaped rocks. Go right down a long sandy hill toward Mono Craters and cross a vast high desert plain surrounded by surreal volcanic forms. In a half-mile the route turns right on a wide road and ends at another dirt road.

Go right toward Reversed Peak. Pass a familiar jeep road to the left and go straight. At the second junction are your original three signs. Go left this time toward the forested ridge and follow the road to a junction by a lone tree.

Go right and climb two switchbacks. Follow the signs left to the forest and right uphill to the three-sign junction. (At this point, there is another overlapping section of trail.)

Again, go left along the ridge a short way. At the junction with two signs, drop steeply down a loose sandy section toward June Mountain. At the bottom, make a sharp left turn and follow the signs through the forest to another steep downhill.

At the bottom of the ridge, the road comes to a junction with a wide dirt road, 1S35, where you turn right toward the Sierra. Follow the signs through two more right turns to your starting point.

CHAPTER 14

Mono Basin

Mono Basin is a magical place. A vast basin shaped by earthquakes, glaciers and volcanic eruptions, that lies on the western edge of the Great Basin, it is bordered on the north and east by high desert hills, on the south by Mono Craters, and on the west by the high peaks of the Yosemite area. Mono Lake, the powerful blue center of Mono Basin is an awe-inspiring sight—the best-known attraction in a little-known land.

Mono Lake dates back to the Pleistocene era, when runoff from giant glaciers created an inland lake 60 times its present size. About 10,000 years ago, after the last ice age, the lake began to shrink. When it no longer had an outlet, alkaline minerals and salts began to accumulate and, over time the lake's waters became a highly concentrated, alkaline soup.

The diversion of water by Los Angeles Department of Water and Power from creeks feeding the lake caused it to shrink to nearly half its modern-day size and the alkalinity to increase. A recent California State Water Board decision has resulted in an increase in flow from the creeks, and the lake is slowly rising.

Mono Lake is a unique ecosystem. The alkalinity and salinity of the water provide a breeding ground for brine shrimp and the pupae of the brine fly. These in turn provide food for over 98 species of water birds that visit the lake. In particular, migratory Wilson's phalarope, Northern phalaropes, and eared grebes, in vast numbers, make a much-needed stop here during migrations. California gulls and snowy plovers nest here; song birds and raptors frequent the marshes and lake shore; coyote, raccoon, deer, and weasels are sustained by the lake and its surroundings.

With its two recently formed volcanic islands and the tufa formations that rise along the shore, Mono Lake is a visual marvel, ever-changing with the light and the seasons.

The Mono Basin has been inhabited for over 5,000 years. The Kuzedika, or Northern Paiutes, camped here to gather brine fly pupae and collect obsidian as well. An Army party first saw the lake in 1852; they were followed by settlers—farmers, ranchers, and miners—in the 1860s. The area is rich in geological and human history.

For information, contact the Mono Basin Scenic Area Visitor Center, 760-647-3044; the Mono Lake Committee, 760-647-6595, or the Lee Vining Ranger Station, 760-647-3044.

1 Moraines and Meadows Loop

Distance: 11.6 miles.
Difficulty: There are difficult uphills and technical downhills.
Elevation: Starting point: 7,200'; highest point: 7,800'.
Type: Loop ride on dirt road, jeep road and broken pavement.
Season: Late spring, summer, and fall.
Facilities: Amenities are available in Lee Vining. Water available at the staging area.
Features: This geologic tour of moraines takes you through high desert and alpine meadows, and to high points for marvelous views of the Sierra and Mono Basin. Glaciers swept down Lee Vining Canyon, pushing aside loose rock that formed moraines. The height of the moraines gives an indication of the depth of the glaciers. Signs mark this USFS- designated route and maps are available at the Mono Basin Scenic Area Visitor Center.
Access: From Lee Vining, go south on Highway 395 to Highway 120. Go west one mile and park by the water tank below the old Lee Vining Ranger Station.

From the parking area at the water tank, go back down Highway 120 to the first road on the right, 1N15, where a sign marks the turn. Follow the road along the side of the moraine past a large water tank and across the front edge of the moraine. Views of Mono Lake and Mono Craters are astounding from here.

At 1.7 miles, the road ends at Horse Meadows Road (1N16); turn right and go up the drainage, climbing the side of the lateral moraine; this part is strenuous. The Los Angeles Aqueduct emerges from a tunnel and contours across the hillside on the left. Continue straight toward a narrow gap.

Above the narrow gap an unusual basin appears, a "hanging valley" created by glaciers, where resistant rock formed a series of shelves. Upper and Lower Horse Meadows are examples of hanging valleys.

1N16 crosses Lower Horse Meadow, covered with rabbit brush, sage, and a blend of grasses. Note that the ridge on the left is weathered, rounded granite—another sign of glacial activity. Cross the creek by

a big Jeffrey pine, go right at a junction, and climb steeply to another shelf.

Enter the forest near Upper Horse Meadows. The lateral moraine lies across the meadow where the vegetation is more alpine, with grasses and wildflowers. Go straight along a ditch and, at a second left, go left up the hill and climb to a saddle, the crest of the ride, where there is a great view of the June Lake Loop area and the Sierra.

From the junction in the saddle, go straight south, the start of a long downhill. Drop down the hill, cross a small creek, then crest a small ridge. Ride in and out of a dry creek down the third gully. Past this dry wash, the road turns toward the base of a big hill, another lateral moraine and follows the creek.

At a forked tree, cross a ditch, continue downhill and cross a second ditch. Then cross the creek by a juniper, ignoring the road to the right, and continuing straight downhill.

At 7.0 miles the road ends at a wide road by the Los Angeles Aqueduct, the world's longest all-gravity aqueduct.

Go left along the base of a hill toward Mono Lake. At a junction by a corral, turn left on a narrow broken pavement road. Follow this road past an old ranch. At a junction with a dirt road, veer left, following the brown paddle signs, and ride along the base of the hill.

At 9.6 miles, Horse Meadows Road (1N16) is on the left. In a quarter-mile, rejoin 1N15, the road on which you began your ride. Climb the front edge of the big lateral moraine; there are excellent views of Mono Lake and Bodie Hills. Continue past the water tank and, at Highway 120, go left (west) and up to the parking area.

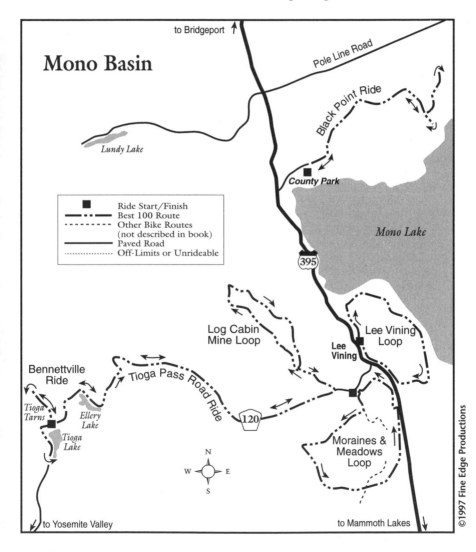

2 Tioga Pass Road Ride

Distance: 22.4 miles.

Difficulty: A long, difficult climb on a paved road. For safety, we recommend that you ride it in spring or fall when there is less traffic.

Elevation: Starting point: 7,200'; Tioga Pass: 9,950'.

Type: Out-and-back on State Highway 120.

Season: Spring and fall. Not recommended during summer tourist season when traffic is at its peak.

Facilities: Store, restaurant, restrooms and water at Tioga Lodge. Carry several bottles of water—a minimum of 2 quarts. Amenities are available in Lee Vining.

Features: Lee Vining Canyon is one of the most scenic bike rides in the Eastern Sierra; a challenging climb through a glacial canyon. Watch for bighorn sheep in the spring.

Access: From Lee Vining, go south on Highway 395 to Highway 120. Go west one mile and park by the water tank below the old Lee Vining Ranger Station.

From the parking area, go west up Highway 120 (Lee Vining Canyon). Note that the huge walls of the canyon are of about equal height on either side—these are the lateral moraines pushed aside by a huge glacier. Continue up the canyon across big meadows, passing two small recessional moraines.

At 2.2 miles, pass a green gate and climb the road up the north wall of Lee Vining Canyon. The Dana Plateau and Sierra Crest come into view as you leave the meadows and forests of the canyon.

A series of pullouts along the way offer the chance to rest and admire the views, each one spectacular. Some pullouts are wildlife viewing areas where you can watch for eagles and bighorn sheep. Down-canyon, you can see the long lateral moraines. This amazing road, blasted into solid granite through impossible terrain, is the highest pass across California's Sierra Nevada range.

Past a knoll to the left, the switchbacks of the old road below are visible. Slender waterfalls cascade down the far wall of the canyon and ahead is the waterfall of Warren Creek. The road enters a side canyon where Warren Fork joins Lee Vining Canyon. A tributary glacier in this canyon left a "hanging valley."

At 6.6 miles, you cross Warren Creek and pass the 9,000-foot marker. The old Tioga Pass road crosses the highway here.

As you climb steeply out of Warren Fork, there is a pullout on your left with a prime view down Lee Vining Canyon, You can see Tioga Pass road all the way to its bottom. Continue up the road along a precipitous section blasted out of sheer granite.

A 8.0 miles you come to Ellery Lake, a reservoir that holds water for the power plant in Lee Vining Canyon. (There are interpretive signs along the road.) Continue around the shore of Ellery Lake, where you can see segments of the old road, pass paved Saddlebag Lake Road where two creeks join, and continue up the highway.

At 9.2 miles you come to Tioga Lodge. The creek runs behind this quaint rustic business, built in 1927.

[**Side trip:** A little farther up Highway 120 you can visit the

Nanatak (Tioga Tarns on some maps) Nature Trail on foot. *No bikes are allowed.* Interpretive displays tell about this fragile ecosystem—an enchanted, stunted forest and alpine meadows.]

Continue up Highway 120 to Tioga Lake past the road to Bennettville (see next ride), marked by an old steam boiler from the ore mill. For the last mile, the road crosses a meadow with stunted trees where wildflowers bloom in early summer. Jagged peaks tower all around the summit of the ride, but Tioga Pass is surprisingly flat after the dramatic ascent. The alpine scenery makes the hard climb worthwhile. At the entrance station to Yosemite Park are two old stone buildings. There is a fee to enter the park.

Your return is a long, fast downhill on good paved road. Watch for cars and *control your speed.* (Careless cyclists have lost their lives on this road.)

3 Bennettville Ride

Distance: 3 miles.
Difficulty: Moderate; a little technical.
Elevation: 9,000' with little gain or loss.
Type: Out-and-back on historic wagon road.
Season: Late spring, summer, and fall. (Seasonal closures may be in effect.)
Facilities: Store, restaurant, restrooms and water at Tioga Lodge. Amenities are available in Lee Vining. Carry several bottles of water and resupply at the lodge. Treat all water from local sources.
Features: Take a pleasant ride on an old wagon road, part of the original Tioga Road, to the ruins of Bennettville, once a community and headquarters for the Tioga Mining District. All that remains are two buildings, a few ruins, and an old mine and ore track.
Access: From Lee Vining, go south on Highway 395 to Highway 120; go west 11.7 miles to the Bennettville marker by the old steam boiler; there is limited parking here.

From the Bennettville historical marker, follow the old highway for 0.1 mile to a cluster of stunted trees and go left on the wagon road. Traverse a meadow, cross a small creek, and pass two small ponds. *Please respect any hikers or equestrians; be courteous and yield the trail.* Since limited singletrack is available to mountain bikes, help keep it open.

You enter a grove of stunted whitebark pines, cross a knoll, and drop down to a creek where there is a great view up Saddlebag Canyon. You climb past several springs along hillsides covered with an abundance of wildflowers.

The trail widens to a road at the pad by the mine. Here you can see the rails exiting the mine shaft, as well as pieces of old mining machinery.

Continue on a singletrack down and across the creek and climb to the two buildings on the hill above the meadow; there are other ruins as well.

Return the way you came in.

4 Log Cabin Mine Loop

Distance: 10 miles.
Difficulty: This is a difficult and challenging ride.
Elevation: Starting point: 7,200'; highest point: 9,600'.
Type: Loop ride on jeep roads.
Season: Late spring, summer, and fall.
Facilities: Amenities are available in Lee Vining. Carry an adequate supply of water.
Features: This ride leads to a nature reserve where you learn about the plants and animals of the area. A side trip visits an historic cabin and mine. The ultimate view of Mono Lake is the finale of the trip.
Access: From Lee Vining, go south on Highway 395 to Highway 120. Go west one mile and park by the water tank below the old Lee Vining Ranger Station.

Start from the water tank and head up Highway 120 for 0.1 mile, and turn right at a jeep road, directly across from the old Lee Vining Ranger Station. There is a sign for the Log Cabin Boy Scout Camp. Head up the steep road on the side of a lateral moraine and pass under a utility line at the first corner. At the next pullout, there is a great view up Lee Vining Canyon with the ranger station and meadow below; you can also see Dana Plateau and the Sierra. Climb to the crest of the moraine that parallels the canyon; the road to the right is marked 1N03. (You will return on this road later.) Go left and across the edge of a meadow lined with aspen. A sign here welcomes you to a private Nature Reserve. *Please stay on the roads.*

On the far side of the meadow, you enter a "cathedral" of tall, straight birch. Across the road are signs which describe plant and animal

Historic log cabin, Mono Basin

life found in this reserve. Above this is a collection of cabins.

You go up Beartrack Canyon on a steep road, enter a mixed forest of aspen and pine, and cross Beartrack Creek. The road passes small meadows. When you cross the creek a second time, the climb tapers off. The high peaks around you are covered with grassy meadows and aspen. Cross the creek a third time and climb a bowl toward the skyline. At 4.6 miles, there is a road on the left to an old mining site and a well-preserved cabin.

[**Side trip:** You can ride up to the old mining site where you can see a sluice and a kiln once used in the mining operations. This side trip is a little over 0.5 mile.]

To continue your trip on the main road, continue to a saddle and a junction. The numerous white stakes you see in this area are active mining claims. (These are private. Please do not disturb.)

At the top of the saddle (4.6 miles), there is a five-way junction and two tin buildings. The left-hand road (signed) leads to the Log Cabin Boy Scout Camp in a forest of stunted whitebark pine. (Water and restrooms available in a limited summer season. Please ask for permission before using.)

Take the road right along the sage meadow past a split in the road. Where the roads rejoin, stop and dismount. Hike 15 yards to the black knoll on the east for the ultimate view of deep blue Mono Lake, its islands standing out in relief. The Bodie Hills lie to the north; Glass Mountain and the ridge to the south.

Back on your bike, follow the green snow stakes down toward Mono Craters in the distance. After a long descent, the road drops off the ridge in eight tight curves; it is technical.

At 6.5 miles, still in the saddle, there is an opportunity for one last view of Mono Lake before the road drops down the south side of the ridge into Beartrack Creek drainage.

The next two miles consist of a fast, steep descent of switchbacks down to the meadow on the top of the lateral moraine. At the junction you passed earlier (1N03), you now go left and descend the switchbacks into Lee Vining Canyon. Drop to Highway 120 and go left 0.1 mile to your starting point.

5 Lee Vining Loop

Distance: 6.7 miles.
Difficulty: Almost easy.
Elevation: Starting point: 6,800'; lowest point: 6,500'.
Type: Loop ride on dirt road, poor pavement and highway.
Season: Year-round, depending on snow conditions.
Facilities: Restrooms and water at Gus Hess Park (seasonal). Amenities are available in Lee Vining.
Features: Terrific views of Mono Lake and the tufa formations. Created where fresh water enters the alkaline, salty lake through cracks or springs, these formations are slow-growing deposits of calcium carbonate. Since tufa forms only underwater, all exposed tufa was once below lake level.
Access: From the Union 76 Station on Highway 395 in Lee Vining, turn east on Main Street and continue straight to Gus Hess Park. Park here.

Lee Vining Canyon

From Gus Hess Park, head north past the baseball fields, passing behind the high school. Follow the pavement to its end at the entrance to the Mono Basin Scenic Area Visitor Center. Directly across is a dirt road that leads down toward the old marina.

At the bottom, go right on a wide dirt road and over a mild rise. There are views of Mono Lake and the first Tufa Reserve to the north. The Mono Lake Basin Visitor Center is above.

Negit and Paoha islands, Mono Lake

Curve south and drop toward Lee Vining Creek and cross it at 2.4 miles. Continue around the base of a hill and climb to a great view of Mono Lake. The second Tufa Reserve is below.

[**Side trip:** Take the road down to the Reserve, park your bike, and wander through the tufa "groves".]

Continue paralleling the lake shore and cross a meadow to the junction with 1N51 by a ranch. Go right on 1N51 and uphill on what becomes a rough paved road. At the top of the hill, ride toward some power lines and follow the road to its end at Highway 395.

Turn right on 395 and ride on the shoulder past the junction of Highway 120. Cross Lee Vining Creek and enter the town of Lee Vining. At the Union 76 station, turn right on Main Street and return to Gus Hess Park.

6 Black Point Ride

Distance: 13 miles.
Difficulty: Almost easy.
Elevation: Starting point: 6,500'; Black Point: 6,958'.
Type: A half-circle ride out-and-back, with a hike to the crest of Black Point.
Season: Year-round, depending on snowfall.
Facilities: Seasonal parking, restrooms, and water at the Mono County Park. Amenities in Lee Vining. Carry a minimum of 3-4 pints of water.
Features: Ride and hike to the top of a recently active volcano, then take a soak in a hot water pond on the way back. Great views along the way.
Access: From Lee Vining, go 4.5 miles north on Highway 395 to Cemetery Road and turn right. Mono County Park is 0.3 mile on the right. Park here.

From the county park, go east on Cemetery Road and follow a fence past the cemetery. The pavement ends at mile 1.2 where you cross Mill Creek. Climb the hill and traverse the north side of Black Point.

You cross a second creek at 2.8 miles, bear right on the east side of Black Point. At the first junction stay left. At a second junction near Dechambeau Ranch, go right, and right again at the next junction. Climb the slope of Black Point toward Mono Lake.

At 5.3 miles a small parking area marks the end of the road. *Bikes are not allowed.* Lock your bike and hike up the trail to the top of Black Point where there are interesting geologic features such as crevasses and tubes.

You have an expansive view of Mono Lake, with Negit and Paoha islands just across a narrow strip of water.

Back at your bike, return the way you came, and take a right at the first junction onto 2N145. Cross a wash. Follow this jeep road toward the Bodie Hills and, at the next junction, go left. There is a parking area ahead and a hot spring with two pools of very hot water. Pass these and continue to two more ponds where the hot water mixes with cold and is a more comfortable temperature.

When you're finished, return past the hot ponds and across the wash. Back at the road to Black Point, turn right and retrace your route to Mono County Park.

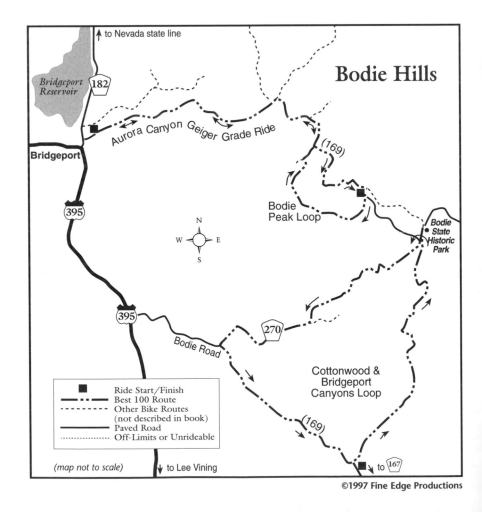

©1997 Fine Edge Productions

CHAPTER 15

Bodie Hills

The discovery of gold in the Bodie Hills heralded the greatest gold bonanza in Mono County history. Although William S. Bodey discovered gold in the area in 1859, it took about 15 years of exploration before a rich vein of gold was found in the Bunker Hill-Bullion area in 1874. By the summer of 1877, the Bodie gold rush began in earnest, and $35 million in gold and silver was mined between 1877 and 1888.

At its peak, the mining camp held as many as 10,000 people, creating a critical shortage of wood for buildings and firewood. Extensive logging of the pinyon pine caused tensions between the miners and the local Paiutes, who depended on the pine nuts for food and considered the pinyons sacred. Later, when logging began in the Jeffrey pine forest near Mono Mills, southeast of Mono Lake, a railroad was built to haul the timber and firewood to Bodie. The roads now leading to Bodie were once historic toll roads serving the town over a hundred years ago.

Bodie was famous for its lawlessness. Murders and robberies were daily events, and the extreme winters and remoteness of the area contributed to its problems. By the late 1880s, the population dwindled as mines closed. Several hundred people remained but the school finally closed in 1940 and the town was abandoned.

Despite fires, snow, and wind that destroyed homes and other buildings, 5% of the original structures remained, making Bodie the largest unrestored ghost town in the West. In 1964, it became a California State Historic Park, encompassing about 450 acres. The town is maintained in a state of "arrested decay," and its buildings are furnished with authentic antiques.

Water and restrooms are the only facilities, and since there is no food available in the area, hikers and mountain bikers must be self-sufficient. The Bodie Hills combine high-desert and alpine plant life in a terrain that seems strange, yet is beautiful. Tremendous views of the Sierra, White Mountains, Sweetwater Mountains, and Glass Mountains can be seen from this area.

In the early 1990s, in order to recognize Bodie's historic values, the Bureau of Land Management designated the viewshed area around the State Park as the Bodie Bowl Area of Critical Environmental Concern (ACEC). This bowl is managed by the BLM, with the California State Parks, to protect its landscape and historic features.

The rides in this chapter follow old toll roads. State Route 270 (the Bodie Road) was once the stage road from Bridgeport; the Geiger Grade was built for freight; Cottonwood Canyon connected Bodie to the farms and ranches in Mono Basin. So, come along and ride the historic routes for fantastic scenery and a visit to a famous ghost town.

Season: Late spring, summer, and fall
Facilities: Water, parking, and restrooms at the ballfield in Bridgeport. Parking, restrooms, and water in Bodie. Amenities are available in Bridgeport or Lee Vining. There is no water along any of the routes described below. Carry at least 2 quarts and refill at Bodie.

Note: Although traffic is restricted to foot travel within Bodie, all county roads are open for public use. For information, call Bodie State Park 760-647-6445.

Bodie Ghost Town in an "arrested state of decay"

1 Aurora Canyon/ Geiger Grade Ride

Distance: 32 miles round trip; 16 miles one way, downhill from Bodie.
Difficulty: Difficult due to distance and elevation.
Elevation: Starting point: 6,500'; highest point: 9,000'.
Type: Out-and-back on dirt road; or one-way downhill with shuttle or sag.
Features: Ride on the historic Geiger Grade Road past the old water flume to Bodie. Visit Bodie Historical Park. There is a fee.
Access/Shuttle: At the junction of Highways 395 and 182 at the south end of Bridgeport, go east on Highway 182 for a quarter-mile. Go right on Aurora Canyon Road to the town ballfields. Park here. For the shuttle, leave a vehicle at the ballfields, then drive another vehicle to Bodie where you start your downhill.

This ride can be done in the reverse as a downhill from Bodie itself, with a sag vehicle dropping you off in Bodie and picking you up in Bridgeport.

Start from the ballfields, ride uphill on Aurora Canyon Road (168), climbing the wide alluvial fan past rabbit brush, sage, and pinyon. The road enters Aurora Canyon and runs up the dry drainage for miles. Occasional willows line the canyon which is narrow in sections, and pinyon trees grow denser with elevation. Imagine, as you ride, that this was once the busiest road in Mono County!

Just past a an open-pit mine, the canyon widens. In spring the slopes here are covered with high-desert grasses and flowers. At 5 miles, ignore a jeep road to the right. (This road is reported to be part of the original Geiger Grade Toll Road.) As you continue up Aurora Canyon Road, you cross several bowls and pass a few springs and meadows.

At the junction of roads 168 and 169 (7 miles), Bodie and Potato peaks dominate the immediate landscape. Bear right onto Geiger Grade Road (road 169), crossing a wide basin toward Potato Peak. Endless views east to Nevada now open up across the sage-covered meadows.

At 9.4 miles, where you come to the crest of the ridge, look back to the north for a great view of the Sweetwater Mountains. You then drop into another basin and cross the meadow to a junction by a creek. (This is the point where the Bodie Peak Loop joins the main road.) You now climb out of this basin and drop down to Rough Creek. Cross the creek and climb to the next saddle. You can see the old Bodie pipeline just above the road from here.

At 14 miles you come to the last crest from where you can look down on Bodie and see evidence of the extensive damage created by past mining activity. You now drop downhill toward Bodie for 2 fast, easy miles to the junction next to Bodie graveyard. Cross the road to the parking area for the State Park, and lock your bike or walk it through the old townsite. Pick up an inexpensive brochure to guide you around town. Return to Bridgeport the way you came.

[**Option:** For a longer ride, return via State Route 270 (the Bodie Road) to Highway 395, go right (north) on Highway 395 and back to Bridgeport.]

2 Bodie Peak Loop

Distance: 9 miles.
Difficulty: Difficult due to elevation, technical trail, and steep road.
Elevation: Starting point: 8,200'; Bodie Peak: 10,195'.
Type: Loop ride on wagon and dirt roads.
Season: Late spring, summer, and fall.
Features: A steep ride on historic wagon roads through high-desert and alpine country with several side trips available. Visit Bodie Historical Park. (There is a fee to enter the park.) Hike to Bodie or Potato Peak for panoramic views of the Sierra Crest from Bishop to Sonora Pass, Glass Mountain, the White Mountains and Mono Basin.
Access: From Bridgeport, go south 7 miles on Highway 395 to State Route 270 (the Bodie Road), turn left (east) to Bodie. From the entrance station at Bodie, follow the bypass road to the junction with Road 169, just past the graveyard. Go left onto Road 169 (Geiger Grade Road), over the saddle and down the other side. Park off the road at the junction with a jeep road to the left, across the road from a square fenced meadow.

Courtesy BLM

Family ride in the Bodie Hills

From the parking area, ride up the jeep road by the cattle trough, cross the old Bodie water pipeline, and climb west to a saddle. Drop into a bowl and stay right at a junction. Notice how stunted the sagebrush is at this elevation.

In a little over a mile you come to a T-junction by a fence where there is a fantastic view of the Sierra. [**Side trip:** Take the road left, up and back, for a good view of Bodie.]

Continue up a steep grade toward Bodie Peak, following the fence line to the crest of the road, the high point of this ride. [**Side trip:** Leave your bike and hike 250 yards up to the summit of Bodie Peak (10,195 feet). Please stay on the path. The fragile plant life has little opportunity for recovery between extreme winters.]

Resuming your ride, follow the fence north toward the low saddle between the two peaks. At the bottom of the saddle, cross through a gate and take the road right up the ridge toward Potato Peak. Take a second right in the meadow and climb to the ridge near Potato Peak. [**Side trip:** Here you can take another hike to the summit of Potato Peak summit (10,236 feet). Although it's more of a scramble than Bodie Peak, the views of Bridgeport Valley and the Sweetwater Mountains are better.]

From the shoulder of Potato Peak, the road drops toward a saddle for a fast ride. At the bottom of the hill, you pass through a gate, bear right through a second gate, cross the saddle, and start down the bowl. This jeep road descends toward Geiger Grade Road (road 169); at 5.1 miles you rejoin it and turn right immediately crossing a creek.

You now climb up to the ridge between Bodie and Potato peaks, and at the crest, you drop into a larger alpine bowl from where you can see Rough Creek below. Drop to the creek, cross it, and climb gradually, paralleling the old Bodie water pipeline, to your starting point by the cattle trough.

3 Cottonwood and Bridgeport Canyons Loop

Distance: 28 miles (includes a side trip to Bodie State Park).
Difficulty: This is a long, challenging ride with a lot of elevation gain, and a technical downhill.
Elevation: Starting point: 6,400'; highest point: 9,000'.
Type: Loop ride on dirt roads, pavement, and jeep roads.
Season: Spring, summer, and fall.
Features: This ride takes you on three historic roads through varied terrain with spectacular scenery. Visit Bodie Historical Park. There is a fee to enter the park.
Access: From Lee Vining go north on Highway 395 for six miles. Turn east on State Highway 167. In seven miles, turn left onto a wide dirt road (Road 169). Park off the road.

Follow the wide dirt road uphill through dense pinyon toward the Bodie Hills, passing a sign: *Ghost town of Bodie 10 miles.*

Follow the fence line to Bodie Peak

In 1.6 miles at the first junction, go right on Cottonwood Canyon Road, past Goat Ranch (at 2 miles). Continue past the corrals climbing the alluvial fan. You then enter Cottonwood Canyon, cross a stream bed, and climb the canyon, losing sight of Mono Lake. Above the canyon, you leave the pinyon behind and enter a vast sage meadow.

At 7.5 miles, you pass several interesting weathered lava formations. In early summer, the bowl ahead has nice displays of Indian paintbrush, California poppies, and wild roses.

At 8.3 miles, there is a junction; Sugarloaf is to the left. Prospects and tailing are scattered across the basin. (There is gold beneath your wheels, but not rich enough to cover the cost of its extraction!) Cross the power lines and climb toward a wide saddle.

From the crest of the saddle at 9.7 miles, you can see Bodie Peak, Bodie Bowl, and the town.

Follow the road to Bodie State Park entrance station (10.3 miles).

[**Side trip:** To visit this fantastic, well-preserved mining town, continue around the edge of Bodie Bowl, past the graveyard, to the parking area where there are restrooms and water. The fee supports the preservation of Bodie. Park and lock your bike or walk it with you as you tour the ghost town. Mileage is *included* for this side trip.]

After the end of your tour, be sure to fill up on water. Return to the parking area (11.9 miles). Go left on the road along the edge of Bodie Bowl, past the Entrance Station and right on State Route 270 (Bodie Road).

Within a mile, you pass a boundary sign for Bodie State Historic Park, and at 14.6 miles, the pavement begins. The road is signed *8% grade* for one mile—this can be fun, but watch out for cars! You drop steeply toward a big basin and at the bottom cross Murphy Spring where the road takes a sharp left curve. Rock ruins of an old stage station can be seen by the

creek. At mile 16.7 you pass Benchmark 8080. Continue down and across Mormon Meadow where a few willows line the creek.

At 20.4 miles you come to the Bridgeport Canyon turnoff. Turn left and parallel Bodie Road for about 100 yards. Turn left again (south) and cross Clearwater Creek, passing a corral and following the side drainage toward a saddle. From the crest of this saddle (23.8 miles), you have great views north as well as south.

You now start down Bridgeport Canyon which follows the old wagon route from Mono Lake to Bridgeport. The route is brushy here, and the road becomes fainter. The road is subject to washouts and you may encounter a sudden drop-off. Continue down the wash in the bottom of the canyon.

Where the canyon opens up, the road becomes more distinct again, descending to a wide graded dirt road where you go left to the junction with Cottonwood Canyon Road. Go right at this junction and downhill to your staring point.

CHAPTER 16

Conway Summit & Bridgeport Valley

Bridgeport Valley lies at 6,400 feet in a basin surrounded by the Sweetwater Mountains, the Sierra Nevada, and the Bodie Hills. Once called Big Meadows, the valley provided rich hunting and gathering grounds for the northern Paiutes. The East Walker River and the Bridgeport Reservoir have helped to keep this a lush green land—prime ranching country.

The town of Bridgeport, Mono County's seat since 1864, was the supply center for Bodie and dozens of other gold and silver mines. (Be sure to take a short historical tour through the town.) Although mining towns came and went, the town of Bridgeport has been sustained by tourism and ranching. Hunters, backpackers, fishermen, OHV riders, and equestrians come to the area for its wonderful recreational opportunities.

Bridgeport Reservoir

Mountain bikers are newcomers to this land where horses have used the trails for over 150 years. Many roads in the area cross private land and access is controlled by the ranchers. The Bridgeport area has avoided "wars" over trail access to date, so please yield to equestrians and hikers with whom you share these non-wilderness roads and trails. Follow the IMBA standards so you can continue to enjoy access to the area.

Most of the roads in Bridgeport Valley were originally built for mining or logging, and there is a history behind each road. Hundreds of jeep roads cross the valley or lead into the Bodie Hills. Since ranches now occupy most of the valley floor, the rides in this area go up into the hills; most require a vehicle to access the starting point.

Note: Conway Summit is an Area of Critical Environmental Concern. Please remain on established roads.

1 Copper Mountain Loop

Distance: 10.8 miles.
Difficulty: Strenuous due to altitude and climb.
Elevation: Conway Summit: 8,138'; high point: 9,200'.
Type: Loop ride on jeep roads.
Season: Late spring, summer, and fall.
Facilities: Nearest facilities are in Lee Vining. Carry a minimum of 3-4 pints of water.
Features: Superlative views of Mono Basin and Bridgeport Valley. You ride past alpine meadows and through dwarf forests. See the remains of Monoville, an early gold-rush settlement and a flume dug in 1860 to deliver its water.
Access: From Bridgeport, go south on Highway 395 for 14 miles to the crest of Conway Summit. From Lee Vining, take Highway 395 north 12 miles to Conway Summit. Park off the road near Summit Inn.

Head up Virginia Lakes Road (Road 021) past the ruins and the flume. At 0.5 mile, by a grove of aspen, you come to the junction with Road 180. Turn left onto 180, and climb steeply up the ridge (the front edge of a lateral moraine) to Jordan Basin. Here you have a view of Conway Summit below and Bodie Hills to the east. Most of Jordan Basin is covered with aspen and clusters of stunted pine and juniper.

Continue up the steady grade past a power line. The view of Mono Basin gets better with elevation. Jordan Basin hangs on the side of spectacular Copper Mountain.

Follow the road along the moraine, past the first junction of 180 and 181. You can see Road 181 looping across the top of the basin, along the far ridge, and back to this point.

Go straight toward the Sierra, still on 180, to the top of the basin. The second junction of 180 and 181 is marked with a sign at 4.0 miles. 180 continues to a dead-end on top of the moraine, but your route goes left on 181, downhill, toward an aspen grove.

Cross the head of the basin through small creeks, meadows, aspen groves, and dwarf forests of whitebark pines. Finally, you reach a saddle at a junction—the high point of the basin. The road to the right leads to a mine on the mountain; from here, you can also see into Lundy Canyon.

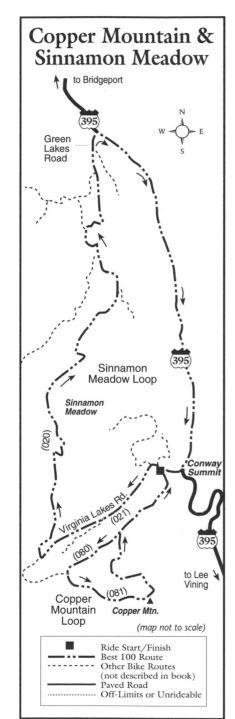

Copper Mountain & Sinnamon Meadow

to Bridgeport

395

Green Lakes Road

N
W — E
S

Sinnamon Meadow Loop

395

Sinnamon Meadow

(020)

Conway Summit

395

Virginia Lakes Rd.

(021)

(080)

to Lee Vining

Copper Mountain Loop

(081)

Copper Mtn.

(map not to scale)

■ Ride Start/Finish
—— Best 100 Route
- - - - Other Bike Routes
         (not described in book)
—— Paved Road
·········· Off-Limits or Unrideable

©1997 Fine Edge Productions

Take the left at the flat pad, follow the road along the crest of the ridge, across a low saddle, and up to a point on a knoll where you have an even better view into Lundy Canyon. Stunted forests line the meadows along the ridge.

Near the end of the ridge is a junction of two jeep roads. [**Side trip:** The road to the right is a spur leading to the ultimate view of Mono Basin. Follow it one half-mile to its end, and take a short walk to the point for a panoramic view of Mono Lake—this is the scenic highlight of a very scenic ride.]

At the junction, descend the switchbacks into Jordan Basin. At a junction, bear left toward the creek and across the basin. After you cross the creek, go straight at the junction and climb to a road on the ridge above.

At the T-junction with road 180, turn right down the ridge and retrace your route. It is all downhill from here and you have stunning views of Mono Lake and Conway Summit on your descent. Go right on Virginia Lakes Road to your starting point.

2 Sinnamon Meadow Loop

Distance: 23.3 miles.
Difficulty: Moderate, but long.
Elevation: Conway Summit: 8,138'; highest point: 9,200'; lowest point: 6,700'
Type: Loop ride on pavement, dirt roads, and highway.
Season: Late spring, summer, and fall.
Facilities: Nearest facilities are in Lee Vining. Carry at least 2 quarts of water.
Features: Traverse several high alpine meadows, ride through forests of aspen and pine, and see the remains of gold rush-era settlements, including Dogtown, home to many Chinese miners.
Access: From Bridgeport, go south on Highway 395 for 14 miles to the crest of Conway Summit. From Lee Vining, take Highway 395 north 12 miles to Conway Summit. Park off the road outside the gate at Summit Inn.

Go west up Virginia Lakes Road (Road 021). Note the foundations, cabins, and corrals, the remains of a gold-rush settlement. The flume you see was dug in 1860 to deliver water to Monoville, site of the earliest gold rush in the area.

Climb the Virginia Lakes Road along the side of a ridge, cross the creek, and climb over the terminal moraine. Continue up the canyon on the paved road.

At 4.5 miles, by the Virginia Lakes Pack Station, go right on Road 020. Follow the road across the gray ridge, past small meadows, and through lodgepole pine forests.

At an intersection with Road 178, stay right on 020 and pass through groves of aspen. The Bodie Hills to the east are stark and impressive, and there are fantastic views in other directions as you cross the open ridge. As you descend to Sinnamon Meadow (named for a local miner), you enter a mixed forest of aspen and pine.

At 8.8 miles, you pass a second junction with Road 178 (Dunderburg Mine Road). Again, continue downhill on Road 020, ignoring all jeep roads, and descending several switchbacks.

At a junction (11.9 miles), go left toward Bridgeport across a plain of sage and sparse grass. Pinyon pines begin to appear. In one mile, at the junction with Green Lakes Road (Road 142), bear right toward Bridgeport on Road 142, through high-desert meadow and pinyon.

At 15.3 miles, the junction of Summers Meadows Road and Green Lakes Road, stay right on the main road. Within a mile you cross the creek by the highway. Go right on Highway 395 into a small canyon past Willow Creek Resort. The Bodie turnoff is above the canyon on the left (19.0 miles); in a short distance on the right is an historical marker at the site of Dogtown.

You now have 5.9 miles of cranking up a long, steady grade to Conway Summit; stop to admire the desert and alpine vistas and the magnificent line of mountains, and drink plenty of water. Keep an eye out for old cabins, tailings, corrals, and ditches, this was once a populated place. At Conway Summit (23.3 miles) you're back to your starting point.

3 Travertine Geologic Ride

Distance: 3 miles.
Difficulty: Easy.
Elevation: 6,480' with little gain or loss.
Type: Out and back on jeep road and graded dirt road.
Season: Year-round.
Facilities: Parking, water, restroom at Bridgeport Ranger Station. Amenities are available in Bridgeport. The Geologic Area is Day Use Only.
Features: Ride through an extensive geothermal area. There are steam vents, hot pools, and hot springs in this boggy basin. See the ridges formed by marble-like travertine that was mined and used in buildings. Terrific views of the Bridgeport Valley.
Access: From Bridgeport, go south on Highway 395, past the Highway 182 junction, to the Bridgeport Ranger Station. Park out of the way.

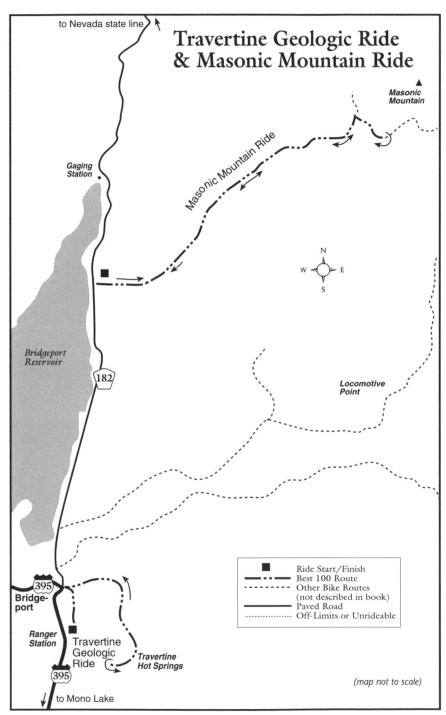

to Nevada state line

Travertine Geologic Ride
& Masonic Mountain Ride

Masonic
Mountain

Masonic Mountain Ride

Gaging
Station

N
W ○ E
S

Bridgeport
Reservoir

182

Locomotive
Point

■ Ride Start/Finish
▪—▪—▪ Best 100 Route
- - - - Other Bike Routes
    (not described in book)
——— Paved Road
·········· Off-Limits or Unrideable

395
Bridge-
port

Ranger
Station

Travertine
Geologic
Ride

Travertine
Hot Springs

395

(map not to scale)

to Mono Lake

©1997 Fine Edge Productions

Note: The Travertine Area has been designated by BLM as an Area of Critical Environmental Concern (ACEC). Please remain on established roads and respect all closures. (See "Travertine—More Than a Hot Tub" at the end of this chapter.)

Immediately south of the ranger station, go left, away from Highway 395, on a narrow paved road. Follow the split-rail fence east past the Cal-Trans maintenance station. The road circles an alkali wetland and leads to the Mono County maintenance yard. Just before the maintenance yard is Jack Sawyer Road on the right. Take this steep wide road past a firing range to the crest of a low hill. Bear right at the junction with Borrow Pit Road.

The road goes along the crest of a low divide, with a view of Bridgeport Valley and the reservoir. The road drops, crosses the edge of an alkali meadow, and ascends to a parking area at the upper hot spring.

There is a round cement pool, with a deck and benches. The source spring of this upper pool is extremely hot, so use caution when you take a dip. Information about this geologic ACEC site is posted on a kiosk nearby.

Just below the parking area, 10 yards on the left, there is a closed road that leads 100 yards downhill to the travertine pool. This historic pool was used by miners who used to stop and bathe before heading to the local dance hall.

There are fantastic travertine formations where the hot water has deposited minerals for centuries. The long ridge (mole) along the spring is an example of this process. At the end of the mole, there are three shallow pools where you can enjoy a hot soak with fantastic views of Bridgeport Valley.

Soak to your heart's content, but leave the area clean. And when you have finished, return the way you came in.

Ruins in the hills below Masonic Mountain

4 Masonic Mountain Ride

Distance: 10 miles.
Difficulty: Moderate.
Elevation: Bridgeport: 6,450'; high point: 8,000'.
Type: Out and back on gravel road.
Season: Spring, summer, and fall.
Facilities: Parking, restrooms, water, and shade at the Fishing Access Day Use Area. Amenities available in Bridgeport.
Features: Terrific views of the Bridgeport Valley; visit the mines on Masonic Mountain, and see sections of an historic toll road.
Access: Just south of the bridge in Bridgeport at the junction of Highways 395 and 182 in Bridgeport (south end), go north on Highway 182, along the shore of Bridgeport Reservoir, for 3.5 miles. Turn left at the *Fishing Access Day Use Area and park.*

Start from the Fishing Access Day Use Area. Cross Highway 182, and go north a short distance to the wide, graded Masonic Road (BLM Road 046). The roads makes a long moderate climb passing through dense pinyon forest. Views of Bridgeport Reservoir and the Sweetwater Mountains get better as you climb.

Continue the steady climb parallel to the canyon. You have views of the Sierra across Bridgeport Valley, as well as of the historic toll road in the canyon below, amid meadows and aspen.

At 4.7 miles you come to a junction with the old wagon road that lead to Masonic Mountain; early Twentieth Century Mines are visible on the mountain. Turn left toward the mountain and climb for about a half-mile. Take the spur road on the right to the old stamp mill. You can explore the many historic sites in this area, but use caution around the mines.

When you're finished exploring, head back to your starting point, the way you came in.

5 Twin Lakes Loop

Distance: 8.4 miles.
Difficulty: Moderate. Some technical singletrack.
Elevation: 7,000' with about 300' gain and loss.
Type: Loop ride on good dirt road, singletrack, and paved road; two miles of singletrack, not well-groomed.
Season: Spring, summer, and fall.
Facilities: Food, restrooms, water at Twin Lakes Resort. Store, restaurant, restrooms, water in Mono Village. Amenities available in Bridgeport.
Features: Ride through beautiful scenery, pine and aspen forest around Twin Lakes.
Access: From the north end of Bridgeport on Highway 395, turn west onto Twin Lakes Road (018). Go 10 miles to Twin Lakes Resort and park in the parking area.

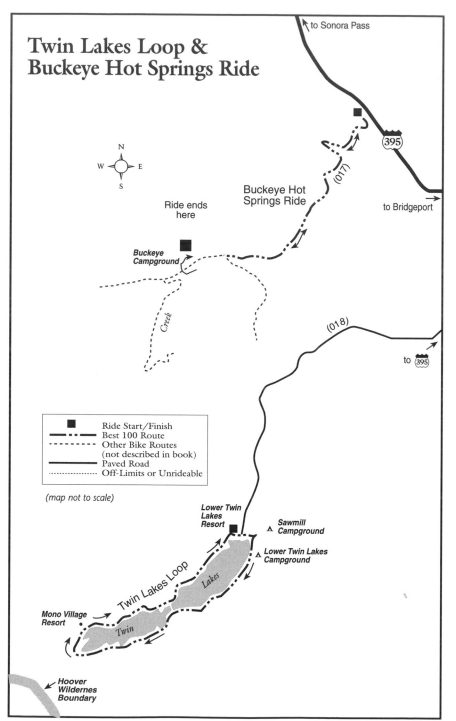

Twin Lakes Loop &
Buckeye Hot Springs Ride

to Sonora Pass

395

Buckeye Hot
Springs Ride

(017)

to Bridgeport

Ride ends
here

Buckeye
Campground

Creek

(018)

to 395

■   Ride Start/Finish
▬ ▬ ▬   Best 100 Route
- - - - -   Other Bike Routes
          (not described in book)
▬▬▬   Paved Road
··········   Off-Limits or Unrideable

(map not to scale)

Lower Twin
Lakes
Resort

△ Sawmill
  Campground

△ Lower Twin Lakes
  Campground

Twin Lakes Loop

Twin Lakes

Mono Village
Resort

Twin

Hoover
Wildernes
Boundary

©1997 Fine Edge Productions

From the parking area at Twin Lakes Resort, go left on Twin Lakes Road back toward Bridgeport for 0.25 mile. Turn right onto Road 044, and cross the bridge over Robinson Creek. There are campsites on both sides of the creek. Bear right along the base of a big lateral moraine; Lower Twin comes into view on your right.

You pass a trailhead with parking and a kiosk. Continue along the road, near the lake and past a few cabins.

At 2.5 miles you pass Cattle Creek Trail. *Off limits to bikes.* Continue along the lake on the graded road through a summer home area and a stand of aspen. At a T-junction, go right downhill. The road curves left and runs by the creek between Twin Lakes. Look for fish; this is a spawning area; *no fishing.*

At 2.8 miles there is a junction with a stone bridge to the right. [Option: For a shorter ride, you can cross the bridge to Twin Lakes Road, go right and follow the shore two miles back to Twin Lakes Lodge.]

For the full loop, take the left road along shore and through the aspen, 0.5 mile to a turnaround, where you'll find a singletrack along the lake shore. This trail is technical and narrow. Pass through stands of fir and cross Cattle Creek, divided at this point into five different channels. *Please walk this series of stream crossings.*

At the end of the lake, the trail drops down along Robinson Creek and splits into several trails—this section takes a little guesswork. (Stay on the best-looking trail.) Find the bridge and cross the creek to the backside of a large campground. Bear right twice and find the entrance station. The store and restaurant here are part of Mono Village Resort.

Pass under the wooden arch and follow the paved road along Upper Twin Lake to the junction at the crest between Twin Lakes. Continue on Twin Lakes Road along the shore of Lower Twin Lake to your starting point.

6 Buckeye Hot Springs Ride

Distance: 9 miles.
Difficulty: Moderate.
Elevation: 6,800' with about 400' gain and loss.
Type: Out-and-back on gravel road.
Season: Year-round, depending on snow conditions.
Facilities: None. Amenities available in Bridgeport. Carry drinking water.
Features: Terrific views of the Bridgeport Valley and a chance to soak at Buckeye Hot Springs. See the ruins of an old sawmill.
Access: From the courthouse in downtown Bridgeport, drive north on Highway 395 for about 3 miles. Directly across Highway 395 from the USFS employee housing, turn left on dirt road 017 and park off the road.

Head southwest up a hill on road 017, passing a helicopter pad and a trailer. It is a long gradual climb. Views left across the Bridgeport Valley are fantastic. The road traverses a long ridge, in and out of small canyons, one of which has a perennial stream (By Day Creek).

As you climb higher you have sweeping views of the surrounding valley, the Sierra Crest, Bodie Hills, and Sweetwater Mountains. The slopes are covered with sage, rabbit brush and pinyon. Below are irrigation ditches and an ocean of grassland where hundreds of cattle graze.

Stay on the wide, well-maintained road and, at 2.8 miles, you enter Toiyabe National Forest. The road now turns up Buckeye Creek Canyon and drops past a triangular parking area at Buckeye Hot Springs (mile 4.7). [**Side trip:** At the triangular parking area, park and lock your bike and take the faint trail leading down the bluff to Buckeye Creek. Hot water from the base of the bluff mixes with the creek water, making a primitive hot spring, very much now as it was when the Indians and pioneers used it. The natural setting in a pine forest is wonderful.]

Continue to a junction with the road to Buckeye Campground; there are meadows and aspen in the canyon. Across the bridge from this junction is an historical marker for an old sawmill. [**Side trip:** Enter Buckeye Campground and ride to the trailhead. It is legal to ride the jeep road only to the wilderness boundary. This trip up Buckeye Creek adds 6 miles and 100 feet of climbing to your total.]

To return to your starting point, reverse your route.

Travertine — *More than a Hot Spring*

Welcome to Travertine Area of Critical Environmental Concern (ACEC). This special place is recognized by the Bureau of Land Management (BLM) and the local community for its important resource values. Throughout this area, unusual geologic ridges extend over a landscape of alkali-encrusted meadows. It is believed that these ridges began over 10,000 years ago as hot underground water rose to the surface and mixed with the air. This water and air interaction continues to produce travertine (calcium carbonate) deposits around the spring source. Through time, this deposition forms long ridges with a fissure down the center where water may continue to flow. The longest ridge is 850 feet long and 15 feet high.

Many people visit Travertine ACEC to enjoy the springs as well as study the area's geology and natural history. Many come to experience the solitude and peaceful surroundings. For everyone's enjoyment of the area, please consider the following:

Did You Know?

The Travertine ACEC is a unique area of sensitive and unusual resources. The area's ridge-like features, hot springs, wetland complex, and wildlife form an interrelated web of natural systems that is rare and easily damaged.

This area has special meaning and value to the local community. Native Americans and others cherish the waters' healing and spiritual properties. *Respect* the area's heritage. Take only pictures during your visit. Cultural resources are protected by Federal and State law and carry penalties for disturbance.

Alkali-covered meadows in the area are important plant and animal habitat. Avoid walking through meadows. Please walk on firm, dry roads and trails.

Respect the Area and Its Users!!

Hot springs can change temperature without notice. Test the water carefully for comfort before entering pools.

Twin Lakes, Bridgeport

You share these pools with many other users. Be considerate, allow others the time and space to experience the pools. Avoid parking within 100 feet of the pools.

Keep your groups small, avoid loud noises, speak softly—experience the solitude.

Poor sanitation can seriously damage area water quality and people's enjoyment of the site. Do NOT wash yourself, utensils, or clothes in pools. Dispose of human waste in a hole far away from meadows, pools, and area ridges.

Carry out all your garbage and trash others have left behind. It shows you care. Remember toilet paper does not decompose easily when buried or left on the surface.

Looking for a Campground?

Select designated campgrounds with public facilities. The Travertine ACEC is not equipped to handle overnight camping. Bathrooms and drinking water are not available.

Check with the U.S. Forest Service office (Bridgeport Ranger Station) on U.S. Highway 395 for nearby campground locations.

Where Can I Take My Vehicle?

You are free to travel on any road not specifically signed *Closed*.

Don't even *think* of going off-road! Where one drives, others will follow. Meadows have been known to swallow vehicles. Towing out a stuck vehicle is expensive!

Resource Protection – It's Up to You!

This area's natural resources produce the quality of your experience. Removing travertine and plants as well as cutting tree limbs reduces the opportunity for others to enjoy the area. It is also prohibited. Do your part to protect your resources

Damage from vandalism or carelessness is expensive and costs you tax dollars. Help protect the area's resources for all to enjoy.

Donate time or financial contributions to support the public's use of Travertine Area of Critical Environmental Concern.

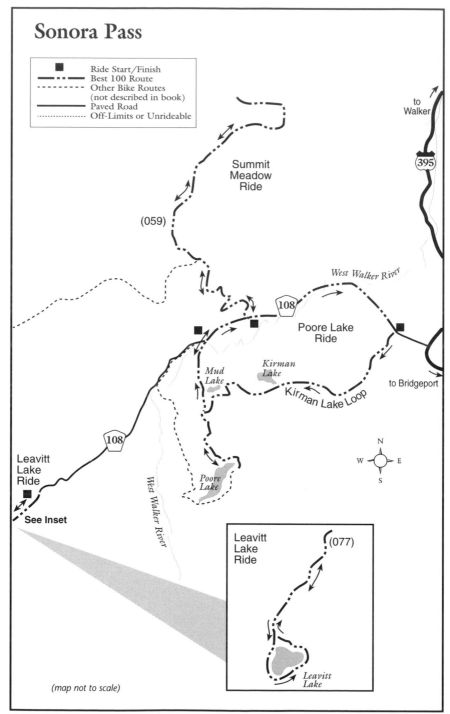

Sonora Pass

Ride Start/Finish
Best 100 Route
Other Bike Routes
(not described in book)
Paved Road
Off-Limits or Unrideable

to
Walker

395

Summit
Meadow
Ride

(059)

West Walker River

108

Poore Lake
Ride

Mud
Lake

Kirman
Lake

Kirman Lake Loop

to Bridgeport

108

N
W   E
S

Leavitt
Lake
Ride

West Walker River

Poore
Lake

See Inset

Leavitt
Lake
Ride

(077)

Leavitt
Lake

(map not to scale)

CHAPTER 17

Sonora Pass

Sonora Pass (Highway 108), which crosses the Sierra Nevada at an elevation of 9,624 feet, was one of the earliest toll roads to be constructed across the range. In response to the Bodie gold rush, it became the main supply route between western California and the Mono Basin. One section along the eastern slope was so precipitous that wagons had to be winched down.

Today, it is a narrow, treacherous road for large trucks or recreational vehicles, and it is always closed by snow in the winter. Most of the area on either side of Sonora Pass is Wilderness, but the highway provides a narrow corridor along which there are limited possibilities for mountain biking.

The eastern slope of the Sierra along Highway 108, which lies within the Toiyabe National Forest, is drained by the Walker and Little Walker Rivers. The only facilities are two USFS Campgrounds and a pack station. Pickel Meadows

Sonora Pass, one of the earliest roads across the Sierra

Mountain Warfare Training Center, a marine base, is off-limits to the public. The nearest stores and gas are located in Bridgeport or Walker.

Three of the rides in this chapter follow historic wagon roads. Sonora Pass is a challenging road ride to a spectacular alpine vista, but *we recommend avoiding it in the summer.*

Note: In 1997, heavy flooding washed out Highway 395 in Walker River Canyon, making access from the north difficult. Access from the south was not affected. Highway 395 will be repaired for through-traffic by mid-June 1997.

1 Kirman Lake Loop

Distance: 11.8 miles.
Difficulty: Moderate. River fording is difficult in spring.
Elevation: Starting point: 6,700'; high point: 7,300'.
Type: Loop ride on dirt road, jeep road, and secondary highway.
Season: Late spring, summer, and fall.
Facilities: Pit toilets and parking at Sonora Bridge Day Use Area. Amenities available in Bridgeport. Carry a minimum of 2 pints drinking water.
Features: This route follows part of the original Sonora Pass Toll Road. There are three inviting alpine lakes and vast meadows along the way.
Access: From Bridgeport, take Highway 395 north to the Sonora Junction (Highway 108). Turn left (west) onto 108 and go one mile. Park off the road by the corrals.

Start at the green gate by the corral, crossing private land. Use the wooden step-over and follow Road 137 toward a second gate and a second metal step-over. Go right, still on Road 137, up a long meadow, and cross Junction Creek.

At a junction, go right, along the base of the dam, across the meadow, and into an aspen-filled canyon. Climb steeply up the gully, pass through a gate *(please keep the gate closed)* and continue up the road. At 2.3 miles, the gully widens to a meadow. Cross to a low saddle; at the crest of this saddle, Kirman Lake is below.

Descend to Kirman Lake whose edges are lined with aspen and tall grasses. This riparian area supports an abundance of bird life; eagles that nest here hunt the high desert meadows.

Ascend through sage meadow to a low ridge and across a small creek. You now descend the drainage to a steep meadow-lined bowl and head toward a red rock outcropping.

At the bottom, at Mud Lake, there is the junction. This lake, which is gradually filling with sediment, has become a pond and will some day become a meadow.

Take the road left to the crest of the ridge and through a gate. The road leads down to a vast meadow. At the bottom, head to a low ridge, cross it, and head toward the long line of black cliffs. After two creek crossings, and at 5.8 miles, Road 137 ends at a T-junction, and you come to a jeep road that runs along the base of the black cliffs. Go right at this junction.

Follow the base of the cliffs along the western edge of Pickel Meadows; small irrigation ditches run along the road here. When you come to a green gate, go through it, being sure to close it.

You come to the Walker River at a wide shallow spot just above an island. *Be cautious:* Before you attempt to cross it, get off your bike and test the depths first—the river may be impassable in early spring.

After you cross the river, go up a small rise and left at a junction that leads to a big green gate with a walk-through. Go right on paved Highway 108 and head toward the Marine Base airstrip. Pass the Marine Base, climb a mild rise parallel to the river, and ride toward a canyon. A short downhill leads to the Sonora Bridge and the Sonora Bridge Day Use Area. There is a lovely picnic area on the far side.

Take the highway uphill past a campground, over a small crest, and drop to the corrals at your starting point.

2 Poore Lake Ride

Distance: 7.2 miles.
Difficulty: Moderate.
Elevation: Starting point: 6,700'; high point: 7,200'.
Type: Out-and-back on jeep roads.
Season: Summer and fall.
Facilities: None. Amenities available in Bridgeport. Carry adequate drinking water.
Features: Travel through vast meadows and see fantastic volcanic and glacial geology. Poore Lake is wonderful for swimming and scenery.
Access: From Bridgeport, take Highway 395 north to the Sonora Junction (Highway 108); turn left (west) and go 4.5 miles to a parking area by a green gate.

Use the step-over, and take Road 061 toward the Walker River. Soon, go right on a spur road down to the river and cross above an island. The river is wide and shallow here but it can be difficult in the early spring. *Be cautious:* Get off your bike and test the depths, first, before you to attempt to cross the river.

Across the river, pass through a green gate, being careful to close it. Continue along a long line of black cliffs toward the upper end of the meadow; small irrigation ditches run along this road.

At the head of the meadow, cross the creek, and follow the road up three switchbacks. Go through the gate at the crest and down to the creek. Cross the creek and climb into a trench-shaped meadow.

Here, the road becomes faint. Bear left, cross the creek again and ride through the meadow toward a lone, tall pine tree. At this point, the road becomes well-defined again and climbs through a juniper grove.

The road crosses the ridge and drops to another trench. Follow the creek, climb a third low ridge, then drop to a meadow. Ride past the base of Poore Lake dam and uphill to its far edge where there is a nice swimming beach.

To return, reverse your route, being careful to close all gates.

3 Leavitt Lake Ride

Distance: 7 miles.
Difficulty: Short, strenuous, and scenic.
Elevation: Starting point: 8,500'; high point: 9,500'.
Type: Out-and-back on jeep road. Singletrack around Leavitt Lake.
Facilities: None. Amenities in Bridgeport. Carry adequate drinking water.
Features: Ride to a beautiful, high-alpine lake with a lovely track around it, and a fast, steep downhill return.
Access: From Bridgeport, take Highway 395 north to Sonora Junction (Highway 108). Turn left (west) and go 11.5 miles to a parking area by an ore loading ramp at the junction of Highway 108 and Leavitt Lake Road (Road 077).

Start at the junction of Highway 108 and Leavitt Lake Road 077. The road runs up a canyon along a stream. There are occasional "pockets" of meadows in the forest, and steep rock walls rise above. Notice that one side of the canyon is granite, while the other side is red volcanic rock.

You enter dense forest and follow the edge of a meadow filled with trees stumps—evidence of extensive avalanches. In summer, this meadow is brilliant with wildflowers.

Cross a creek, climb a low divide, and cross a second, larger creek. Continue up the edge of a large square meadow where the road gets steeper and enters a forest of stunted white pine. Now you climb a long lateral moraine.

Continue the steep climb to the top of the moraine, riding along a stream. Enter a fantastic alpine meadow with volcanic peaks on three sides. Leavitt Lake is directly ahead, and

Leavitt Lake, in a beautiful high-Alpine bowl

there is a great view down the canyon.

Drop to the outlet of Leavitt Lake where a road leading to a mine crosses the creek. *This road is closed to all vehicles and bicycles beyond this point.*

Go to the right on a faint jeep track that narrows to a great singletrack around Leavitt Lake. This is mountain bike paradise, and you may want to do more than one lap around the lake.

After circling the lake, cross the outlet creek on logs, and climb the mild hill to the right. Cross the meadow on the shelf and begin the steep, fast downhill. Enjoy the great scenery on your return trip downhill, but *control your speed.*

[**Option:** For an easy, scenic ride, drive to Leavitt Lake and bicycle around the lake. It is a little over a mile and almost level. The views are spectacular.]

Summit Meadow, worth the "pain" to get there

4 Summit Meadow Ride

Distance: 18.2 miles.
Difficulty: Very strenuous; a steep and technical ride.
Elevation: Starting point: 6,700'; highest point: about 9,500'.
Type: Out-and-back on graded dirt road.
Season: Late spring, summer, and fall.
Facilities: None. Amenities available in Bridgeport. Carry at least 2 quarts water.
Features: This is a challenging ride that parallels the Emigrant Wagon Road to a remote alpine bowl surrounded by mountains; great views of the Upper Walker River and Sonora Pass area.
Access: From Bridgeport, take Highway 395 north to the Sonora Junction (Highway 108). Turn left (west), go 4.0 miles on Highway 108. Park by the corrals across the highway from the Marine Base. (The road between the base and the airstrip is Road 059, Silver Creek Road.)

Emigrant Wagon Road

red cliffs, enter a narrow gully and cross Silver Creek. *The route is extremely steep to the top of the gully.*

At the top of the gully is the Silver Creek junction. Take 059 to the right for a second steep climb up the long narrow meadow toward a saddle. This section is brutal—a 900-foot climb in 1.4 miles. The Emigrant Wagon Road runs parallel to 059. At the saddle, you can see into the bowl of Summit Meadow, surrounded on three sides by mountains.

Drop down from the saddle toward Summit Meadow. Lost Cannon Peak (11,099') is on the left. Pass a logging pad and cross the edge of a wet meadow—the wagon trail crosses here, too.

Head toward the open side of the basin—this is the top of the world from where you can see Walker Canyon to the east.

The road traverses the big meadow through forest of whitebark pine and aspen. After crossing a creek, the road follows a small ditch. Observe the "arborglyphs" (carvings) in the bark of the aspen.

(At the far eastern edge of the basin, a road to the right leads past a logging camp and to a singletrack that drops to Grouse Meadows. This is the route for the option described below.)

The main road (Road 059) curves back toward Lost Cannon Peak. This high basin holds the headwaters of Lost Cannon Creek, and—according

Head up Silver Creek Road (Road 059) between the airstrip and the Marine Base. Climb one very steep mile to a shelf where the grade eases and you have a great view into Pickel Meadows. You come to the historic Emigrant Wagon Trail, which crosses the road here, and which you'll see several times on the ride. Continue up Silver Creek Road.

At 1.7 miles is a junction with Road 023, on the right. Continue left on Road 059, up through sage and alpine meadows. The road climbs steadily toward a line of red cliffs, and the Sweetwater Mountains now come into view.

At a triangular junction (2.9 miles), bear right up Road 059 to the to local lore—the place where a cannon from the Fremont-Carson Expedition was buried.

Drop past two gates, climb slightly, then drop into the forest on the edge of a huge meadow. At a junction, bear left, cross the creek, and climb. Then drop to a camp at the end of the road by Lost Cannon Creek. Blazes on the trees, up and down the creek, mark the Emigrant Wagon Road. This area is designated as a Wilderness Study Area (WSA). *Bicycles are not allowed.*

Return on Road 059 the way you came in. It is 13 miles to the top of the high saddle. From there, you have a fast five-mile downhill to Pickel Meadows and your starting point.

[**Option:** At the open end of Summit Meadow, take a road to a logging camp and find Grouse Meadow Trail which leads off the shelf into the upper end of Mill Creek. Go left on the road at the bottom of the trail, climb out of the canyon onto a shelf, and bear right twice at two junctions. Pass through a gap and descend to wide, well-graded Road 023. Go right and follow a wide shelf overlooking Pickel Meadows and the Walker River. Continue until you reach Road 059 on which your ride started. Go left downhill to your start.]

Sheep-herding burro, Sonora Pass

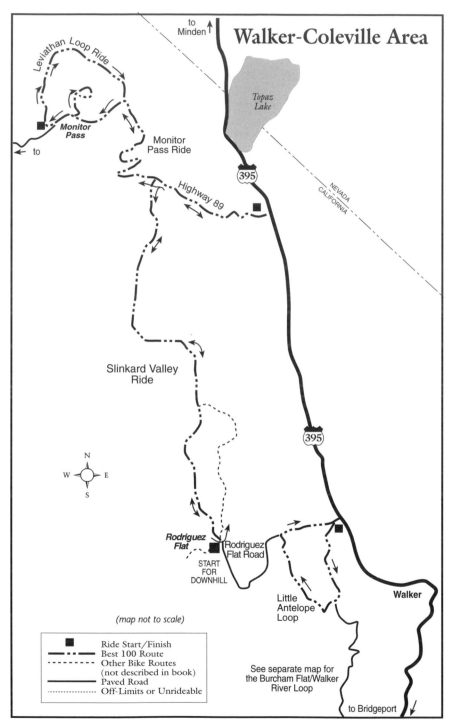

Walker-Coleville Area

to Minden

Leviathan Loop Ride

Monitor Pass

to

Monitor Pass Ride

Highway 89

Topaz Lake

395

NEVADA
CALIFORNIA

Slinkard Valley Ride

395

N
W · E
S

Rodriguez Flat

Rodriguez Flat Road

START FOR DOWNHILL

Little Antelope Loop

Walker

(map not to scale)

■	Ride Start/Finish
—·—·—	Best 100 Route
- - - -	Other Bike Routes (not described in book)
——	Paved Road
··········	Off-Limits or Unrideable

See separate map for the Burcham Flat/Walker River Loop

to Bridgeport

©1997 Fine Edge Productions

CHAPTER 18

Walker-Coleville Area

The Walker-Coleville area in northern Mono County lies in the Antelope Valley at the outlet of Walker River Canyon. Here the high desert meets the volcanic, post-glacial northern Sierra, encompassing both temperate and alpine zones. The mountains appear to be islands in an ocean of sage. Two large valleys in the area—Slinkard and Little Antelope—have been designated as Winter Deer Range by the Department of Fish and Game.

Although gold and silver were found on both sides of Antelope Valley, farming and ranching have been the predominant way of life for over 100 years. The massive cottonwoods still standing testify to the age of the area ranches.

The town of Walker, and the Walker River, were named by the Fremont-Carson Expedition in honor of Joseph Walker, leader of the first American expedition to California in the 1830s.

Little Walker River

The rides in this chapter reflect the history of the area, as well as the astounding contrasts of climate and plant life. Monitor Pass is an historical wagon road that leads to the mines on the Carson River. Leviathan Loop is a tour of alpine meadows. Slinkard Valley is a classic glacial valley and Winter Deer Range. Little Antelope Valley Loop offers abundant bird life and contrasting plant life. Burcham Flat Ride follows the probable route of the Fremont-Carson Expedition.

1 Burcham Flat/Walker River Loop

Distance: 31 miles.
Difficulty: Moderate, but long.
Elevation: Starting point: 5,400'; highest point 7,700'.
Type: Loop ride on dirt road and pavement.
Season: Spring, summer, and fall.
Facilities: None. Some amenities available in Walker. Carry a minimum of 2 quarts of water. Treat all water from local springs.
Features: For much of the ride, you closely follow the route of the Fremont-Carson Expedition. There are wonderful views from the high places, and the Walker River Canyon is rugged and beautiful.
Access: Begin at the south end of Walker at the junction of Highway 395 and East Side Lane. (Please see the note at the end of the chapter regarding a possible detour.) For information contact the Bridgeport Ranger Station (seasonal hours) at 760-932-7070.

Go north on East Side Lane, the upper end of Antelope Valley. Cross a bridge over the Walker River, and ride up a grade along the foothills of the Sweetwater Mountains.

At a junction, bear right toward the Indian Reservation Housing. Below this subdivision, go right on a dirt road along the power lines. Views of Antelope Valley and the Walker River Canyon open up. Pass a sign: *Deep Creek 6 mi.; Burcham Flat 11 mi.* Road 031 makes a long gradual uphill traverse above Walker Canyon, eventually veering away from the main canyon and dropping into a side canyon. At 3.4 miles, the road divides. Take the left uphill, out of the gully, and climb the ridge. There are views of Highway 395 below.

At 5.6 miles, the road crests, then drops to a creek and crosses it. Climb the ridge and drop into a second larger drainage. Cross Deep Creek and climb out of the canyon. At the crest you can see the Sierra Nevada.

At 9.3 miles, pass a jeep road on the left. You continue straight up the ridge and climb through sage toward a saddle where you have glimpses of the Sweetwater Mountains.

At 11.3 miles is the crest of the saddle—the top of the ride. Views of the Sonora Pass Area and the Upper Walker River Canyon and Little Walker Canyon are outstanding. Burcham Flat is a vast desert-alpine bowl below.

Start the long downhill on the wide dirt road (031), crossing Burcham Creek in a big meadow. A

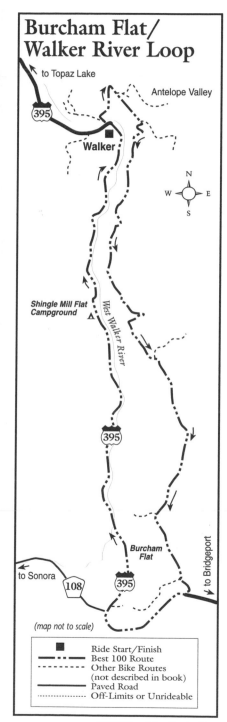

Burcham Flat/ Walker River Loop

to Topaz Lake

Antelope Valley

(395)

Walker

N
W · E
S

Shingle Mill Flat Campground

West Walker River

(395)

(395) **Burcham Flat**

to Sonora

(108) (395)

to Bridgeport

(map not to scale)

■	Ride Start/Finish
—·—	Best 100 Route
- - -	Other Bike Routes (not described in book)
——	Paved Road
······	Off-Limits or Unrideable

©1997 Fine Edge Productions

Tight turns in a beautiful canyon

Courtesy BLM

line of aspen follows the creek up the canyon. Climb a minor crest, then descend to Highway 395, cross under a power line at a sharp corner, and follow a creek to the paved highway. (Please refer to the note in the chapter introduction regarding Walker River Canyon.)

Go right on Highway 395 and follow the creek. In one mile, the creek is joined by the Little Walker River. Pass a big meadow at Sonora Junction and within a mile you pass the Cal-Trans Maintenance Station.

At 20 miles, cross the bridge and enter the Walker River Canyon. This deep rift cuts between the Sierra and Sweetwater ranges. It is a fishing paradise and a very scenic canyon.

Pass several campgrounds along the river. There are numerous places to rest and admire the view. The ride back is a long and gradual downhill.

Big walls of granite tower above and Jeffrey piness line the river.

At 27 miles, you can see the old wagon road on both sides of the canyon. The stonework of the narrow hand-built road is amazing. Near the bottom, the canyon opens up into Antelope Valley. Continue down the highway to the junction with East Side Road and your starting point.

2 Little Antelope Valley Loop

Distance: 7.3 miles.
Difficulty: Moderate, almost easy.
Elevation: Starting point: 5,200'; highest point 5,800'.
Type: Loop ride on graded dirt and jeep roads.
Season: Late spring, summer, and early fall. Because this is winter range for deer, people are discouraged from late October to late April.
Facilities: None along the route. Gas, water, food, and restrooms in Walker. Carry all drinking water.
Features: This is a tour of meadows and irrigation ditches, a dramatic contrast between high desert and grassland. Many species of birds can be seen.
Access: Drive 2 miles north of Walker on Highway 395, turn left (west) by the sign for Mill Creek Canyon Road. Park off the road.

Ride up Mill Creek Canyon Road through a narrow canyon that opens up at the junction of Roads 099 and 028. There is a kiosk and a register here for the California Department of Fish and Game. Please fill out a card. This ride passes through the Little Antelope Valley Deer Winter Range Reserve.

7Go left across the creek onto 028 and follow it uphill along the edge of a vast meadow. Pass by a ranch—the DFG headquarters for the Reserve. Go past two ponds, over a cattle guard, and past a small ditch.

At 2.4 miles, you come to a large corral. Go right on a jeep road along the ditch and through a double gate. Cross Lost Cannon Creek and head downhill. The road leads to a triangle of fences near a big dry ditch. Pass through a gate and go right downhill. About a half-mile down, pass through another gate and parallel the creek down the valley.

At 3.9 miles, by a square of cottonwoods and the ruins of an old ranch, continue straight along the ditch. Notice the stark contrast between the desert above the ditch and the meadow below. Willows and tall grasses line the ditch, and many species of birds live here. This area is set aside for deer, and it benefits the entire wildlife community.

At 4.9 miles, cross through a gate, leave the ditch, cross a small creek, and climb toward a knoll. On the knoll by the "Artists Cabin," take a right to Rodriguez Flat Road (099; Golden Gate Road on some maps) just above a big corral. Turn right and go downhill. Descend through vast meadows to the junction by the kiosk. Here you go straight down the short canyon to Highway 395 and your starting point.

3 Slinkard Valley Ride

Distance: 28.4 miles; 14 miles downhill with shuttle.
Difficulty: Moderate with steep sections.
Elevation: Starting point: 5,100'; highest point 8,500' with gain and/or loss along the route.
Type: Out-and-back on paved and dirt roads or one way downhill with shuttle.
Season: Late spring, summer, and early fall. Because this is winter range for deer, visitors are discouraged from late October to late April.
Facilities: None. Carry snacks and a minimum of 2 quarts of water.
Features: This ride takes you through a fantastic glacier-carved valley—a deer refuge that is off-limits to motorized vehicles.
Access/Shuttle: Out and back ride: starts at the junction of Highway 395 and Highway 89. For the shuttle, leave one vehicle at this junction. Drive south on Highway 395 to Mill Creek Canyon Road. Turn right (west), drive a quarter mile, and turn right again on Rodriguez Flat Road (Road 099). Follow this steep road for about 3 miles to a large green gate at a sharp left-hand corner of the road. There is a sign for Slinkard Valley Reserve. Park here.

Note: BLM public lands that flank the valley have been designated as an Area of Critical Environmental Concern (ACEC) to protect the area's wildlife and scenic values. The mountain range immediately west of the valley has been designated a Wilderness Study Area (WSA).

From the junction at 395 and 89, climb Highway 89 through the narrow canyon and into Slinkard Valley.

At 3.3 miles, turn left onto Road 203 which drops into the valley and crosses a small creek. A short climb brings you to a gate with a walk-through 20 feet uphill. A sign says: *California Department of Fish and Game Deer Winter Range.* Motorized vehicles are prohibited; bicycles are restricted to roads. Use is discouraged from late October through early March to allow the deer to bear their fawns undis-

Slinkard Valley looking south

Slinkard Valley from the North

turbed. This refuge has greatly bene-fited the bird life in the area. Please sign the register and stay on the roads.

You pass through a pedestrian gate. Continue south up the classic glacial valley. A barn next to a large irrigation pipe with running water is your next landmark. The road dips across a creek drainage by the elevated pipe, climbs steeply up the valley, and crosses the pipe, ascending several shelves and paralleling a power line. It is a sustained ascent with ever-improving views. Small water pipes irrigate this side of the valley.

At 7.4 miles, there is a road on the right to a green cabin with a corral. There is a level area with picnic tables, a fire pit, outhouse.

Past the cabin, still on Road 203, turn sharply left at a corner, go through a gate and downhill toward a large corral. Control speed on this sandy downhill. At the corral, pass through another gate and cross an irrigation ditch.

At 8.7 miles you cross Slinkard Creek. The road turns up the valley and parallels the creek and the power lines. Ascend the vast meadow up Slinkard Valley through two gates. A large irrigation pipe runs on the other side of the valley. Pass a trough by a large erratic boulder, go through a third gate, and cross the valley toward a second green cabin. Several pipe sections are scattered near a second corner as the road turns up the valley again.

At 11.7 miles there is a spur to the second cabin—the view from its porch is spectacular. The source of Slinkard Creek starts from this section of the valley.

The ride from here is steeper. You cross a small gate, pass through a big green gate, and enter a canopy of aspen. You pass through a second green gate, then cross a small stream. The road becomes extremely steep and there is evidence of logging.

Finally, the road crests by a third

big green gate. A sign marks the boundary of the DFG Reserve. (This is where you parked for the shuttle.) The gate is in a curve of the Rodriguez Flat Road. This is the turn-around point.

To complete this ride, return the way you came. It is a fast downhill ride; be careful to monitor your speed.

4 Monitor Pass Ride

Distance: 19.4 miles.
Difficulty: Difficult and non-technical.
Elevation: Starting point: 5,100'; Monitor Pass: 8,314'; Leviathan Peak: 8,960'.
Type: Out-and-back on paved and dirt road.
Season: Late spring, summer, and fall.
Facilities: None. Carry snacks, extra clothing, and at least 2 quarts of water.
Features: A challenging road ride through beautiful scenery. In Slinkard Valley, see the irrigation pipes that were installed for cattle in the 1950s. Today, the California Department of Fish and Game irrigate the valley to provide winter food for deer. Leviathan Peak is the visual climax to the ride; the fast, dangerous downhill its cycling climax.
Access: At the junction of Highways 395 and 89, park off the road near the fire station fence. *Note:* In 1998, the fire station may be moved from its present location. The first kiosk of the newly designated Highway 395 Scenic Byway will be placed there.

Start at the junction and go west on Highway 89 where the road immediately enters a steep canyon. Use extreme caution in this section—there are no shoulders along the road. Enjoy the contorted rock walls and the lush growth around Slinkard Creek; bird life is abundant in this area.

At 1.5 miles the canyon opens up by a corral into a wide valley. Continue up a steady grade toward the switchbacks, pass the Slinkard Valley Road on the left, and into pinyon pines.

At 4.4 miles you enter a forest of tall Jeffrey pines where the road crosses the creek twice in wide curves. There are shady resting places where you can picnic before the first of several switchbacks. At the first corner of the switchbacks, there is a pullout where you have outstanding views of Topaz Lake, the Sweetwater Mountains, and Antelope Valley.

Continue up the grade and around a knob. At 6.9 miles there is another pullout where you can look down into Slinkard Valley and up at Leviathan Peak. Continue up the highway through an alpine wonderland, leaving Mono County and crossing into Alpine County at 7.8 miles.

At the sign for Leviathan Peak Fire Tower, go right and follow the road up two switchbacks and over a gap to the loop at the top. The walkway around the outside of the tower is always open and the views are panoramic, stretching from Carson Valley to the Sweetwater Mountains. The immediate foreground is covered by meadows and aspen. Monitor Pass is also visible. In the 1860s, this was the route wagons took to carry food and hay from Antelope Valley to the

Carson River mines.

To return, reverse your route. *Be careful of your downhill speed and watch for cars.* Stop at the overlooks to cool brakes and rims, and be realistic about your skills.

[**Option:** The Leviathan Loop Ride can be added to extend this ride.]

Note: Each summer, the Markleeville Death Ride which covers five passes—16,000 feet of altitude gain-and-loss in 140 miles, crosses Monitor Pass twice, descending and ascending this road.

Fire tower, Leviathan Peak, from Monitor Pass

5 Leviathan Loop Ride

Distance: 7 miles.
Difficulty: Moderate; some short technical sections.
Elevation: Starting point: 8,100'; Leviathan Peak: 8,960'.
Type: Loop ride on jeep roads with a finish on paved road.
Season: Late spring, summer, and fall.
Facilities: Water and parking at Topaz Fire Control Station.
Features: This ride circumnavigates Leviathan Peak through a wonderland of meadows, flowers, and aspens. Wildflowers are abundant in May and June. Vistas are at the top of each climb.
Access: At the junction of Highway 395 and Highway 89, go west on Highway 89 for ten miles, just past Monitor Pass. There is parking for several cars by two small ponds.

Start in a big meadow by the two small ponds. Follow Road 083 to the right of the ponds, over a saddle and through alpine meadows and sage.

(Well-signed Road 083 leads you around Leviathan Peak.)

At a three-way junction, take the middle fork along a fence line over

Alpine meadow, Leviathan Peak

roller coaster dips. At the next junction, stay left along the fence. Leviathan Peak is on the right. Drop into a wide bowl toward the Sierra and cross a meadow lined with aspen.

Road 083 continues to curve toward the east around Leviathan Peak. The view of Leviathan Peak with the meadow and aspens in the foreground is impressive. The road follows the drainage down into a grove of aspen. At the bottom of the drainage, go right and up to the top of a ridge.

At 3.3 miles, you reach a saddle at the crest of the ridge where there are outstanding views. Eagles soar over the meadows, and numerous wildflowers brighten the scene in early summer.

The descent ahead is the steepest and most technical part of the ride. We recommend walking this section. Drop into aspen, ignore the road to the left, then climb up the drainage into a meadow by a spring and a pond. Ignore a second left as well. The meadow is a lake of flowers in the early summer.

The road joins Highway 89 at 4.8 miles. Go right on Highway 89 toward Leviathan Peak. Aspen groves accent the rolling terrain. Continue west to the grove of aspen at the summit of Monitor Pass (indicated by an historical marker). It is a short descent to your starting point at the twin ponds.

Note: In January 1997, melting snow, combined with rain, caused Walker River to jump its man-made course washing out much of Highway 395 in Walker River Canyon. There was heavy flooding in the towns of Walker and Coleville, and many people lost their homes and farms. Highway 395 is scheduled to reopen in June 1997. (As an alternate route the Walker area can be accessed by connecting with Highway 395 north of Topaz Lake. From the Bridgeport area, Highway 182 east connects with Nevada 338, north to Nevada 208, and then west to Highway 395, just north of Topaz Lake. From this point, you can head south on Highway 395 to Walker.)

APPENDIX

References

Chalfant, W. A. *The Story of Inyo*, revised edition, Bishop: Chalfant Press Inc., 1933.

Dodd, K. *Guide to Obtaining USGS Information*, U.S. Geological Survey Circular 900, 1986.

Embrey, Sue Kunitomi, Editor. *The Lost Years 1942–1946*, Los Angeles: The Manzanar Committee, 1972.

Hall, Clarence A., Jr., Editor. *Natural History of the White-Inyo Range*, Berkeley and Los Angeles: University of California Press, 1991.

Irwin, Sue. *California's Eastern Sierra, A Visitor's Guide*. Los Olivos: Cachuma Press, 1991.

Little, Elbert L. *Audubon Society Field Guide of North American Trees*. New York: Alfred A. Knopf, 1980.

MacMahon, James A. *Deserts*. New York: Alfred A. Knopf, 1985.

Peterson, P. Victor, and Peterson, P. Victor, Jr. *Native Trees of the Sierra Nevada*. Berkeley and Los Angeles: University of California Press, 1975.

Putman, Jeff, and Smith, Genny, Editors. *Deepest Valley, Guide to Owens Valley*. Mammoth Lakes: Genny Smith Books, 1995.

Russell, Israel C. *Quaternary History of the Mono Valley, California*. Reprinted from the 1889 U.S. Geologic Survey. Lee Vining: Artemisia, 1984.

Shelton, John S. *Geology Illustrated*. San Francisco: W. H. Freeman and Company, 1966.

Smith, Genny, Editor. *Mammoth Lakes Sierra*. Mammoth Lakes: Genny Smith Books, Sixth Edition, 1993.

Stegner, Wallace and Stegner, Page, *American Places*, "There It Is: Take It." New York: Greenwich House, 1983. (a good reference for understanding the history of water problems in the Eastern Sierra)

Stellenberg, Richard, *Audubon Society Field Guide of American Wildflowers— Western*. New York: Alfred A. Knopf, 1979.

Eastern Sierra Agencies & Resources

Bishop Chamber of Commerce
& Visitors Center
City Park
690 N. Main
Bishop, Ca 93514
Tel: 760-873-8405

Bodie State Historical Park
P.O. Box 515
Bridgeport, Ca 93517
Tel: 760-647-6445

Bridgeport Ranger District
Toiyabe National Forest
P.O. Box 595
Bridgeport, CA 93517
Tel: 760-932-7070

Bureau of Land Management*
(BLM), Bishop Resource Area
785 N. Main St., Suite E
Tel: 760-872-4881
Fax: 760-872-2894

BLM Lone Pine-Ridgecrest
Resource Area
Tel: 760-384-5400

California State Park
Touch-tone Information
Tel: 916-653-6995

Cerro Gordo
contact: Jodi Stewart to arrange
overnight accommodations (advance
reservations needed)
Tel: 760-876-4154

Eastern Sierra Museum
155 N. Grant
Independence, CA 93526
Tel: 760-878-0364

Interagency Visitor Center
Highways 395 and 136
Lone Pine, CA 93545
Tel: 760-876-6222

Inyo County Parks Information
224 N. Edwards
Independence, CA 93526
Tel: 760-878-0272

Laws Railroad Museum
& Historical Site
Laws
Bishop, CA 93514
Tel: 760-873-5950

Lee Vining Chamber of Commerce
Lee Vining, CA 93541
Tel: 760-647-6629

Lee Vining Ranger Station
Visitor Information
Tel: 760-647-3044

Lone Pine Chamber of Commerce
126 S. Main
Lone Pine, CA 93545
Tel: 760-876-4444

Mammoth Adventure Connection
P.O. Box 353
Mammoth Lakes, CA 93546
Tel: 760-934-0606;
800-228-4947, ext. 3606

Mammoth Lakes Visitors Bureau
P.O. Box 48
Mammoth Lakes, CA 93546
Tel: 760-934-2712

Mammoth Ranger Station
& Visitor Center
Highway 203
Mammoth Lakes, CA 93546
Tel: 760-924-5500

Mono Basin Scenic Area
Visitor Center (USFS)
Highway 395
Lee Vining, CA 93541
Tel: 760-647-3044

Mono County Information
Tel: 760-932-5300

Mono Lake Committee
P.O. Box 29, Highway 395
Lee Vining, CA 93541
Tel: 760-647-6595

Mono Lake Tufa Reserve
(California State)
Tel: 760-647-6331

Mt. Whitney Ranger Station
P.O. Box 8
631 S. Main St.
Lone Pine, CA 93545
Tel: 760-876-6200

USFS, Inyo National Forest
873 N. Main St.
Bishop, CA 93514
Tel: 760-873-2400

White Mountain Ranger Station
& Visitor Center
798 N. Main St.
Bishop, CA 93514
Tel: 760-873-2500

*The Bureau of Land Management (BLM) office in Bishop, California, conducts a unique environmental education program in the Eastern Sierra for interested individuals and groups. The program originated about five years ago when the BLM received donated mountain bikes from Dr. Al Farrell, a noted mountain bike philanthropist. Dr. Farrell's support motivated bike industry representatives such as Specialized GT Bicycles, Bike Nashbar, Rock Shox, Yakima Products, and Fine Edge Productions to support the program. Since then, the BLM has coordinated dozens of educational bike trips for organizations, academic institutions, and interested parties. With this approach, the BLM has successfully used mountain bikes as a way to connect others to our environment. For further information on this program, contact the BLM at 760-872-4881.

Basic Skills for Mountain Biking

by R. W. Miskimins

Everybody knows how to ride a bike—at least almost everybody can ride around the neighborhood. But with the advent of the mountain bike, riding a two-wheel pedal-powered machine has gotten more complicated. Watch a pro-level mountain bike race and the need for "technical skills" will become obvious. Can you handle steep hills, big rocks, creeks, muddy bogs, loose sand, big tree roots, deep gravel, or radical washboards? These are the kinds of factors that differentiate mountain biking from road riding and that demand skills and balance above and beyond those required to ride around the neighborhood. The key to acquiring these abilities is practice—start easy and work diligently until you achieve high-level control of your bike.

1. BICYCLE

All mountain bikes are not created equal. Some are better suited to staying on pavement. They have too much weight, too long a wheelbase, ineffective braking systems, sloppy shifting, too smooth tread on the tires, poorly welded frames, and so on. As a general rule, the mountain bicycles marketed by the discount store chains, department stores, and sporting goods stores are only suited to on-road, non-abusive use. Bicycles from bike stores, excepting their least expensive models, are generally suited to heavy duty, skilled off-road use. They should be relatively light (under 30 pounds), and have a fairly short wheelbase and chainstay (for agility), moderately steep head angle (again for agility), strong and dependable braking and shifting systems, well-made frames, and knobby/aggressive tires.

For details on choosing the right bike for you, consult the experts at your local bike shop. They can help you not only with selecting a bicycle, but also with various accessory decisions, in such areas as suspension forks, bar ends, and gear ratio changes. And of extreme importance, whatever bike you decide on, get the right size for you. If a bike is too big for your height and weight, no matter how hard you try, you will never be able to properly handle it. If you are in doubt or in between sizes, for serious off-road riding opt for the smaller bike.

2. FUNDAMENTAL PRINCIPLES

There are some very general rules for off-road riding that apply all the time. The first, "ride in control," is fundamental to everything else. Balance is the key to keeping a bike upright—when you get out of control you will lose your ability to balance the bike (that is, you'll crash). Control is directly related to speed, and excessive speed for the conditions you are facing is the precursor to loss of control. When in doubt, slow down!

The second principle for off-road riding is "read the trail ahead." In order to have time to react to changes in the trail surface and to obstacles, you should be looking ahead 10 to 15 feet. Especially as your speed increases, you want to avoid being surprised by hazardous trail features (rocks, logs, roots, ruts, and so

on)—if you see them well ahead, you can pick a line to miss them, slow down to negotiate them, or even stop to walk over or around them.

The third principle is to "stay easy on the grips." One of the most common reactions by novices in tough terrain is to severely tense up, most noticeably in a "death grip" on the handlebars. This level of tightness not only leads to hand, arm and shoulder discomfort but interferes with fluid, supple handling of the bike. Grip loosely and bend at the elbows a bit—don't fight the bicycle, work with it!

The last general principle to be presented here is "plan your shifting." If you are looking ahead on the trail, there should be no shifting surprises. Anticipate hills, especially steep ascents, and shift before your drive-train comes under a strong load. Mountain bikes have a lot of gears and their proper use will make any excursion more enjoyable.

3. CLIMBING

Mountain bikes were originally single-speed, balloon-tire cruisers taken by truck or car to the top of a hill and then used for exciting and rapid descent. After a few years, they were given gears to eliminate the shuttle. Today's off-road bikes have 18 to 24 speeds, with a few extremely low gears so they can climb very steep hills. One of the keys to long or difficult climbs is attitude; it's a mental thing. You need to be able to accept an extended, aerobic challenge with the thoughts "I can do it" and, above all, "This is fun."

Your bike is made with hill-climbing in mind. Find a gear and a pace that is tolerable (not anaerobic) and try to maintain it. Pick a line ahead, stay relaxed, and anticipate shifting, as noted earlier. In addition, be alert to problems in weight distribution that occur when climbing. It is best to stay seated, keeping your weight solidly over the traction (rear) wheel if possible. However, if the slope is so steep that the front wheel lifts off of the ground, you will have to lean forward and slide toward the front of the saddle. Constant attention to weight distribution will give you optimum traction and balance for a climb. And make sure your saddle height is positioned so when your foot is at the bottom of a pedal stroke, your knee is very slightly bent—a saddle too low or too high will significantly reduce both power and control on a steep and difficult climb.

4. DESCENDING

This is where most serious accidents occur, primarily because a downhill lends itself to high speed. It is unquestionably the most exciting part of mountain bike riding—expert riders reach speeds over 60 mph! For descents, the "stay in control" and "read the trail ahead" principles can be injury-saving. Know your ability and don't exceed it. And be certain your brakes are in good working order—don't believe the slogan "brakes are for sissies." On steep and difficult downhills everyone has to use them. Regarding braking, always apply the rear brake before the front (to avoid an "endo"—that is, flying over the handlebars), and if possible, brake in spurts rather than "dragging" them. On easy hills, practice using your brakes to get comfortable with them.

As was the case for steep uphills, steep descents require attention to weight distribution. Many riders lower their saddle an inch or two prior to descending (to get a lower center of gravity). All cyclists quickly learn to lift their weight slightly off the saddle and shift it back a few inches to keep traction and to avoid the feeling of being on the verge of catapulting over the handlebars. Practice this weight transfer on smooth but steep downhills so you can do it comfortably later on obstacle-laden terrain. Finally, it is possible to go too slow on a difficult downhill, so slow you can't "blast" over obstacles. Instead, because of lack of momentum, hazards can bring you to an abrupt stop or twist your front wheel, and both of these results can cause loss of control.

5. TURNING

A particularly treacherous time for mountain bikers is high speed or obstacle-laden turns. The first principle is: don't enter a curve too fast. Turns often contain loose dirt and debris created by all the mountain bikes that preceded you. Slow down before you get there; you can always accelerate during the turn if you choose. Lean around the turn as smoothly as possible, always keeping an eye out for obstacles. It is common for the rear wheel to skid in turns. To take the fright out of that phenomenon, go find a gentle turn with soft dirt and practice skidding to learn how you and your bike will respond.

6. OBSTACLES

If you get into the real spirit of off-road cycling, you will not ride just on smooth, groomed trails. You will encounter rocks, roots, limbs, logs, trenches, ruts, washboards, loose sand (or dirt or gravel), and water in a variety of forms from snow and ice to mud bogs to free-flowing springs and creeks. Obviously, the easiest means for handling an obstacle is to go around it; however, you can't always do that. For raised obstacles, those you need to get up and over, riders need to learn to "pop the front wheel." To practice this, find a low curb or set out a 4x4 piece of lumber. Approach it, and just before the front wheel impacts it, rapidly push down then pull up the front wheel. The wheel lift is enhanced if you simultaneously lower and raise your torso and apply a hard pedal stroke. After your front wheel clears the obstacle, shift your weight up and forward a little so the rear wheel can bounce over it lightly.

If you encounter "washboards," the key to relatively painless negotiating is to maintain a moderate speed and get into a shock absorbing posture—slightly up and off the saddle, knees slightly bent, elbows slightly bent, loose grip on the handlebars, and relaxed. Soft spots in the trail can make your bike difficult to control and create an instant slowdown. If you have to deal with loose, deep sand, dirt or gravel, the key is to go slower but "power through." Shift your weight back a little (for better traction), then keep your bike straight and keep pedaling. Maintaining momentum and a straight line is also important in mud holes; be certain to do any shifting prior to soft spots or muddy bogs (otherwise you will lose momentum). Sharp turns can present a particular problem in these conditions—you will be much more prone to losing the rear wheel to a slide out, so be extra cautious in sandy or muddy curves.

Going through water can be a lot of fun, or it can be a rude awakening if you find yourself upsidedown on a cold February afternoon. Before any attempt to cross a waterway, stop and examine it first. Make sure it isn't so deep that it will abruptly stop you, then find the route that has the fewest obstacles (look for deep holes, big rocks, and deep sand). Approach the crossing at a fairly low speed and plan on pedaling through it (rather than coasting) for maximum traction and control. Be aware of the potential for harmful effects that riding through water can have on your bearings (if they are not sealed) and exposed moving parts. Plan on lubricating your chain, derailleurs, inner wires, and so on, when you return home. Finally, regarding snow and ice, stay away from it as much as possible. Snow riding can be fun but if it's deep, it can be very laborious. Maintaining momentum and avoiding buried obstacles are the two major tasks for snow riders. Also, the difficulty of steep ascents and descents are significantly magnified by a few inches of snow. Most mountain bikers riding on snow prefer flat or nearly flat terrain.

The Care & Feeding of a Mountain Bike

by R. W. Miskimins

ROUTINE CHECKUPS FOR YOUR BICYCLE

The key to years of fun and fitness from your mountain bike is giving it check-ups on a regular basis. You need to know how to clean it, lubricate a few places, make simple adjustments, and recognize when something needs expert attention. For the average rider, most bike shops recommend tuneups once a year and complete overhauls every two to three years. All of the maintenance in between your trips to the bike shop you can do yourself. Given below is a nine-step checkup procedure—a list to run through after every extensive ride—before you head back out into the hills again.

1. CLEANUP

Unless the frame is really filthy, use a soft rag and a non-corrosive wax/polish such as Pledge to wipe off the grime and bring the old shine back. If you need to use water or soap and water prior to the polish, don't high-pressure spray directly at any of the bearing areas (pedals, hubs, bottom bracket or head set). You should clean all your components, too (including the chain and the rear cogs), but use a different rag and a lubricant such as Tri-Flow or Finish Line for wiping them down. Do not use polish or lubricants to clean your rims—an oily film will reduce your braking ability. Instead, wipe off the rims with a clean dry rag. If you need to remove rubber deposits from the sidewalls of the rims use acetone as a solvent.

2. INSPECTION

After you get the grit and grime off, check out the frame very carefully, looking for bulges or cracks. If there are chips or scratches that expose bare metal (especially when the metal is steel), use automotive or bicycle touch-up paint to cover them up. Your inspection should also include the components. Look for broken, bent or otherwise visibly damaged parts. Pay special attention to the wheels. When you spin them, watch the rim where it passes the brake pads. Look for wobbles and hops, and if there is a lot of movement, the wheel needs to be trued at home (or take it to a bike shop) before using it. Look for loose or broken spokes. And finally, carefully check your tires for sidewall damage, heavy tread wear, cuts and bulges, glass and nails, thorns, or whatever.

3. BRAKES

Grab the brakes and make sure they don't feel mushy and that the pads are contacting the rim firmly (be certain the brake pads do not rub against the tires!). If the brakes don't feel firm, there are barrel adjusters at one or both ends of the wire cables that control the brakes—turn them counterclockwise to take up some of the slack. If you are unsure as to the dependability of your brakes, for safety's sake let a bike shop check them.

4. BEARING AREAS

Most cyclists depend upon professional mechanics to fix any problems in the pedals, hubs, bottom bracket or head set, but they should be able to recognize when something is wrong. Spin the wheels, spin the crankarms (and the pedals) and move the handlebars from side to side. If you feel notches or grittiness, or if you hear snapping, grating or clicking noises, you have a problem. Check to make sure each of the four areas is properly tightened. To check for looseness, try to wiggle a crankarm side to side or try to move a wheel side to side. Check your headset adjustment by holding the front brake, rocking the bike forward and backward, and listening for clunking sounds.

5. SHIFTING

Presuming your bike has gears, check to make sure you can use all of them. The most common problem is the stretching of the inner wire that operates the rear derailleur. If your bike is not shifting properly, try turning the barrel adjuster, located where the cable comes out of the derailleur. Turn it just a little; usually a counterclockwise direction is what you need. Unless you know what you are doing, avoid turning the little adjustment screws on the derailleurs.

6. NUTS AND BOLTS

Make sure the nuts and bolts which hold everything together are tight. The handlebars and stem should not move around under pressure, and neither should your saddle. And make certain that the axle nuts or quick-releases that hold your wheels are fully secure—when a wheel falls off, the result is almost always crash-time. If you have quick-release hubs, they operate as follows: Mostly tighten them by holding the nut and winding the lever, but finish the job by swinging the lever over like a clamp (it's spring-loaded). Do not wind them up super tight as you would with a wingnut—for safe operation they must be clamped, and clamped very securely, with considerable spring tension! If you are at all uncertain regarding the use of quick-releases, go by a bike shop and ask for a demonstration.

7. ACCESSORIES

Make sure all your accessories, from water bottles to bags to pumps to lights, are operational and secure. Systematically check them all out and if you carry flat-fixing or other on-the-road repair materials or tools, make sure you've got what you need and you know how to use what you carry. Statistics show that over 90% of all bicycle breakdowns are the result of flat tires, so it is recommended that you carry a pump, a spare tube, a patch kit, and a couple of tire levers with you whenever you ride.

8. LUBRICATION

The key to long-term mechanical happiness for you and your bike is proper and frequent lubrication. The most important area of lubrication is the chain—spray it with a Teflon-based or other synthetic oil (WD-40, household oil, and motor oil are not recommended), then wipe off all the excess. You can use the same lubricant for very sparsely coating the moving parts of your brakes and derailleurs.

9. INFLATION

You now are ready for the last step. Improper inflation can lead to blowouts or pinch flats. Read the side of your tires to see what the recommended pressure is and fill them up. If there is a range of pressures given, use the high figure for street cycling, the low figure or near it for off-road riding.

After going through these nine steps of getting your bike ready you've earned another good long ride!

Roadside Repairs
by R. W. Miskimins

Cyclists who take a little time to prepare for equipment failure before riding will get the most enjoyment out of their bicycle. Although there are dozens of things that can go wrong on a ride, especially if you crash, most of them happen so rarely that it doesn't make a lot of sense to worry about them. The chance that you will need to replace a bent axle or replace a wheel with a dozen broken spokes or tighten the lock ring on your cassette (rear sprockets) or replace a defective shift lever is always there, but thankfully these are not the common trailside problems. For these kinds of difficulties, most cyclists ride, carry or coast the bike back to their car, any way they can, and head for a bike shop.

It has been written that more than 95% of all trailside or roadside repairs involve either fixing flats or simply tightening something that has rattled loose. With this in mind, consider the following as insurance against long walks home.

PRE-RIDE PROTECTION

Bicycles arrive from the factory with regular tubes and no added protection to cut down on the possibility of flats. There are three different approaches to minimizing the possibility of air loss while riding your bicycle. The most popular over the years has been "thorn resistant" tubes (they used to be called "thorn proof"). They do help, but are not very effective against much of what might create problems for you. Two more effective products are tire liners (plastic or Kevlar and plastic strips that go inside the tire, between the tire and the tube) and sealants (goo that goes inside the tube and seals the holes that thorns, staples, and so on make). Some cyclists employ two and sometimes three of these measures to minimize flat tires. Bear in mind that each of them adds a significant amount of weight to your bike, so it is best to select one and hope for the best. Short of using solid, airless tubes (which is not recommended), nothing is foolproof. Always be prepared to fix flats.

BICYCLE BAGS

Whatever you choose to carry in the form of tools and spare parts will require a comfortable means to haul them. Although you could carry what you need in a fanny pack or backpack or even in your pockets, the most popular kinds of bike bags are those that fit under the rear of your saddle (underseat bags). They do not interfere with mounting or dismounting or handling and they carry a remarkable amount of gear. The best ones have some form of plastic clips, rather than just straps, to attach them to the bike. The extremely small ones are best suited to racing since they carry very little. The extremely big ones are best suit-ed to slow, nonaggressive riding; they tend to bounce around on rough terrain and, when full, add too much weight. Other forms of bags include the frame pack, which doubles as a shoulder strap when carrying your bike; handlebar bags, which are suitable when off-road handling is not an issue; and bags that attach to racks (either on top or hanging down alongside the wheel), which are most often used for long-distance touring.

REPAIR KIT

Once you have chosen a bag for your bike, consider the following as essentials to put in it: a spare tube (whenever possible, put patches on punctured tubes at home rather than in the outback), a patch kit to cover you if you get more than one flat on an outing, tire levers (plastic tools for getting the tire off and back on the wheel), and a set of Allen wrenches—especially 4mm, 5mm and 6mm—to tighten up loose stem, saddle, handlebar, shifters, and so on. Be certain, before you go riding, that you know how to take your wheels on and off and how to replace a bad tube. A lot of people carry the right repair materials but don't know how to use them.

These suggestions will take care of a remarkable number of trail/road repairs. At many shops this is all that is recommended for the typical cyclist to carry. There are a few other tools, however, that some cyclists—especially mountain bikers who ride far from civilization—like to carry. Again, if you bring these tools along, be sure they will work for your specific bike and that you know how to use them.

Consider the following possibilities: crescent wrench (needed if both your wheels are not quick release), chain tool to repair damage to the chain by taking out a link or two, spoke wrench for straightening slightly bent wheels, crank wrench for tightening loose crankarms, small screwdriver for derailleur adjustments, cone wrench for tightening loose hubs, or socket wrenches (8mm, 9mm, or 10mm) to use for brake adjustments and the like. In addition, some long-distance cyclists carry spare parts such as cables, brake pads, and a rag to wipe their hands.

BICYCLE PUMPS

Since flat tires are the primary problem for cyclists, a pump becomes important. It doesn't do any good to replace a punctured tube with a new one if you cannot inflate it. There are basically three kinds of bicycle pumps.

Floor pumps are generally too awkward to carry on a ride; but since they pump high volumes of air and fill tires rapidly, they are perfect for home and shop use.

For many years, most cyclists have carried frame-fit pumps on their bikes for emergency use. With the proper size they can be squeeze-fit on to a bicycle frame with no additional hardware needed. If you use a frame-fit pump on a mountain bike and you like to ride rough terrain, however, consider a secondary velcro tie or something similar to ensure that the pump doesn't fly off the bike as you negotiate bumps. Also, consider placing the frame-fit pump behind your seat tube rather than in the usual position below the top tube, so it is not in the way if you need to carry your bike.

Mini-pumps, the third type, have become most popular for mountain bikers over the past few years. They are very small and can fit into out-of-the-way places on your bike, such as alongside a water bottle cage. This requires special hardware, but it is a very tidy application. The down side to these pumps is that they move very small volumes of air at a time. Many of them now are "double shot," meaning they move air when both pushed and pulled. Since pumps are for emergencies, inflating a tube beats hours of walking, no matter what size your pump.

Finally, be aware that there are two different kinds of valve stems on bicycles now. The "regular" ones, like those on cars, are called Schrader valves. The skinny metal ones are Presta valves or French valves, and they require that you first unscrew the little gadget on the top before applying a pump. All the standard pumps now can be altered to work for either type of valve. Also available at a very nominal cost are adaptors that allow you to use Presta valves at a regular gas station pump connection.

Below is a checklist for the most basic, inexpensive roadside repairs:

☐ tire liners	☐ patch kit	☐ mini pump
☐ underseat bag	☐ tire levers	☐ Allen wrenches
☐ spare tube	☐ Presta adaptor *(if needed for your bike)*	

Route Index

Andrews Mountain Loop, 55
Artesian Wells Loop, 84
Aurora Canyon/Geiger Grade
    Ride, 182

Baker Creek Loop, 52
Bald Mountain Lookout Ride, 154
Banner Ridge Loop, 93
Bennettville Ride, 175
Big Smokey Loop, 151
Black Mountain Ride, 60
Black Point Ride, 179
Blind Spring Valley Ride, 97
Bodie Peak Loop, 183
Buckeye Hot Springs Ride, 195
Burcham Flat/Walker River
    Loop, 208
Buttermilk Country Loop, 77

"Cabo San Crowley" Ride, 116
Cactus Flat Ride, 21
Cerro Gordo/Swansea Loop, 27
Copper Mountain Loop, 188
Cottonwood and Bridgeport
    Canyons Loop, 185
Coyote High Sierra Traverse, 74
Crater Mountain Loop, 49
Crowley Lake Loop, 111

Darwin Loop, 22

Geiger Canal Loop, 83
Geothermal Loop, 146
Geothermal Staging Area, 145
Glass Flow Ridge Loop, 163

Glass Mountain Ridge Ride, 159
Grandview Mine Ride, 61
Great Wall of Owens Gorge Ride,
    The, 110
Haiwee Reservoir Ride, 20
Hard Core Ride, 130
Hartley Springs Loop, 165
Hogback Loop, 34
Horseshoe Lake Loop, 143
Horton "Roubaix" Ride, 81
Hot Creek Ride, 147

Independence Historical Tour, 40
Inyo Craters Loop, 132

June Lake Loop, 167

Keough's Hot Ditch Loop, 58
Kirman Lake Loop, 200
Knolls Blue Diamond Loop, 123
Knolls Loops, 121
Knolls Triangle Loop, 124

Lake Mary Loop, 142
Lakes Basin Staging Area, 139
Laurel Canyon Ride, 136
Leavitt Lake Ride, 202
Lee Vining Loop, 177
Leviathan Loop Ride, 214
Little Antelope Valley Loop, 210
Little Smokey Loop, 149
Log Cabin Mine Loop, 176
Lone Pine Station Ride, 35
Lookout Mountain Loop, 151
Lower Rock Creek Trail Ride, 101

Mammoth Creek Park Staging
    Area, 133
Mammoth Creek Trail Loop, 135
Mammoth Mountain Bike
    Park, 144
Masonic Mountain Ride, 193
Mazourka Canyon Ride, 43
McGee Canyon Ride, 114
McMurry Meadows Loop, 50
Minaret Vista Ride , 128
Monitor Pass Ride, 213
Moraines and Meadows Loop, 172
Mount Tom Loop, 90
Mountain View Ride , 127
Movie Road Loop, 32

North Village Staging Area, 126

Old Mammoth Road Ride, 138
Owens Gorge/Rock Creek
    Loop, 104

Panorama Dome Loops, 140
Panorama Trail Loop, 169
Patriarch Grove Ride, 64
Pleasant Valley Loop, 87
Poore Lake Ride, 201

Red Rock Canyon Ride, 95
Reward Loop, 39
Rock Creek Loop , 102

Sagehen Summit Loop, 156
Sand Canyon Loop, 107
Sawmill Meadow Ride, 157

Sawmill Road/Mammoth Creek
    Loop, 125
Scenic Loop Road Ride, 131
Shady Rest Forest Loop, 120
Shady Rest Park Loop, 120
Shady Rest Staging Area, 119
Sherwin Creek Loop, 135
Silver Canyon Ride, 62
Sinnamon Meadow Loop, 189
Sky Meadow Loop, 105
Slinkard Valley Ride, 211
Smokey Bear Flat Staging Area, 149
South Alabama Hills Loop, 32
Summit Meadow Ride , 203

Taboose Creek Loop, 44
Tinemaha Loop, 46
Tioga Pass Road Ride, 174
Tobacco Flat Ride, 115
Tour De Joshua Loop, 25
Town Bike Path, 119
Town Bike Trail Loop, 134
Travertine Geologic Ride, 190
Tungsten Hills Loop, 79
Twin Lakes Loop, 193

Uptown/Downtown Singletrack
    Loop, 126

Volcanic Tableland Ride, 89

Westgard Pass Road Ride, 54
White Mountain Ride, 67
Wildrose Canyon Loop, 160
Wyman Canyon Ride, 69

Acknowledgments

The authors wish to thank the many people who shared their knowledge or gave their help, in the past as well as the present, with routes and rides: Shirley Braxton of Missoula and the late Sam Braxton who rode the Bodie routes with us; Tim Ford for checking out some foul routes; Pete Lewis for his help in describing Horton Roubaix and Coyote High Sierra Traverse routes; Jim King for his input regarding Upper Rock Creek; and Mickey McTigue and Richard Mason for their help in exploring some really remote areas.

We would like to thank, in particular, the staff of the Bureau of Land Management, Bishop Resource Area and the Inyo National Forest who took the time to read the manuscript and to add their invaluable suggestions and corrections.

Special thanks to Joe Pollini for his help beyond the call of duty in reading our manuscript and offering cogent suggestions.

Thanks, too, to the many cyclists and agency employees who volunteered a favorite trail or rounded up much-needed photographs.

And last, but never least, we owe our deepest thanks to our production crew, without whose long hours we would never have been able to bring this project to a conclusion: Melanie Haage, Sue Irwin, Cindy Kamler and Pat Eckart.

About the Authors

Réanne Hemingway-Douglass, the principal author of this book, has lived at the head of the Owens Valley since 1980. As an owner of Fine Edge Productions, she has written or edited more than 20 mountain bike trail guides. In the 1980s she led the first women's bicycling team across Tierra del Fuego and her articles have appeared in numerous outdoor magazines. Along with her husband Don, Réanne was active in forming the International Mountain Bicycling Association (IMBA) and in putting on the first-ever Kamikaze race on Mammoth Mountain in 1985. The Douglass's *Mountain Biking Inyo and Mono Counties* (Guides #1 and #2) have been consolidated and updated with the help of Mark Davis in this larger, more comprehensive book.

Mark Davis is a Mammoth Lakes resident active in the local Mammoth Area Mountain Bike Organization (MAMBO) and in local public land access issues. He is an expert on Eastern Sierra bicycle trails. Mark has hiked the entire Pacific Crest Trail twice and has ridden his bike in all 48 contiguous states. As he says, "I live to ride my bike."

Outdoor Publications from Fine Edge Productions

RECREATION TOPO MAPS
FROM MOUNTAIN BIKING PRESS™

(with Mountain Biking, Hiking and Ski Touring Trails. 6-color, double-sided, includes trail profiles & route descriptions)

Eastern High Sierra-Mammoth, June, Mono, 2nd Ed., ISBN 0-938665-21-9	$9.95
Santa Monica Mountains, ISBN 0-938665-23-5	$9.95
San Bernardino Mountains, ISBN 0-938665-32-4	$9.95
San Gabriel Mountains—West, ISBN 0-938665-13-8	$8.95
North Lake Tahoe Basin, 2nd Ed., ISBN 0-938665-34-0	$8.95
South Lake Tahoe Basin, 3rd Ed., ISBN 0-938665-35-9	$8.95

Laminated copies – $10 surcharge.

MOUNTAIN BIKING GUIDEBOOKS
FROM MOUNTAIN BIKING PRESS™

Mountain Biking North America's Best 100 Ski Resorts, ISBN 0-938665-46-4	$16.95
Mountain Biking Northern California's Best 100 Trails by Fragnoli & Stuart, ISBN 0-938665-31-6 (classic routes, 80 detailed maps, 300 pages)	$16.95
Mountain Biking Southern California's Best 100 Trails, Douglass & Fragnoli, eds., ISBN 0-938665-20-0 (classic routes, 80 detailed maps, 300 pages)	$14.95
Mountain Biking The Eastern Sierra's Best 100 Trails, by Hemingway-Douglass, Davis, and Douglass, ISBN 0-938665-42-1	$18.95
Mountain Biking the San Gabriel Mountains' Best Trails, with Angeles National Forest and Mt. Pinos, ISBN 0-938665-43-X	$14.95
Mountain Biking North Lake Tahoe's Best Trails, Bonser & Miskimins, ISBN 0-938665-40-5	$14.95
Lake Tahoe's 20 Best Pavement & Dirt Rides, by Miskimins, ISBN 0-938665-36-7	$6.95
Guide 3A, Lake Tahoe South, 3rd Ed. by Bonser & Miskimins, ISBN 0-938665-27-8	$10.95
Guide 4, Ventura County and the Sespe, 3rd Ed.,by McTigue, ISBN 0-938665-18-9	$9.95
Guide 7, Santa Monica Mountains, 3rd Ed. by Hasenauer & Langton, ISBN 0-938665-38-3	$11.95
Guide 10, San Bernardino Mountains, by Shipley, ISBN 0-938665-16-2	$10.95
Guide 11, Orange County and Cleveland N.F., 2nd Ed. by Rasmussen, ISBN 0-938665-37-5	$11.95
Guide 13, Reno/Carson City, by Miskimins, ISBN 0-938665-22-7	$10.95

NAUTICAL BOOKS

Cape Horn—One Man's Dream, One Woman's Nightmare, by Hemingway-Douglass, ISBN 0-938665-29-4	$22.50
Exploring the South Coast of British Columbia, ISBN 0-938665-44-8	$39.95
Exploring the North Coast of British Columbia, ISBN 0-938665-45-6	$49.95
Exploring the Inside Passage to Alaska—A Cruising Guide, ISBN 0-938665-33-2	$49.95
Exploring Vancouver Island's West Coast—A Cruising Guide, ISBN 0-938665-26-X	$39.95
Sea Stories of the Inside Passage, by Lawrence, ISBN 0-938665-48-0	$13.95
GPS—Instant Navigation, by Monahan and Douglass, ISBN 0-938665-47-2	$24.95
GPS Waypoints: British Columbia, by Douglass, ISBN 0-938665-50-2	$19.95
Exploring California's Channel Islands, an Artist's View, by Gates, ISBN 0-938665-00-6	$6.95

OTHER GUIDEBOOKS & MAPS

Favorite Pedal Tours of Northern California, by Bloom, ISBN 0-938665-12-X	$12.95
Ski Touring the Eastern High Sierra, by Douglass & Lombardo, ISBN 0-938665-08-1	$8.95

To order any of these items, see your local dealer
or order direct from Fine Edge Productions.
Please include $2.50 for shipping with check or money order.
California residents add 7.25% tax.

FINE EDGE PRODUCTIONS,
Route 2, Box 303, Bishop, California 93514
Fax: 760-387-2286
email: fineedgepr@aol.com
Visit our web site: **www.fineedge.com**

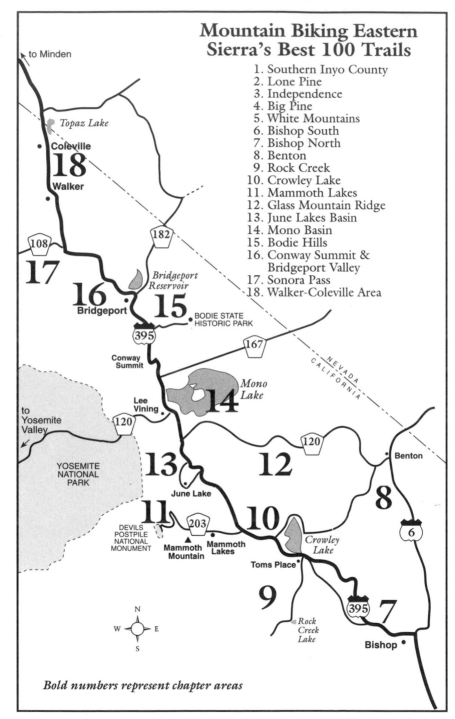

Mountain Biking Eastern Sierra's Best 100 Trails

1. Southern Inyo County
2. Lone Pine
3. Independence
4. Big Pine
5. White Mountains
6. Bishop South
7. Bishop North
8. Benton
9. Rock Creek
10. Crowley Lake
11. Mammoth Lakes
12. Glass Mountain Ridge
13. June Lakes Basin
14. Mono Basin
15. Bodie Hills
16. Conway Summit & Bridgeport Valley
17. Sonora Pass
18. Walker-Coleville Area

Bold numbers represent chapter areas